An Introduction to Religious and Spiritual Experience

An Introduction to Religious and Spiritual Experience

Marianne Rankin

With love and very best wishes for your future studies

from

Marianne

continuum

Continuum International Publishing Group
The Tower Building   80 Maiden Lane
11 York Road   Suite 704
London SE1 7NX   New York NY 10038

www.continuumbooks.com

© Marianne Rankin 2008

All rights reserved. No part of this publication may be reproduced or transmitted in any form or by any means, electronic or mechanical, including photocopying, recording, or any information storage or retrieval system, without prior permission in writing from the publishers.

British Library Cataloguing-in-Publication Data
A catalogue record for this book is available from the British Library.

ISBN 10: HB: 0-8264-9820-5
         PB: 0-8264-9821-3
ISBN 13: HB: 978-0-8264-9820-5
         PB: 978-0-8264-9821-2

Library of Congress Cataloging-in-Publication Data
Rankin, Marianne.
Introduction to religious and spiritual experience/Marianne Rankin.
p. cm.
Includes bibliographical references (p.).
ISBN 978-0-8264-9820-5 – ISBN 978-0-8264-9821-2
1. Experience (Religion) 2. Religions. 3. Spiritual life. I. Title.

BL53.R28 2009
204'.2–dc22   2008021938

Typeset by Newgen Imaging Systems Pvt Ltd, Chennai, India
Printed and bound in Great Britain by Cromwell Press Ltd, Trowbridge, Wiltshire

In memory of my Mother and Father.

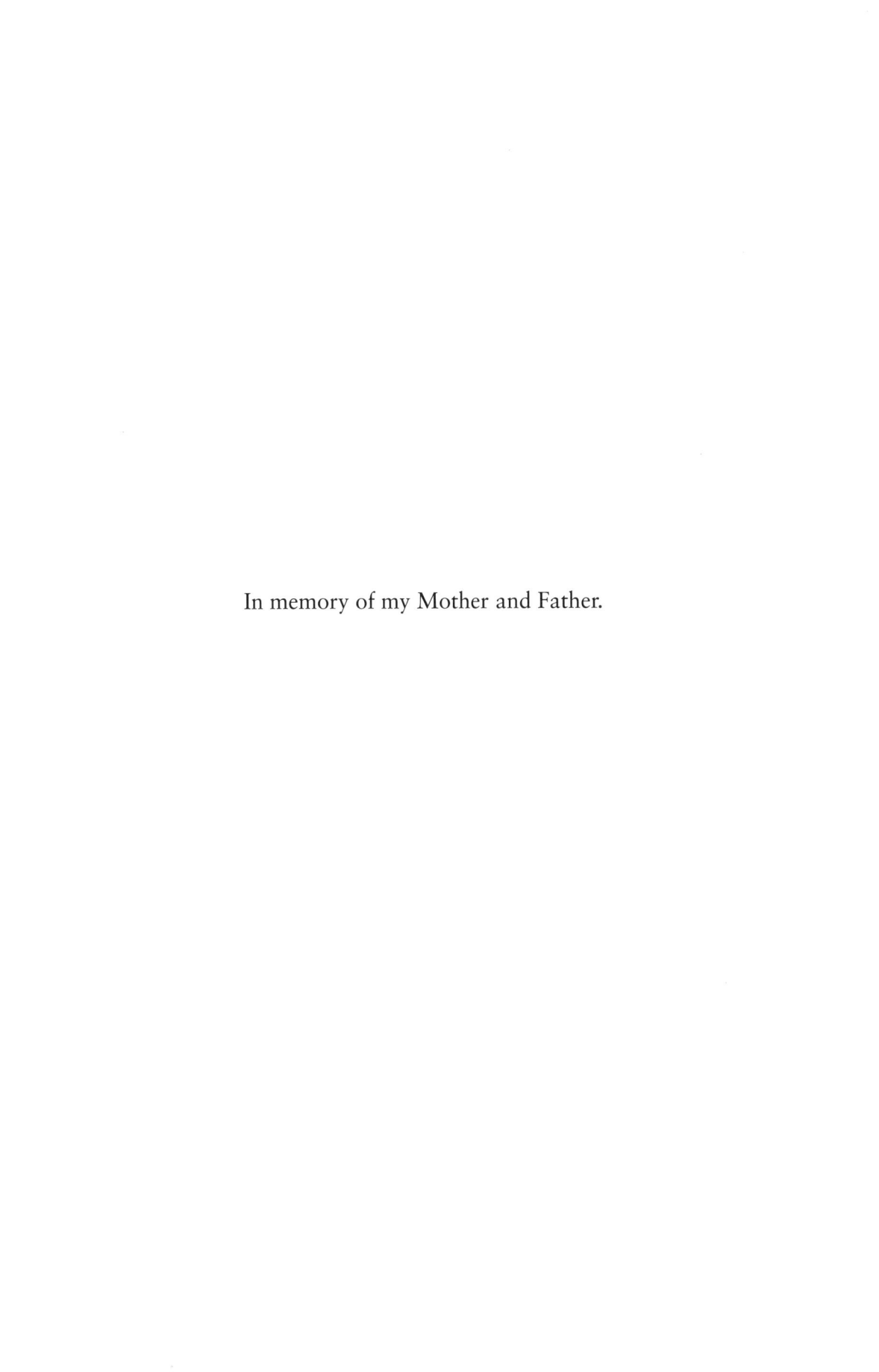

Contents

Preface	xiii
Acknowledgements	xv
Introduction	1
1 What is a Spiritual Experience?	5
2 Terminology	11
Religious Experience	11
Spiritual Experience	13
Transcendental Experience	14
Paranormal Experience	14
Exceptional Human Experience (EHE)	15
Peak Experience	15
Limit Experience	15
Ecstasy	15
Cosmic Consciousness	16
Mystical Experience	16
Absolute Unitary Being	16
Out of the Body Experience (OBE)	17
Near Death Experience (NDE)	17
3 Spiritual Experience and Religions	18
Founders/Messengers	18
Texts	19
Development	22
New Religious Movements	23
New Age Movements	23
Interfaith Movements	23
Quasi-Religions	24
Marxism	25
Humanism	25
4 Experiences of the Founders/Messengers of the Major Religious Traditions	27
Hinduism	27
Zoroastrianism	30

Contents

Jainism	30
Buddhism	31
Daoism (Taoism)	32
Confucianism	33
Judaism	33
Christianity	35
Islam	36
Sikhism	38

5 Experiences of the Founders/Messengers of Less Well-Known Religious Traditions — 40
- Brahma Kumaris — 40
- Brahmo Samaj — 40
- Baha'i — 41
- Quakers — 42
- Christian Science — 43
- Church of Scientology — 43
- Mormons — 44
- Theosophists — 44
- Anthroposophists — 45
- Unitarians — 46
- Gurus — 47
  - Sai Baba (1835–1918) — 47
  - Satya Sai Baba — 47
  - Ramana Maharshi (1879–1950) — 48
  - Maharishi Mahesh Yogi (1911–2008) — 48
  - Lord Sri Caitanya Mahaprabhu (1486–1533) — 48
  - Prabhupada (1896–1977) — 49
  - Mother Meera (1960–) — 49
- Alternative Paradigms — 50
  - Neale Donald Walsch — 50
  - Eckhart Tolle — 50
  - Fritjof Capra (1939–) — 50
  - Deepak Chopra (1946–) — 51

6 Religious Triggers of Spiritual Experience — 53
- Worship — 53
- Festivals and Religious Ceremonies — 54
- Prayer — 56
- Contemplation — 62
- Meditation — 63

Contents

Blessing	66
Silence	67
Darshan	67
Renunciation	68
Sacred places	69
Pilgrimage	70
Fasting	73
Chanting	74
Yoga	74
Interfaith	75
Search	76

7 Non-Religious Triggers of Spiritual Experience — 78

Place	78
Illness and Prospect of Death	79
Accident	80
Despair	82
Depression	83
Fear	85
Anger	86
Nature	86
Music	88
Sound	89

8 Types of Spiritual Experience — 93

Spiritual Experience in Childhood	93
Initiatory Experiences	99
Conversion	99
Regenerative Experiences	102
Healing	103
Miracles	107
Guidance	107
Solitary	108
Communal	110
Visions	111
Light	113
Love	118
Voices	119
Tongues	121
Angels	123
Dreams	125

Contents

	Shamanic Journey	127
	Shamanic Healing	129
	Soul Retrieval via the Internet	129
	Drugs and trips	131
	Synchronicity	132
	Sense of Presence	133
	The Numinous	136
	The Dark Night of the Soul	138
	The Dark Side – Negative Spiritual Experiences	139
	Dangerous Aspects of Spiritual Movements	141
	The People's Temple	142
	Branch Davidians	142
	Irreligious Experiences or De-Conversion	143
9	**Dying and Death**	**146**
	Dying	148
	End of Life Experiences	151
	Out of the Body Experiences	154
	Near Death Experiences (NDE)	155
	Post-Death Experiences	164
10	**Mystics**	**171**
	Dionysius the Areopagite	173
	Dame Julian of Norwich (1342–Circa 1416)	174
	Rumi (1207–1273)	177
	Swami Paramahansa Yogananda (1893–1952)	180
	Contemporary Accounts	182
	Mysticism Across Religions	186
	Hinduism and Christianity	186
	Buddhism and Christianity	189
	Mystical Experience within All Religions	191
	Mysticism with No Religious Tradition	193
	Direct Path	194
11	**Spiritual and Mystical Experiences of Well-Known People**	**196**
	Plato (427–347 BCE)	196
	St Paul (Circa AD 10–67)	198
	C. G. Jung (1875–1961)	200
	William Wilberforce (1759–1833)	202
	Sir Francis Younghusband (1863–1942)	204
	Mahatma Gandhi (1869–1948)	205
	Mother Teresa (1910–1997)	206

Contents

Dietrich Bonhoeffer (1906–1945)		207
Chad Varah (1911–2007)		208
Elisabeth Kübler-Ross (1926–2004)		210
Dame Cicely Saunders (1918–2005)		212
His Holiness the Dalai Lama (1935–)		213
Nelson Mandela (1918–)		214
Aung San Suu Kyi (1945–)		215
Yusuf Islam (1948–)		218
Eric Clapton (1945–)		218
12	**Fruits of Spiritual Experience**	**220**
	Paintings of Ken Butler-Evans	222
	The World's Largest Book: Kuthodaw Pagoda	222
	Charities	223
	The Müller Orphan Houses	223
	The Prison Phoenix Trust	224
	The Allan Sweeney International Reiki and Healing and Training Centre	225
	Religious Orders	226
	St Benedict (480–543)	227
	St Francis of Assisi (1182–1226)	227
	Outside the Walls: the Beguines	228
	Repentance and Forgiveness	228
	The Truth and Reconciliation Commission	229
13	**Spiritual Experience Research**	**231**
	The Religious Experience Research Centre	231
	Contemporary Research	233
	Research Worldwide	234
	China	235
	Turkey	236
	India	237
	Consciousness Studies	238
14	**The Interpretation of Spiritual, Religious and Mystical Experience**	**240**
	Friedrich Schleiermacher (1768–1834)	241
	Rudolf Otto (1869–1937)	241
	William James (1842–1910)	242
	Lynn Bridgers (1956–)	243
	Evelyn Underhill (1875–1941)	244
	Martin Buber (1878–1965)	245

Contents

Aldous Huxley (1894–1963)	245
A. J. Ayer (1910–1989)	246
W. T. Stace (1886–1967)	247
Steven Katz (1944–)	247
Ninian Smart (1927–2001)	247
Robert Sharf (1953–)	248
Richard Swinburne (1934–)	248
Caroline Franks Davis	249
Pluralism	250
John Hick (1922–)	250
Keith Ward (1938–)	251
Implicit Religion	252
Edward Bailey (1935–)	252
Don Cupitt (1934–)	252
Daniel Dennett (1942–)	253
Richard Dawkins (1941–)	253
D'Aquili (1940–1998) and Newberg (1966–)	254
Recommended Reading	254
Peter Donovan	254
Paul Marshall	255
Grahame Miles	255
Conclusion	256
Notes	258
Bibliography	268
Index	275

Preface

In the twenty-first century religion is a contentious matter. Many rational thinkers had assumed that as humans evolved, religion would be left behind as no longer necessary, God would not only be dead but all transcendent beliefs would be buried by the scientific, materialist paradigm. This has, however, not proved to be the case, and whether for good or ill, religion remains a powerful force in today's world.

Spirituality on the other hand is getting a much better press. People feel that they are spiritual beings, whether or not they follow any particular religion. Many are exploring alternative spiritualities, as attested by the growth of Mind, Body and Spirit sections in bookshops, new magazines and gatherings of many kinds of alternative groups all over the country. The decline in church worship in Britain does not indicate a nation of convinced atheists, rather a population unsure of what to believe, and interested in exploring the options. The experiential side of religion has an important role in that search for meaning, with practices such as yoga, meditation, tai chi and circle dancing now very much part of the mainstream.

A lively engagement was triggered in 2007 by Richard Dawkins' bestseller *The God Delusion* with ripostes such as Alister McGrath's *The Dawkins Delusion* and debates nationwide. The renowned broadcaster John Humphreys had the biggest postbag of his career in response to his Radio 4 series *Humphreys in Search of God* in which he interviewed religious leaders about their faith, as part of a personal search. People remain deeply interested in spirituality and religion, whether they are for or against. Young people in particular, although often eschewing formal worship, which in general means little to them, and often critical of what they see as the gap between religious teaching and practice, do have a holistic understanding of the interdependence of humanity and the planet, not found in previous generations. Profoundly aware of the enormous inequalities of standards of living, they become involved in projects at home and abroad to help others. They travel the world and are concerned about how what we do affects the earth's future and so are conscious of environmental issues. Those who engage in spiritual exploration do so

Preface

with an unprecedented awareness of the great variety of religious traditions in existence. The number of students opting for Religious Studies is growing, as they enjoy thinking about the Big Questions. This book is primarily for them.

My presentation does not focus on the texts, institutions or practices of any religious tradition, but on experiences which indicate a deeper or transcendent level of existence. Although the actual experiences cannot themselves be shared, the accounts given reflect their importance to people and the profound effects on their lives. As we cannot know the divine directly, it is through such stories that it is possible to approach the spiritual dimension. This may be experienced within the individual through introspection and meditation; or beyond, through relational consciousness; or through wonder at the universe and intimations of something beyond it. However experienced, it is that awareness, the experiential heart of religion which is explored in this book.

This is a wide-ranging introduction to the subject and aims to encourage further, deeper study. My presentation is set out in short sections making it suitable for reference, although it may be read as a continuous text. I record moments which have been of deep significance to people, life-changing events. I also recount less dramatic, longer-term experiences which have brought comfort and awareness of a constant Presence. There are negative experiences too and even experiences of people rejecting religion with joy. As the field is vast, this is inevitably a personal selection, enhanced by the experiences shared with me during the time I was writing the book.

We cannot know the true nature of ultimate reality but sometimes it seems as if the clouds part and there is a glimpse of something beyond which touches people's lives, whether our own or those of people we know or have read about. These biographical snippets are records of such happenings. They point the way to understanding what it means to be truly human.

Acknowledgements

So many people on hearing about this project, immediately shared their experiences with me and allowed me to quote them. I am deeply grateful to all who have contributed to the book in this way as these accounts are very precious and many had not been shared before. Most of the new accounts are now recorded in the Alister Hardy Religious Experience Research Centre Archive held at the University of Wales, Lampeter and are quoted anonymously by reference number. My thanks also go to those who have sent their accounts to the RERC over the years, as I have been able to make use of the archive for this book. I have also been able to include data from the RERC Global Project. For information on China I thank Professors Paul Badham and Xinzhong Yao; for data and accounts from Turkey, Professor Cafer Yaran of the University of Istanbul and for details of the Tamil Nadu project in India, Revd Jonathan Robinson.

Very special thanks are due to Peggy Morgan, for her encouragement in my studies and for her role in my involvement with the Alister Hardy Society, as well as for her invaluable advice after reading the first draft of the book. Three professors have been particularly supportive: my former tutor Keith Ward in Oxford, Paul Badham in Lampeter and Hal French in South Carolina and I am deeply indebted to them. I am also most grateful for the suggestions made by Dr Wendy Dossett and Dr David Hay. I thank all at the RERC for their co-operation, particularly Jean Matthews for her patient work in adding so many new accounts to the archive, and to the members of the Alister Hardy Society for their companionship on my journey.

My husband John and daughter Eleanor lived with the idea of this book for a long time and I am deeply grateful to them both for their enthusiasm and support. Above all, I thank John for all his help while I was writing. I am particularly grateful to him for his comments on the text, but most of all for his constant love and encouragement.

Introduction

In this book I seek to answer some fundamental questions. What exactly is meant by the terms religious and spiritual experience and are they synonymous? Are such experiences the same as mystical or psychical experiences and how do they differ from what we might call ordinary experiences? Who has what kind of experiences and how are they interpreted? What do they tell us about spirituality, religion and human consciousness? Might such events in fact be a common thread linking humans on a spiritual level, bringing the different religions together in a shared recognition of the transcendent, however interpreted or worshipped? If so, could such an approach perhaps contribute towards a more tolerant and peaceful understanding of the different religions, viewing them as a variety of responses to one all-embracing spiritual reality?

Spirituality may be understood as an awareness of another level of existence. Such an awareness of a higher, all-encompassing reality is often the result of an experience which cannot be explained merely with reference to the everyday world. Such experiences are at the heart of the religious traditions, many of which can be traced back to life-changing moments of revelation and transformation. Those are perhaps the most intense and best known, but accounts of such occurrences come to us from all ages and cultures. People of all religions and none have had such experiences. They still do. Are these events simply unexplained but perfectly natural occurrences, which science has yet to understand or do they indicate the existence of a transcendent level of reality? Might our present definition of human consciousness need to expand to include another level of awareness?

Many of the most admirable leaders of religious movements have experienced the power of wisdom, love and compassion. Here, I present a wide range of religious traditions from the personal, experiential point of view of such people, so far as these are known. Thus a series of biographical portraits is sketched, focusing particularly on the transformative events in their lives. Inevitably brief, the accounts do not deal with the development of the religious traditions from the original vision, nor is the context of the experiences considered in detail. This way of looking at religions does, however, go right to the heart, to the starting point of the tradition. I also consider the experiences of particular individuals linked to the traditions – saints, mystics, *gurus* (teachers) and *avatars* (incarnations).

Throughout the book, I also include a variety of extraordinary experiences of ordinary people. Some come from the RERC archive, others from books and websites as I would like to introduce the reader to the wide range of material available. However, many have been recounted to me since I began writing, simply as a result of my talking about this book. Most of these are life-enhancing and greatly treasured but I also consider the downside – negative experiences, de-conversion experiences and cases of spiritual abuse. In addition to the accounts of experiences themselves, I look at the triggers and effects. It is extremely difficult to classify these experiences, as researchers from Alister Hardy onwards have found. Triggers merge with experiences, a vision can lead to a conversion – so under which heading should such an event come? I have simply used the headings as guides, to help the reader to find different types of experience but in my view there are no clear boundaries and I propose no formal categories.

There will always be uncertainty where personal accounts of inner experiences are concerned, as to the veracity of the reports and the role played by expectation and interpretation. There is a vast literature on the subject, which I introduce.

Many people maintain that any religious belief is misguided and that such delusions should simply be eradicated. This has in fact been attempted, notably in communist countries such as the Soviet Union and China. That didn't work, as is attested by the research cited in this book. Religion survived suppression and resurfaced as soon as permitted. Indeed, spiritual values were often harnessed in opposition to political oppression.

Attempts to explain away spirituality as wishful thinking, childhood brainwashing or as a kind of mental virus seem inadequate in the face of the wisdom shown by people inspired by a spiritual attitude to life; the comfort derived from religion; the great works of music, literature, art and architecture inspired by faith; and the many charitable organizations established through religious conviction. Yet in these days of religious extremism, terrorism and warfare, perhaps a new approach is needed, one based on an understanding of all religions as differing but universal responses to one transcendent reality. As spiritual experiences are found throughout history and in contemporary accounts all over the world, the phenomenon seems to be common to humanity as a whole. Humans seem to be hard-wired to relate to a spiritual dimension which

Introduction

leads to compassion and wisdom. If so, such a power needs to be harnessed to enable people to live in harmony with their neighbours. We need to co-operate to ensure the survival of the planet. If we are able to understand humans as finite but within an infinite dimension, we may be able to see the world in a different perspective and live in peace.

* * *

The book has its roots in the work of the Religious Experience Research Centre, now at the University of Wales, Lampeter, but set up in 1969 at Manchester College, Oxford by Sir Alister Hardy as the Religious Experience Research Unit.

Sir Alister Hardy (1896–1985) was a Darwinian biologist, who studied under Julian Huxley and later became professor at Hull, Aberdeen and eventually Linacre Professor of Zoology at Oxford. There, interestingly, he taught Richard Dawkins. Hardy was Chief Zoologist on the *Discovery* voyage to the Antarctic in 1924–1928 and was knighted for his services to biology. In 1963–1964 he gave the Gifford Lectures, later published as *The Living Stream: A Restatement of Evolution Theory and its Relation to the Spirit of Man* and *The Divine Flame*. He was awarded the Templeton Prize for his work on religious experience.

Hardy thought of humans as spiritual animals, and of religious experience as a natural phenomenon of evolutionary value. He felt that in exploring their environment, humans had become aware of something beyond it, a transcendent presence which met them in a different way from their everyday experience. In other words, he believed that spirituality was a natural part of consciousness.

In order to acquire data in support of his theory, Hardy began a collection of the experiences of ordinary people, which he obtained first through a press agency. He collected experiences related to the spiritual aspects of life but not to formal religion. He then placed adverts in the religious press, but met with a disappointing lack of response. So he turned to the secular newspapers, the *Guardian*, *Observer*, *Times* and *Daily Mail*. There, after a short article or example of a spiritual experience, he posed what is now known as 'The Hardy Question':

> Have you ever been aware of or influenced by a presence or power, whether you call it God or not, which is different from your everyday self?

There was an overwhelming response to his appeal, as readers sent in accounts of experiences they had never dared share with anyone before, for fear of being thought abnormal. This was the beginning of what is now an archive of about 6,000 accounts held at the RERC in Lampeter. Alister Hardy always thought that spiritual experience was a natural human trait and so would be universal. He began the research in the UK and wanted it to be extended to other cultures and other faiths. This is now happening as today the work is going forward in China, India, Turkey, Japan, the USA and South America, enabling the archive to reflect experiences from all over the world.

* * *

There are many interesting cross-references within the text, as people and ideas appear in different sections. The work became rather like Indra's Net, an infinite net said to hang above the palace of the king of the Vedic gods. At each node of the net there is a jewel, each one reflecting all the others. I have decided to let the reader find these connections, rather than indicate them in the text. Alternatively, good use might be made of the index.

All dates are CE (Common Era) unless otherwise stated.

1. What is a Spiritual Experience?

A spiritual experience may be thought of as an experience which points beyond normal, everyday life, and which has spiritual or religious significance for the person to whom it happens. Whatever form it takes, such an experience gives an indication of a greater reality underlying the physical world of the senses. Reductionists explain away religion as a delusion and are convinced that in our experience of life 'what you see is what you get', that there is no more to life than meets the eye, or direct sense experience. Spiritual experience counters this, indicating another dimension which is different from ordinary reality or a deeper level of experience within that reality. Spiritual experiences occur with or without religious practice. Various surveys have shown that between half and one-third of the populace feel that they have had some kind of experience of spiritual significance.

Interpretation of similar events varies, of course, according to the secular or spiritual standpoint of the experient. There are non-religious people who would lay claim to such experiences but interpret them as part of being human, an aspect of the natural world. They do however, recognize them as qualitatively different from ordinary experiences.

Such experiences can arrive out of the blue and happen to people with or without any kind of religious faith. Those who have such experiences are frequently convinced that they have been touched by a higher power, either in a single incident or continuously throughout life, in a constant awareness of a relationship with this power. Although in some of these experiences there is no immediately obvious connection to any particular religious tradition and descriptions are given which are open to different interpretations, others tell of visions of a loving, comforting figure, whom they recognize as Jesus, Krishna or a Bodhisattva.

Many people try to induce such experiences, but they cannot be invoked to order, although intense religious practice may well result in a deepening awareness and openness.

In *The Spiritual Nature of Man* Alister Hardy defined religious experience as,

> a deep awareness of a benevolent non-physical power which appears to be partly or wholly beyond, and far greater than, the individual self.

Religious and Spiritual Experience

He describes the ways in which such a power might become manifest.

> To some, the presence of this abstract non-physical power is strongest when contemplating natural beauty or listening to music: others feel it when they paint or create. Awareness of its presence affects the way man looks at the world, it alters behaviour and changes attitudes. Knowledge of this wider dimension to life may be seen by the individual as life-enhancing, or he may recognize it as a special force which gives him added confidence and courage. As a result of their experiences many are led to prayer and to religion.
>   People experience the abstract power in a wide variety of ways. Some may describe their feelings in terms of trust, awe, joy, or bliss; exceptionally they may reach the heights of ecstasy. Others may have sensory impressions, see lights, hear voices, or have feelings of being touched.... however diverse the kind of experience, spiritual awareness appears to be universal to human kind ... [1]

When beginning his research, Alister Hardy used the spiritual experience of the socialist reformer Beatrice Webb (1858–1943) to illustrate what he was looking for.

> Beatrice Webb was conscious of experiencing a sense of reverence or awe – an apprehension of a power and purpose outside herself – which she called 'feeling' and which was sometimes induced by appreciation of great music or corporate worship. But the experience went further than this nebulous, fleeting 'feeling' – because as a result of it she achieved a religious interpretation of the universe which satisfied and upheld her and enabled her to seek continuous guidance in prayer – and this without compromising her intellectual integrity. [2]

Let us look at a few more examples. The first two are taken from the Alister Hardy Trust website: www.alisterhardyreligiousexperience.co.uk

The numbers in brackets throughout the book refer to the archive at the Religious Experience Research Centre at the University of Wales, Lampeter:

> I was out walking one night in busy streets of Glasgow when, with slow majesty, at a corner where the pedestrians were hurrying by and the city traffic was hurtling on its way, the air was filled with heavenly music; and an all-encompassing light, that moved in waves of luminous

What is a Spiritual Experience?

colour, outshone the brightness of the lighted streets. I stood still, filled with a strange peace and joy, the music beat on in its majesty and the traffic and the pedestrians moved through the light. They passed on their way, but the music and light remained, pulsating, harmonious, more real than the traffic of the streets. I too moved on . . . till I found myself in the everyday world again with a strange access of gladness and of love. [0208]

I was sitting one evening, listening to a Brahms symphony. My eyes were closed and I must have been completely relaxed for I became aware of a feeling of 'expansion', I seemed to be beyond the boundary of my physical self. Then an intense feeling of 'light' and 'love' uplifted and enfolded me. It was so wonderful and gave me such an emotional release that tears streamed down my cheeks. For several days I seemed to bathe in its glow and when it subsided I was free from my fears.

I didn't feel happy about the world situation but seemed to see it from a different angle. So with my personal sorrow. I can truly say that it changed my life and the subsequent years have brought no dimming of the experience. [0071][3]

Some experiences are dramatic. Here a desperate woman who had decided to commit suicide shouts to a God she is not at all sure she believes in,

. . . at that moment I let out a loud challenge into that dark and lonesome night, into that desolation of land and soul and I shouted:
. . . IF THERE IS SUCH A THING AS GOD THEN SHOW YOURSELF TO ME – NOW . . . and at that very instant there was a loud crack, like a rifle shot (coming from the bedroom) . . . I stumbled through the open door to my bedroom. I fell into the bed shaking and then something forced my eyes upward to the wall above my bedside table and where I had a very small photograph of my father hanging. . . . The picture had gone – I just looked at the empty space . . . but on looking closer I saw the photograph, face down, on the little table and the narrow frame was split apart, the glass broken and from behind the cardboard on the back there had slipped out . . . the last letter [my father] had written me . . . When I picked up that letter and read over and over the words of this beloved caring father of mine, I knew that was HIS help to me, and God answered me directly in the hour of my soul being in anguish.[4]

Religious and Spiritual Experience

Here is a description of a lifetime of awareness of another dimension,

I think from my childhood I have always had the feeling that the true reality is not to be found in the world as the average person sees it. There seems to be a constant force at work from the inside trying to push its way to the surface of consciousness. The mind is continually trying to create a symbol sufficiently comprehensive to contain it, but it always ends in failure. There are moments of pure joy with a heightened awareness of one's surroundings, as if a great truth had been passed across. [00651]

Some people live strengthened by such a spiritual awareness,

My main religious experience has been of God's guiding my life according to His plan. I have had some terrible experiences and frustrations, and suffered defeats and failures and humiliations since childhood, but I have always been able to see the wise and loving purpose of God behind them, turning evil to good account and leading me onwards to do what He has for me to do here and to fulfil my destiny. This is particularly true of my marriage ... and the birth of my son; and also true of my vocation and my work.

I have experienced the Holy Spirit as the Giver of Light, and the One who guides into Truth, especially the truth about myself, in psychoanalysis and through dreams.

I have experienced the power and help of God, most particularly when I have had to do tasks and have personal encounters which I have feared. When I have really prayed about them beforehand and remembered His presence, they have become such as I could cope with.

I have had the vision of the Christian Way as the way of love and release from ego-centricity; it is still a vision which I can only approximate to in the reality of living; but I am sure it saves me from succumbing to its opposite: at least it counterbalances the pull of self. In prayer and meditation, I find continuing light and inspiration of this sort, and also judgement and challenge. [001397]

A similar comfort is described by a mother,

About ten years later I began to pray for my children's safety, and this became a habit which I have never lost, and often the answer to such a prayer is spectacular. Now I've evolved a belief which is identical with Beatrice Webb's: 'I find it best to live as if the soul of man were in communion with a superhuman force which makes for righteousness'. May I add that since this belief grew in me I feel as if I had grown, as if my mind had stretched to take in the vast universe and be part of it. [00854]

Sometimes we know what is right and wrong, but such experiences reinforce a moral code.

One day when I walked around, I found some money. Although an inner voice said to me not to take it, I could not dominate my selfish desires and took it. However, just ten minutes after I put the money into my wallet, I found out that I lost my wallet. Oddly enough, there was nobody with me. Then I thought and realized that Allah had punished me. Because that money did not belong to me and, who knows, it was earned with how much difficulties.[5]

Some people beg for help in extreme circumstances and in return, make a vow to live for God if only God will spare them.

When I was twelve, my family were living on the outskirts of London and experiencing occasional visits from German bomber planes. One night, when I had been confined to bed for six weeks and was unable to walk because of some illness, I heard the roar of a German bomber overhead. (We knew the sound all too well.) This one was being chased by British fighter planes and the pilot must have decided to drop the bombs at random to make it easier to escape. The whine of a close bomb is ear-splitting and I just knew this one was going to hit us.
    I ducked my head under the eiderdown and I desperately prayed aloud: 'Dear God, save me now and I will serve you all the days of my life.' The bomb landed in the back garden and blew the roof off the bungalow. All the windows were blown in, of course, and I was smothered in broken glass – but shielded from injury by the eiderdown. My life was saved. This incident made God very real to me and I am very much aware of God's presence in my life now, as well as when I look back. Of course one has to get on with life and its fascinations – but I do try to keep that vow to serve God. It is all too easy to drift away, especially in adolescence. But I know that even if, at times, I have lost God, God has never lost me. Deo gratias! . . . To me, God is pure love and uses us to convey that love to all His creatures. [005445]

As a result, God remains important in this person's life and she eventually became ordained.

The course of Alister Hardy's life and work was set by a vow,

> At the outbreak of World War One, he made a vow that, if he lived through it, he would do all in his power for the rest of his life to reconcile the purely materialistic view of evolution with his own experience of what he could only call spirit.[6]

Some people find such experiences linked to art, music or nature, and they may interpret them as aesthetic, although the loss of sense of self, of time or place as one is totally absorbed in creativity may be felt to be a spiritual experience. It is often while creating something that an awareness of one's own creator may be felt, or oneness with creation itself. Whether active or passive, in a religious setting or not, spiritual experience can be triggered in many ways. Some people feel an awareness of God or the divine in nature:

> Just occasionally when I was sure no-one could see me, I became so overcome with the glory of the natural scene that for a moment or two I fell on my knees in prayer – not prayer asking for anything, but thanking God, who felt very real to me, for the glories of his kingdom and for allowing me to feel them. It was always by a running waterside that I did this, perhaps in front of a great foam of Meadow Sweet or a mass of Purple Loosestrife.[7]

Often these experiences are not written down until long afterwards. Alister Hardy was 88 years old before he noted down the above which, despite his great interest in the subject, he had never told anyone before.

It is so often the case that these experiences remain unshared. People treasure them as highly personal messages and are often reluctant to talk about them. They are precious and fear of ridicule is a potent factor in keeping such events to oneself. Yet once people feel that they have a sympathetic ear or a helpful companion to share the experience with, they are able to talk freely about it and the effects it had on their lives.

2. Terminology

There have been many attempts to define just what is understood by religious and spiritual experience. Experience itself may be considered a modification of consciousness and the great variety of spiritual experiences, their varying intensity and the wide range of interpretation is reflected in the different terms given to them. It may be helpful to think of a continuum of different types of awareness, ranging from a momentary experience of awe or an awareness of 'Something Beyond' right across the spectrum to perhaps the most intense form of all, the mystical experience.

Religious Experience

This is a particularly appropriate term for experiences which either confirm or conform to the tenets of a religious tradition or which take place during religious observance or practice or are the result of lengthy preparation or devotion, of mental training, prayer or fasting. Such experiences may be communal, taking place within a setting of worship or ritual or may be solitary.

Religious Experience was the term used by William James (1842–1907) in his Gifford Lectures on Natural Religion of 1901 and 1902, subsequently published as *The Varieties of Religious Experience*. From the perspective of a psychologist, he looked at the religious propensities of

> individuals for whom religion exists not as a dull habit, but as an acute fever rather.[8]

He calls such people 'geniuses' in the religious line, unusual folk who have traits often considered pathological. James divides religion into two main categories: the institutional – including church, theology and worship; and the personal, experiential side. It is the latter which concerns him in his lectures:

> ... the feelings, acts, and experiences of individual men in their solitude, so far as they apprehend themselves to stand in relation to whatever they may consider the divine.[9]

Religious and Spiritual Experience

In *The Meaning and End of Religion*, Wilfred Cantwell Smith (1916–2000) proposes that we reconsider the definition of religion.

> The proposal I am putting forward can, at one level, be formulated quite simply. It is that what men have tended to conceive as a religion, can more rewardingly, more truly, be conceived in terms of two factors, different in kind, both dynamic: a historical 'cumulative tradition', and the personal faith of men and women.[10]

It is that personal aspect which is the subject of this study.

Ninian Smart (1927–2001) viewed religion as composed of seven different dimensions, one of which was the Experiential and Emotional Dimension. This was exemplified in the experiences of people such as Muhammad and the Buddha and also in the feelings of practitioners of religion. According to Smart, the experiential dimension brings life and emotional enhancement to the other dimensions: ritual, doctrinal, narrative, ethical, material and social.

> A religious experience involves some kind of 'perception' of the *invisible* world, or involves a perception that some visible person or thing is a manifestation of the invisible world.[11]

Another perspective is that of finding a deeper significance in life, as expressed by the former Director of the RERC, Peggy Morgan,

> . . . religious experience . . . is 'ordinary, everyday experience in depth'[12]

Most religious people experience the reality of their beliefs through their practice and in their daily lives. Many feel that they are in a relationship with the divine. Without this, the doctrines would be empty and have no lasting effect. For a religion to thrive, more than formulae and historical tradition is necessary. The on-going experience of worship, meditation or living a life in harmony with others generally gives comfort and stability, but more importantly, it often leads to a more selfless way of life.

It must not be forgotten, however, that some religious practitioners are wary of or even condemn extraordinary experiences as misleading or even dangerous and in many traditions it is made clear that they are not to be sought and should even be ignored. In fact it is important that the focus is not so much on the experience per se, but on its meaning and effects. The value of religious experience is in the response and transformation of the individual – a process however it is brought about, which is essential for spiritual growth. The results of the experience are what matter and the guiding principle to tell false from genuine religious manifestations is given by Jesus in his Sermon on the Mount,

> . . . you will know them by their fruits. (Matthew 7:20)

Spiritual Experience

A more general term, spiritual experience may be preferred for experiences which do not reflect any specifically religious beliefs, but which give an indication of an influence which is inexplicable in any down-to-earth way. Such events often lead to a wide, all-embracing view of the spiritual dimension of life. They might lead to a search within religious traditions, or may simply be absorbed into the lives of the experients as an underlying acceptance of this other dimension, often felt to be one of love, comfort and guidance. However, the experience might bring awareness of dissatisfaction with the everyday, triggering spiritual unrest and leading to a spiritual search.

This category is perhaps the most numerous, in that many people do not in fact find that the experiences are limited to any particular religious tradition. Some people are concerned to stress that their experiences are not religious but spiritual,

> My experience occurred when I was a child between ten and eleven years of age. Each day I was drawn to stand at a bedroom window at the back of our family terraced house in Pont-y-moel. I looked out between the sidewalls of the house across a narrow valley to the lower mountain levels of Mynydd Maen, which then rose steadily towards Twm Barlwm. For a year I was compelled to stand and wait and watch.
>
> On a day in March a column of luminous light appeared from one of the empty levels cut into the mountain which had been used for pigeons cots. It enclosed a figure, grew upwards and as it touched the clear blue sky disappeared, the waiting was over. I had no need to return to the window. I was not surprised at the 'appearance' but I was surprised that the intense need to go to the window had gone. This 'appearance' is as clear to me today as it was then, and I know that I experienced in that moment, true reality. It is the single most important experience of my life.
>
> I do not consider this to be a religious but a spiritual experience. The difference in definition is fundamental to the journey of self-discovery I have taken through my art.

> My experience has been the single most important influence on my life and work. I believe it was a glimpse of a true reality. My work as an artist and writer has been an exploration of the relationship between an inner world and the outer world through visual and written language. [100053]

Transcendental Experience

Another term often used to designate this type of experience, is Transcendental Experience. Alister Hardy, although frequently referring to religious experience, also uses the term as it enables him to distinguish the experience of a power beyond the individual self from the concept of religion.

> At certain times in their lives many people have had specific, deeply felt, transcendental experiences which have made them all aware of the presence of this power. The experience when it comes has always been quite different from any other type of experience they have ever had. They do not necessarily call it a religious feeling. It often occurs to children, to atheists and agnostics and it usually induces in the person concerned a conviction that the everyday world is not the whole of reality: that there is another dimension to life.
>
> . . .
>
> Some people feel a personal devotional relationship with the power after their experience; some call it God, some do not. Some see it as an aspect of their wider self through which such an experience has come, whilst others see it as part of man's general consciousness.[13]

The term has also been used by Michael Paffard in his research for *Inglorious Wordsworths* in which he elicited descriptions of such experiences from his sixth form boys using Wordsworth's *Tintern Abbey* as a stimulus.[14]

Paranormal Experience

Another term for psychical experience is Paranormal Experience, which usually refers to powers which have not yet been explained by science and are seen as beyond the norm. This includes such events as telepathy, telekinesis and clairvoyance. Psychical research concentrates on the experiences as evidence of the paranormal rather than considering the effects on the lives of the experients. Spiritualists concern themselves with communications from beyond the grave and are often appealed to in times of bereavement. However, most of these experiences lack the spiritual dimension.

Exceptional Human Experience (EHE)

This term was coined by Rhea White, an American parapsychologist, to denote these out of the ordinary experiences. Inspired by her own Near Death Experience, she studied parapsychology to learn more, and subsequently founded the Exceptional Human Experience Network to study all kinds of anomalous experiences. She provided a bibliography of books and articles on the subject notably with Laura Dale in *Parapsychology: Sources of Information*.

Peak Experience

Abraham Maslow used this term to stress its secular connotation. He saw such an experience as indicating a sense of expansion of the self, offering an understanding of the ultimate unity of all things and leading to personal growth and fulfilment, with no need for a religious context or spiritual interpretation. In his view everyone could and should be encouraged to cultivate such experiences for their therapeutic value.

Limit Experience

Revd. Dr. Andrew Greeley, researching in the USA, used the term Limit Experience to indicate that these experiences point 'towards a limit or horizon of life' while hinting that there may be something beyond this horizon. In Australia Dr. Paul McQuillan availed himself of the term to interview high school students for research, thereby avoiding specifically religious language. In this way he was able to elicit the students' responses to the spiritual without limiting their thinking to formal religion. [15]

Ecstasy

This was how Marghanita Laski designated the sensation of being outside time and in contact with the transcendent spirit in *Ecstasy in Secular and Spiritual Experiences.*[16] By means of a questionnaire and literary and religious experiences from secondary sources she investigated experiences resulting from withdrawal inward, as well as intensity experiences triggered by external conditions. She also looked at the similarities and differences between natural ecstasy and experiences induced by alcohol and drugs and at the effects of such experiences in people's lives. Above all, she was concerned to include the experiences of non-religious people although admitting that the language in which such events were described was usually religious.

Cosmic Consciousness

R. M. Bucke used this as the title of his book published in 1901. The term indicated the final stage of the development of consciousness, in a progression from instinctual to self-consciousness and ultimately to cosmic consciousness.

Mystical Experience

A mystical experience is often described as an intense experience of the unity of all things or a state of achieving unity with the divine. There are mystical movements and techniques within most religious traditions, examples being the Sufis of Islam and the Kabbalists and Hasidim of Judaism. In 1899 Dean W. R. Inge noted that there were twenty-five different definitions of mysticism, and it is an elusive concept. The term is also occasionally used as a generic term for all such experiences, whatever the focus or intensity. William James suggested that all personal religious experience had its roots in mystical states of consciousness and he identified four features in his lectures on mysticism, published as *The Varieties of Religious Experience.*

Essentialists consider all mystical experience to be the same or of the same transcendent reality, seeing a common core. Empiricists focus on the differences between mystics as they deny any unmediated experience and maintain that the mystic's cultural and linguistic milieu are formative of the experience itself.

Absolute Unitary Being

AUB and Hyperlucid Unitary State are terms used by Eugene d'Aquili and Andrew B. Newberg in *The Mystical Mind, Probing the Biology of*

Religious Experience for experiences arising from meditation, religious ritual and spontaneous spiritual events, with AUB referring to the most extreme state of mystic union. Theirs is a neuropsychological approach to theology, which they call neurotheology. They studied the mind/brain relationship to spiritual experience, by monitoring the brain activity of people involved in spiritual practice.

Out of the Body Experience (OBE)

At times people feel themselves to be separate from their own body, usually watching it from the outside, often above. This is known as an Out of the Body Experience and tends to happen at times of stress or during accidents and traumatic situations. Such experiences lead to a consideration of what human consciousness is, challenging the materialist paradigm as the OBE seems evidence of some kind of mind-body dualism.

Near Death Experience (NDE)

This is often preceded by an OBE and takes place when the individual is clinically dead but has a coherent experience before being revived. An NDE can occur during an accident, cardiac arrest or in times of massive stress. Other phenomena around death are Death Bed Visions, End of Life Experiences and Post Death Appearances. All such experiences seem to indicate a continuation of consciousness after clinical death and to hint at an afterlife. First brought to the world's attention in 1975 by Raymond Moody in *Life After Life,* these experiences are still the subject of much research.

Perhaps these OBEs and NDEs may be thought of as psychical rather than spiritual, particularly if they are merely interpreted as being unusually different from day-to-day reality in a way which may be explained in the future. However, their lasting effect is often a spiritual one, as many people change their lives as a consequence of such an experience, becoming more aware of others and often changing their profession and attitudes. Many also begin a spiritual exploration, triggered by the event. OBEs and NDEs also seem to indicate that the mind or spirit can exist outside the body, which is very much part of a religious view of life and death, so they need to be included in the range of experiences to be considered.

3. Spiritual Experience and Religions

Spiritual experiences can lead to a perspective that life is set within the context of a greater reality. This may well imply an underlying moral order entailing reverence for all living beings, in particular love of one's neighbour, expressed in the Golden Rule of 'do as you would be done by'. There is frequently an emphasis on inner peace and perhaps meditation. It will be obvious that many of these attitudes can also be found at the heart of the world's religious traditions. While religions are composites which include doctrines, practices and communities, here our concern will be with the foundational experience and the resulting texts.

Founders/Messengers

Although not true in every case, many religious traditions trace their origins to the experiences of a remarkable individual. As William James put it, although referring to 'churches', the same may be taken to apply to religions other than Christianity,

> Churches, when once established, live at secondhand upon tradition; but the *founders* of every church owed their power originally to the fact of their direct personal communion with the divine.[17]

The Buddha, Abraham, Moses, Jesus, Muhammad and Guru Nanak began movements of followers which have stood the test of time, although inevitably changing over the years. Within religious traditions, certain individuals have stood out such as Francis of Assisi or Mahatma Gandhi. Gurus, or teachers, also inspire followers, like Maharishi Mahesh Yogi, who started the Transcendental Meditation or TM movement, which made meditation known to vast numbers in the West. His best-known disciples were the Beatles. Other spiritual leaders such as the Pope or the Tibetan Buddhist leader, the Dalai Lama, have world-wide influence. Much can be learned from their spiritual experiences.

Spiritual Experience and Religions

Traditions have grown out of personal experience and faith in various ways. In Judaism it was in the form of the giving of a law and initiation of a covenant. Islam was the result of the giving of the message of the Qur'an. In Christianity the revelation came in the form of the incarnation in the life, death and resurrection of Jesus Christ. These experiences of revelation have led to the establishment of major religions. Other religious revelations have come in the form of prophecy or communication from the divine, miracles, visions or voices.

Individuals whose message has had this kind of transformative effect are sometimes called founders but other terms are often used. John Macquarrie's book *The Mediators* takes nine such figures who have 'brought that conception of God to the people'.[18] He has taken the term from the eighteenth-century German theologian Schleiermacher, whose *Speeches on Religion to its Cultured Despisers* strongly advocates an experiential approach to religion. In *Six Religions in the Twenty-First Century* by W. Owen Cole and Peggy Morgan, these key figures are not seen as founders, as the foundation for most religions is considered to be transcendent rather than human, so they use the term messengers.

Texts

Sacred texts are treated with respect within places of worship and some of the most beautiful books ever made are of religious writings: scrolls of the Torah, illuminated Gospels and intricately decorated copies of the Qur'an. The production and care of these texts were acts undertaken with reverence. The scriptures contain the teachings on which the religious traditions are based, and are consulted for inspiration and also for practical advice on how to live.

Sikhs revere their holy book, the Adi Granth, as a teacher, for it replaced the power inherent in the line of Gurus, to mediate between human and divine. The book is an object of devotion in the Sikh gurdwara (temple), kept on a raised platform and covered when not being used. If kept at home, the book must have a special room to itself. Problems can be solved or strength given to face them through consultation of the book.

> We would go to a person, actually, or seek the guidance of the Guru Granth Sahib. We do that because it's a book full of all sorts of information; and then, if sometimes you cannot read, then you ask a granthi or a priest who will help. What happens is that they open the book at random and read what is on that page: specially sometimes there are some solutions.[19]

Some revelatory experiences have taken the form of instructions to write, leading to texts which are then respected as special teachings or even revered as holy writ. According to Muslims, Muhammad was instructed to read or recite, which is what *Qur'an* means. What he recited was not written down until some years later.

> Alone in the cave of Hira, Muhammad continued to search for truth and meaning. Then the Angel Gabriel suddenly appeared to him and ordered: 'Read!' Muhammad answered: 'I am not of those who read.'[20]

In an entirely different situation, in 1976, a militant atheist, Dr. Helen Schucman, was extremely unhappy to receive instructions to take down material which continued to be given over a seven-year period. This inner dictation led to the composition of *A Course in Miracles*,[21] a manual of spiritual development.

It is a matter of debate just how far texts may be accepted as direct revelation, how far the authors felt that they were merely recording the words of the Lord and to what extent the process was a human interpretation of divine inspiration. Translation has been an important issue for texts deemed to have been directly revealed. The Vedas are often regarded as having been given in the holy language of Sanskrit. They were not translated for years to preserve their authenticity. As the Qur'an is generally believed by Muslims to have been received by Muhammad in Arabic from the Angel Jibril (Gabriel), it was not translated for many years, so that this direct communication was not compromised. Greater difficulties arise when considering texts which have been built up over time such as the Bible, where it is more difficult to maintain that words from the divine have been accurately recorded and preserved.

Neither Jesus nor the Buddha wrote anything down. Their experiences were recorded by those who either knew them or of them and were inspired by them. The Christian and Buddhist texts recount the original experiences of the founders of the traditions, their teachings and the early history of the movements which grew up around their memory. They are thus a testament to the effect of the revelation on the early followers, who composed the texts. Their motivation in setting down such material was faith in the vision of the founder, so the accounts cannot be taken as neutral. The Gospels were composed by followers of Jesus in order that the events of his life and death and his teaching should not be lost. It was the Buddha's cousin Ananda, who accompanied him on his journeys, and was influential in setting up the *Sangha* or community of monks, who recited the Buddha's sermons which were later recorded in written form for posterity.

Spiritual Experience and Religions

The issue of literal interpretation versus a metaphorical or more liberal reading is an ongoing debate across and within religious traditions. While some believers base their lives on an exact reading of scripture, others are of the view that myth and fact are hard to separate in books which have evolved slowly, often only written down after a lengthy period of oral tradition. Within most religious traditions there are literalists who take the scripture at face value and focus on the actual wording, while others take a more open, liberal view of their scripture, focusing on the overall message. These differences of approach are often as deep as those between liberals of different religious persuasions.

Modern historical research into the origins of many of the sacred texts shows how their development over lengthy periods of time indicates that too literal an interpretation is not justified. A more critical response is called for. It may be more accurate to accept that divine revelation has come through the medium of a human being and is therefore inevitably influenced not only by the culture and place of the original revelation, but also by the authors, and the place and culture of the time of writing. An understanding that the text itself should not be seen as infallible would be helpful when differences between religions lead to dispute.

Another factor to be considered with regard to scripture is the limitation of language, any language, in expressing spiritual experience. Scriptures may be read on different levels, with historical fact and legend mingling in a way which opens the way to various levels of interpretation.

Oral traditions such as those of Africa, North America and Australia thrive as they maintain their cultural heritage, rituals and beliefs, which often have deep links to nature. There is often a shamanic element, that is contact with sprits within nature and of the dead by means of a medium or shaman. These are potent, experiential traditions of spirituality and after much suppression are now being increasingly valued. In Japan, Shinto has no founder and no scriptures, but the spiritual reality of *kami*, which means sacred power, is inherent in the universe. It can be found in nature or in people, and the Emperor, for example, is regarded as manifesting kami.

The relationship between experience and religious text is well described by Fr Bede Griffiths,

> ... there is a mode of experience which transcends both body and soul, an experience of the Spirit, which is not merely rational and so dependent on the senses, but intuitive – a direct insight which comes not from the soul and its faculties but from the Spirit himself, the absolute, which is present in the ground of the soul of everyman and reveals itself to those who seek him. Yet when we begin to speak

of that experience, we have once more to use the language of sense and reason, and the reality of that which we have experienced can never properly be expressed.

This limitation imposes itself on all human language. The language of the Vedas, the Upanishads and the Bhagavad Gita, ... goes as far as it is possible to go towards breaking down this barrier. ... The Bible is often described as the word of God, but it is the word of God expressed through the words of men with the inevitable limitation of all human words. ... The Bible habitually uses the language of myth and symbol and even when there is a historical basis for a story, it is worked over by the imagination and transformed into a myth, that is, into a symbolic expression of ultimate reality. [22]

Development

The experiences of the founders or key figures at the origin of the major religious traditions not only took place within a certain civilization and historical and cultural context but also often within the context of an existing religion. The aim of many of those who had the revelatory experience was often not to found a new tradition at all, but rather to amend the existing order. However, there were times when the overwhelming insights gained by a few extraordinary individuals led not merely to a reappraisal of the existing religious tradition but to the creation of a new religion. Jesus, a Jew, did not intend to found Christianity.

Many of the great religious traditions owe their inspiration to people who had experiences so profound that they appeared to their contemporaries to have extraordinary spiritual insight and authority. They attracted followers during their lifetime and after their deaths, movements of people emulating their lives and following their teachings emerged. Often, however, as these movements develop and the organization grows, human dynamics take over and schisms arise. There is a tendency to rely too heavily on texts, ritual and doctrine rather than on the original vision. There is a risk of stagnation, what Durkheim calls 'the routinisation of charisma' in his *Elementary Forms of Religious Life*. New insights are then needed to revitalize the tradition and these sometimes come to saints and mystics who may find themselves on the edge of their tradition. Yet their influence often moves the religion in a different direction. In a few cases this may actually lead to the establishment of another tradition. This can also happen as a result of traditions affecting each other, absorbing insights and practices from one another. Religions are fluid and evolving entities.

Spiritual Experience and Religions

Apart from the mainstream religions, there are groupings or movements which are of interest as they blend spiritualities in new, innovative ways and are often more concerned with the experiential side than with the more formal aspects of faith.

New Religious Movements

The term New Religious Movement covers a wide range of organizations. Often born of a reaction to entrenched, formal religion, but not repudiating it entirely, or from a fusion of two or more religions, these religious movements are not usually entirely new. In many parts of the world, under colonialism, religions were imposed on indigenous peoples. Later a fusion of the original spiritual tradition and the imported one resulted in the creation of New Religious Movements.

New Age Movements

New Age Movements arose in the West through a fascination with the religions of the East, meditation and yoga and in the counter-culture of the 1960s. Adherents eschew formal, hierarchical religion preferring direct experience and a creative spirituality. New Agers take elements from various traditions, often incorporating esoteric and paranormal trends, creating an eclectic fusion to suit themselves. More recently an interest in the occult and paganism has arisen, along with sessions of channelling, where contact with a deceased spiritual teacher or luminary is made and messages received. An interest in healing and shamanism is often part of this view and a holistic vision of the individual and of the planet is typical, often leading to specific dietary preferences and vegetarianism.

New Agers constitute a loose fellowship of individuals and small groups with a wide variety of interests and beliefs. Magazines abound and all over the country there are numerous courses and gatherings of all kinds of alternative spiritualities and holistic practices. New Age ceremonies are often held outside or at ancient spiritual sites. The internet provides a good linking mechanism for such movements.

Interfaith Movements

In recent years there has been a growth of interfaith dialogue between leaders and members of different faith traditions, with many different organizations coming into being. Many major events in Britain, such as the Service of Remembrance on 11 November at the Cenotaph in London now routinely include the leaders of different religious traditions, who often know each other well, as their paths cross frequently these days. Co-operation between faith communities is a fact of life and often goes unreported.

The First World's Parliament of Religions was held in Chicago in 1893. Four thousand people from all over the world gathered there, a colourful sight as the bright robes of different religious traditions mingled. Two further events were held there, in 1933 a gathering called the Second World Parliament of Religions was organized by the World Fellowship of Faiths. In 1993 there was a centennial celebration of the first Parliament. The Parliament of the World's Religions then moved, to Cape Town, South Africa in 1999 and to Barcelona, Spain in 2004. At these events representatives of over a hundred different religions shared news, views and generally got to know each other in an atmosphere of joyful exploration and harmony. The Council for a Parliament of the World's Religions plans the next Parliament in 2009 in Melbourne, Australia.

There are many interfaith organizations, some working internationally for peace, others at a local level on social projects, The World Congress of Faiths, The International Association for Religious Freedom, United Religions Initiative, Temple of Understanding, the Inter-Faith Network UK and the North American Interfaith Network to name but a few. Many hold conferences and organize discussion groups to explore each other's beliefs and practices. The aim of them all is to promote dialogue and constructive efforts in mutual understanding and co-operation at all levels of society. An overview of the movement is to be found in *Faith and Interfaith in a Global Age* by Marcus Braybrooke and his *A Heart for the World* looks at the depressing world scenario of materialism, terrorism and environmental desecration and suggests an interfaith alternative.

For some people, interfaith has become a faith in itself and Interfaith Ministers are now being ordained, to perform services of worship which are all-inclusive, blending insights from the major world traditions and embracing a generalised spirituality.

Quasi-Religions

Although religions usually have a transcendental focus, there is a view that would include other worldviews as religious. These days football has become an overwhelming passion for many, breaking through divisions of sex, age and class and splintering into allegiances to clubs and teams but within a shared community of fans. When people die, their support of their team is frequently quoted as part of their identity. This is a kind of implicit religion, which is found in many secular aspects of life, with communal rituals and shared beliefs forming a cohesive community.

The worldviews of Marxism and humanism can be considered to function as religions unless the definition of religion is thought necessarily to include an awareness of another dimension.

Marxism

Karl Marx (1818–83) reasoned that it was the ruling classes who gained from the illusory happiness of religion, 'the opium of the people' which kept the oppressed lower orders content and maintained the social equilibrium which served them well. Marx predicted that religion would die out if social inequality were to be overcome, as real happiness for the working classes would supplant the illusion offered by religion. He was followed rather like a religious leader and communist countries have been run with this underlying worldview. The twentieth century however has seen the fall of communism and the rise of religious fundamentalism, despite increased equality and prosperity, giving the lie to the Marxist viewpoint.

Although it is evident that prosperity has not dispelled religion, Liberation Theology which began in Latin America, maintains that the insights gained from Marx on power and aggression are still relevant. The analysis is that developed countries are kept rich by the poor remaining oppressed and that Christians need to become engaged in the struggle to change this.

Humanism

There are many different humanisms: Christian, Cultural, Literary, Modern, Philosophical, Renaissance, Religious and Secular. They trace their roots to Ancient Greece and Socrates in particular. All share a view of life as all in itself, with no transcendent level of reality and no continuity of any kind after death. They accept an evolutionary view and humanity as responsible for the fate of the species and the planet. Theirs is a reason-based ethic, independent of any transcendent good. Humanists may think of themselves as religious or secular, depending on their view of what constitutes religion. Many take part in ceremonies to mark the major transitions of birth, marriage and death without recourse to any religious tradition, even providing humanist officiants to lead non-religious funerals.

4. Experiences of the Founders/Messengers of the Major Religious Traditions

Religions are not neat compartments with clear demarcations; they are living, changing, adapting and often splintering movements of groups of people, linked by their perception of a vision which they share to a greater or lesser extent. This must be borne in mind when reading the accounts below. Labels have been used for convenience and to enable the possibility of forming a coherent, if somewhat generalized overview.

Let us look at the insights or revelations of some of the messengers or founders of the major religious traditions in so far as they are known. It is not easy to distinguish fact from fiction, particularly looking further back in time, where one has to contend with lengthy periods of oral tradition. Subsequent embellishment leads to history, myth and legend becoming inextricably interwoven. It is a matter of interpretation as to how far these biographies can be taken as factual accounts and how far they should be read as spiritual patterns. However, towards modern times more accurate reports of the lives of the founders become available, although again, leaders of spiritual movements are particularly susceptible to hagiography or vilification. The following accounts give the main spiritual experiences in the lives of these key figures as accurately as possible. What is important is that these people seem to have transcended everyday reality and seen the world from a new perspective which not only changed their own lives but also resonated with their contemporaries. It is an account of the origins of religious traditions from a personal, experiential standpoint. Much can be learned about spirituality by considering the experiences, lives and even the myths surrounding these unusual people.

Hinduism

The word 'Hindu' was originally used to refer to the people who lived beyond the Indus River, and later used by the British to designate

Religious and Spiritual Experience

Hindustanis, who lived in North West India. Later still it was a term used by Indians in opposition to colonial rule and nowadays it is still a term of political identification. However, in religious terms, the Hindu tradition refers to a group of religious people with a vast array of beliefs and practices, many of whom would not see Hinduism as a religion at all, but a spiritual way of life, entailing an acceptance of many different religious paths. Many prefer the term *sanatana dharma*, meaning the eternal truth.

In this tradition, there was no revelation to any particular individual. It was the rishis (seers) who composed the revelatory texts, known as the four *Vedas* (the word means knowledge) in Sanskrit between 1500 and 500 BCE. The oldest of these was the *Rig Veda* and the others the *Sama, Yajur* and *Atharva*. These were revealed directly (*shruti*) to the rishis, and the very words of these texts were revered as holy and often recited as mantras. The *Vedas* comprise hymns, ritual, esoteric, mystical and philosophical texts, which originally accompanied the fire sacrifices, performed by the Brahmins, the priestly caste. The *Brahmanas, Aranyakas* and *Upanishads* (hidden teachings) were interpretations of these texts.

Later texts were distinguished from these original Vedas, by being designated as *smriti*, meaning 'memory'. The principal teachings were that this eternally changing world is not reality itself, which is unchanging and eternal. The ground of all being, Brahman, is *sat, cit, ananda* – being, consciousness and bliss – and is identical with the individual soul, *atman*.

> This whole world is the perishable and the imperishable, the manifest and the unmanifest joined together – and the Lord bears it, while the self (*atman*), who is not the Lord, remains bound because he is the enjoyer. When he comes to know God he is freed from all fetters. . . . The one God rules over both the perishable and the self (*atman*). By meditating on him, by striving towards him, and, further, in the end by becoming the same reality as him, all illusion disappears.[23]

Brahman is worshipped as Shiva, Vishnu and Brahma and as the Goddess in the forms of Kali, Durga, Parvati or Lakshmi. Theistic movements such as Vaishnavism developed for the worship of Vishnu, who protects the universe and is often depicted with four arms or being transported on a bird, his garuda. Shaivism is the adoration of Shiva. Often shown as a dancing figure, Shiva does not generally have avatars or incarnations, although he can manifest himself at will. He is seen as the destroyer of the world but is also worshipped as an erect phallus and the consort of Parvati.

If there is one personality who is representative of Hinduism, it is Krishna. He is regarded as an avatar of Vishnu, traditionally thought to be the eighth. Although his actual existence is still disputed, it is said that he was born in the third century BCE in Mathura, between Delhi and Agra. Legend has it that he was born a Prince, but to avoid envy at court, was brought up by the daughter of a cowherd. There are tales of his mischievous youth and later dallying with milkmaids as well as of his skilful flute playing and miracles. His love of the maids or *gopis* is interpreted as the love of God toward souls.

In the *Bhagavadgita* (*The Gita*) section of the *Mahabharata* epic, Krishna joins Arjuna on the eve of battle between two related dynasties, the Kauravas and the Pandavas. Arjuna sees his own relatives on both opposing sides and is full of anxiety. Disguised as his charioteer, Krishna explains how one should follow one's calling in life and for Arjuna this is as a warrior. Humans experience repeated lives and deaths and Krishna expounds upon the transmigration of souls. He also reassures Arjuna that the divine love ensures that God will manifest in any epoch when humans are in need of illumination.

Arjuna asks Krishna to show himself in his divine manifestation. Krishna explains that Arjuna needs 'mystic eyes', in other words spiritual vision for this, and then reveals himself as the Lord of the universe, which is described by Arjuna in the text,

> Your form is difficult to see because of its glaring effulgence, spreading on all sides, like blazing fire or the immeasurable radiance of the sun. Yet I see this glowing form everywhere, adorned with various crowns, clubs and discs.
>
> You are the supreme primal objective. You are the ultimate resting place of all this universe. You are inexhaustible, and You are the oldest. You are the maintainer of the eternal religion, the Personality of Godhead. This is my opinion.[24]

Krishna shows himself in other manifestations and explains different spiritual paths such as action in Karma Yoga, and the meditation of Dhyana Yoga but the practice of devotion or bhakti is considered the highest.

> He who meditates on Me as the Supreme Personality of Godhead, his mind constantly engaged in remembering Me, undeviated from the path, he, O Partha, is sure to reach me.[25]

Such devotion to Krishna continues, particularly in the International Society for Krishna Consciousness (the Hare Krishnas).

Zoroastrianism

Zarathushtra (Zoroaster) lived in Persia, probably in the 7th Century BCE. He was a priest, married with children and had a series of illuminating visions, which led to new teachings.

> When he was thirty years old, one early morning, he went to fetch some water from the river. It was around dawn. The sky had just turned colour and the sun was about to rise. As he had gone into the waters of the river, Vohu Mana (the angel of the Good Mind) appears to him, and opens the portal to the Divine Light of Ahura Mazda. This was the first moment of Illumination and the first Revelations of Zarathushtra.
>
> In his vision, he perceived Ahura Mazda as the Wise Lord of Creation, and the six emanations of Ahura Mazda, the Amesha Spentas as the guardians and artisans of this physical world. He perceived the laws upon which the universe operated, and understood the inter-relationship between Ahura Mazda, the Amesha Spentas and the Creation.[26]

Although he converted some members of his family, his teachings were initially rejected and he left his home. After many years of persistence, he managed to convert Kavi (King) Vishtaspa, in northern Persia, and the new religion was launched, which subsequently spread throughout the Persian Empire.

Zarathushtra initiated the worship of 'Ahura Mazda' the one God, who was opposed by Angra Mainyu. The world was seen as offering a choice between the forces of good and evil. Worship took place in temples where fires, burning continuously, symbolized the light of the One God and rituals included purification and the singing of hymns known as *Gathas*, which still survive.

Zoroastrians still prefer not to bury their dead, avoiding pollution of earth, air and water. The corpses are exposed on so-called Towers of Silence for vultures to devour. Priests were called Magi and it is thought that the wise men who visited Bethlehem when Jesus was born may have been Zoroastrians. Today the main followers of Zoroastrianism are the Parsis in India.

Jainism

The founder was known as Mahavira, which means 'Great Hero'. It is said that he was a Prince who probably lived in the 6th or 5th Century BCE in the Ganges valley. He left home at the age of 30 and spent the next twelve and half years practicing meditation and fasting, freeing himself from desires, feelings and attachments. After a time, he also freed himself from clothes, and went about naked.

In the thirteenth year he achieved enlightenment, the clarity of insight known as *kevala*. Mahavira spent the next 30 years travelling around India preaching about the eternal truth. His ultimate objective was to show how to attain total freedom from karma – rebirth according to one's just deserts – and achieve *moksha* or liberation. He was considered to be the 24th and last *Tirthankar* or 'Fordmaker' providing humans access to salvation. On his death at the age of 72 he was considered to have become a *Siddha* or pure consciousness, having attained *Nirvana*.

His teachings were based on a view of the universe as eternal, uncreated. Mahavira enjoined complete non-violence, or *ahimsa*, and his teaching of not harming any form of life led monks to sweep the ground before walking to ensure no loss of insect life and even to wear a mask to avoid swallowing any living creature. His teachings were written down after a period of oral transmission as the *Agam Sutras*.

It was into this religious world, in about 500 BCE in India, that the Buddha was born.

Buddhism

It is known that the Buddha lived for 80 years and most probably from c484– c404 BCE.[27] Siddhartha Gautama was born a prince of the Sakya clan in Kapilavastu, in modern Nepal. Because of a prophecy at his birth that he would either become an emperor or a holy man, his father, in order to avoid the latter, ensured that he remained in the palace, protected from the realities of life. He was surrounded by luxury and had a beautiful wife and a son. However, aged about 30, he left the palace with his charioteer to explore the outside world. He discovered the 'Four Signs': he saw an old man, a sick man and a corpse and learned that age, sickness and death were a normal part of everyone's life. He then saw a sannyasin or holy man and it was explained that this man was searching for a way to understand and overcome these states.

This changed his life. As a result, in what became known as the Great Renunciation, Siddhartha left his wife, child and family to go out into the world to seek the wisdom to overcome age, sickness and death. After much fruitless exploration and years of ascetic practice he sat down under a fig tree, vowing to remain until he gained Enlightenment.

There, he had a profound experience of insight into the nature of life, death and human suffering and what is needed to overcome this. Thus he became the Buddha, One who is Enlightened or Awake and the tree became known as the Bodhi Tree (Tree of Enlightenment). Siddhartha had awoken to the human predicament, to an awareness of the roots of human suffering, which lie in enslavement to greed, hatred and delusion. It is said that Mara, a representation of evil, attempted to thwart Gautama's efforts but was ultimately unsuccessful.

The Buddha's first sermon was preached in the Deer Park in Banaras (Benares), to a group of friends, who had accompanied him on his ascetic search. This was later referred to as the first turning of the Wheel of the Dharma, and marked the beginning of his teaching life, which lasted about forty years. He taught the Four Noble Truths:

The reality of suffering in life;
The cause – selfish desire;
The possibility of overcoming this;
The means, through the Noble Eightfold Path:
 right views, right thoughts, right speech, right action, right livelihood, right effort, right mindfulness, right concentration.

Gautama is regarded as one of a series of Buddhas or enlightened beings to appear on the earth. He is the Buddha for our age, but another, Maitreya, is expected, and many have existed before in previous ages.

Buddhists follow the Buddha's teachings, whether in the Mahayama, Theravada or Vajrayana schools, which have given rise to other movements such as Zen and Pure Land Buddhism in Japan. When Buddhism spread to China, two philosophies or spiritual movements already held sway, Daoism or Taoism and Confucianism. Little is known for certain about the founders of these traditions, although there is no shortage of legends.

Daoism (Taoism)

Laoze (Lao-Tsu), meaning 'Old Master', was said to have been the author of the *Daode Jing* (*Book of the Dao* or *Way and Its Virtue*) some time between the sixth and fourth century BCE in China. Legend has it that the wise teacher was so disillusioned with humans that he was on his way into exile when the city gatekeeper asked him to write down the principles of his philosophy before he left.

The Dao or Tao is a mystical work advocating a way of life in harmony with nature as well as society, a way of spontaneous action and inner peace. This may be summed up as *wu wei* or going with the flow of life and the natural world. *Feng shui*, meaning wind and water, is a method of aligning dwelling and working places in harmony with nature in order to bring prosperity and good health. From the Dao we have the principles of Yin (feminine, passive, dark, associated with the moon and night) and the opposite, Yang (masculine, active, bright, associated with the sun and day). The concept of Qi (Chi) meaning air, breath and energy is also important. Energy permeates the universe and also human beings, and qigong is a way of getting oneself into harmony with this essential energy. In Oriental art the brushstrokes used in calligraphy, writing and painting are infused with Qi and the paintings include spaces for the energy to flow. The Dao or Tao is a mystical work which points beyond the everyday world, and this is expressed in its well-known opening sentence,

The Tao that can be told is not the eternal Tao.[28]

Confucianism

Generally accepted as being a younger contemporary of Laoze, K'ung Fu-tzu (Confucius) (551– 479 BCE) was a Chinese sage whose teachings were eventually brought together by his disciples into the Five Classics three centuries after his death. These works include the *I-ching* or *Book of Changes*.

Biographical details are sketchy but it is thought that Confucius was of noble birth but became a civil servant. He left Lu where he was born and travelled throughout China for many years, promulgating his moral teachings. His sayings and actions were later recorded in *Lun Yu (The Analects)*. He was mainly interested in ethical and political matters and *The Analects* comprise a guide to living with compassion for others. His message was one of *li* or moral rectitude, social cohesion, study and ritual piety, perhaps more philosophical than religious. It is from Confucius that we have the Golden Rule of *jen* or virtue: 'What you do not wish for yourself, do not do to others'.

Judaism

At its heart, Judaism is a religion founded on the relationship of a covenant between God and his chosen people with the terms set out in the *Torah*, the first five books of the Bible, also known as the Pentateuch.

In the book of Genesis, the story of the first covenant is told, that between God and Noah, a covenant wider than just with the Jewish people. At the time of a great flood, sent by God to destroy his creatures because of their wickedness, Noah followed God's instructions in building an ark and he and his descendents were saved. The sign of the covenant was that of a rainbow.[29]

The second covenant was with Abraham, formerly Abram or Avram. He left Ur of the Chaldees in Mesapotamia for Canaan and was to be the father of the nation. The twelve tribes of Israel are his descendents through his grandson Jacob. According to the book of Genesis, Abraham conceived his first child at 99 years old. His obedience to God was tested when he was instructed to sacrifice his son Isaac, who was only spared at the last minute.[30]

Although Abraham is seen as the first monotheist, it is Moses who is usually accepted as the founder of the Jewish religious tradition, as it was to him that the Torah was given. Moses was born in the 13th Century BCE, while the people of Israel were captive in Egypt. As a baby, Moses was hidden in a basket among the reeds and was discovered and adopted by an Egyptian princess. His loyalties were, however, with his own people, and he killed an Egyptian who had beaten a Hebrew slave. He subsequently fled Pharaoh's court, and became a shepherd. It was while tending sheep that Moses had his first recorded spiritual experience, of seeing a burning bush, which was not consumed by the fire and of hearing the voice of God instructing him to liberate the Israelites and to lead them to the promised land. This was the land of Canaan, nowadays known as Israel or Palestine. Assisted by his brother Aaron, Moses brought down extraordinary plagues upon Egypt to convince Pharaoh to let the people go. The Exodus is still commemorated by Jews today at *Pesach* (Passover).

The covenant between God and his people was fully revealed to Moses on Mount Sinai with the commandments recorded in the *Torah* (which means 'divine instruction'). Moses was seen as standing before God in a unique way, subsequently reflecting the glory of God.

> And the Lord said to Moses, 'Write these words; in accordance with these words I have made a covenant with you and with Israel.' And he was there with the Lord forty days and forty nights; he neither ate bread nor drank water. And he wrote upon the tables the words of the covenant, the ten commandments.
>
> When Moses came down from Mount Sinai, with the two tables of the testimony in his hand as he came down from the mountain, Moses did not know that the skin of his face shone because he had been talking with God.[31]

Major Religious Traditions

Moses is revered not only by Jews, but also by Christians. Muslims too hold him in high esteem, referring to him as Musa, one who conversed with God. Both these religious traditions have their roots in the Jewish tradition. After the time of Moses, the Prophets of Israel including Elijah, Elisha, Isaiah, Jeremiah and Ezekiel, reported revelations from God, giving warnings and advice. Jesus too was considered to be a prophet in this line, but one whose entire will was so submitted to God, that he was later called the Son of God.

Christianity

Jesus was born in Palestine, probably around 6 CE and his life was lived in close communication with God, whom he called 'Abba', a familiar term for father. Despite the Christmas stories, which link the birth of Jesus to Bethlehem and the lineage of King David, little is actually known of his life. It is recorded that he was baptized in the River Jordan by John the Baptist. There he had a vision of the heavens opening and heard the voice of the Father proclaiming

> Thou art my beloved son; with thee I am well pleased.[32]

This heralded the beginning of his ministry. First he withdrew into the wilderness to contemplate this role and to face the temptations it might bring. Subsequently he taught in parables and preached the coming of the Kingdom of God, that the will of God should be followed on earth. He performed healing and other miracles, such as the feeding of the five thousand. His main teaching was given in the 'Sermon on the Mount' which included the Beatitudes and the 'Lord's Prayer'. Jesus lived a simple life, dependent on God for his needs and preached accordingly,

> 'Consider the lilies of the field, how they grow; they neither toil nor sin; yet I tell you, even Solomon in all his glory was not arrayed like one of these. But if God so clothes the grass of the field, which today is alive and tomorrow is thrown in the oven, will he not much more clothe you, O men of little faith? Wherefore be not anxious, saying, "What shall we eat?" or "What shall we drink?" or "What shall we wear?" For the Gentiles seek these things; and your heavenly Father knows that you need them all. But seek first his kingdom and his righteousness, and all these things shall be yours as well.' [Matthew 6:28–33]

Religious and Spiritual Experience

He travelled with 12 disciples, chosen from among his countrymen and his ministry lasted for about 3 years before he arrived in Jerusalem. There he was arrested, tried by Pontius Pilate and crucified at the time of the Feast of the Passover. According to the Gospels, Jesus had previously indicated his acceptance of his fate. After his death his followers had extraordinary experiences convincing them that Jesus had been raised from the dead. They seemed to meet him and he reassured them that he was still with them. The disciples then had the experience of Pentecost,

> When the day of Pentecost had come, they were all together in one place. And suddenly a sound came from heaven like the rush of a mighty wind, and it filled all the house where they were sitting. And there appeared to them tongues as of fire, distributed and resting on each one of them. And they were filled with the Holy Spirit and began to speak in other tongues, as the spirit gave them utterance. (Acts 2: 1–4)

They then went outside to preach. At the time there were people from many different countries in the city, and everyone, whatever their own language, was able to understand what the disciples were saying. The apostles, or early followers of Jesus, began worshipping and preaching Jesus as the risen Messiah, the Christ, meaning 'the Anointed One'. He was seen as the Son of God and his death a sacrificial act on behalf of humanity,

> For God so loved the world that he gave his only Son, that whoever believes in him may have eternal life. [John 3:16]

As the word was spread, notably by St Paul, the movement grew away from Judaism and the Christian Church was established. Accounts of these early days and the life of Jesus were eventually written down as the Gospels within the New Testament as a continuation of the Hebrew Scriptures to make the Bible.

The faith became the official religion of the Roman Empire in 381 CE and eventually spread worldwide. It later split into three main branches, Roman Catholic, Protestant and Eastern Orthodox.

Islam

Muhammad is considered by Muslims to be the last of the prophets of the Bible, beginning with Adam right through to Jesus. Muslims believe that Muhammad was sent by God to rectify misunderstandings of followers in this line, and so he is revered as the seal of the prophets.

Born in Makkah (Mecca) around 570 CE, Muhammad lost his father before he was born and his mother when he was six years old. He was cared for first by his grandfather then his uncle. He worked for and later married Khadija, a widow some fifteen years older. It was she who helped and supported Muhammad when he had doubts about his revelations.

Muhammad used to go into a mountain cave to meditate and it was when he was about forty years old that he began having visions. On what became known as 'the Night of Qadr' (Power or Glory), recorded in *Surah* (Section) 97 of the Qur'an,

> We revealed this on the Night of Qadr. Would that you knew what the Night of Qadr is like!
> Better is the Night of Qadr than a thousand months.
> On that night the Angels and the Spirit by their Lord's leave come down with each decree.
> That night is peace, till break of dawn.

He had a vision of the Angel Jibril (Gabriel), who instructed him to 'Read' or 'Recite' (*Qur'an* means recitation). This is recorded in Surah 96 of the Qur'an, which begins,

> In the name of God, the Compassionate, the Merciful
> Recite in the name of your Lord who created – created man from clots of blood.
> Recite! Your Lord is the Most Bountiful One, who by the pen taught man what he did not know.

According to Muslims, Muhammad was illiterate, but the word of God was imparted directly to him. It was a message to Jews and Christians as well as to the pagan polytheists of Arabia, to bring them back to the essential message, to the worship of God alone. He received the *Qur'an* over a period of 23 years, committing it to memory. It was not written down until after Muhammad's death when it is generally held that Abu Bakr compiled the surahs, arranging them by length, beginning with the shortest.

For 12 years Muhammad taught the supremacy of the all-powerful, merciful creator Allah, establishing Islam, which in Arabic means 'submission' (to the will of Allah). There was much hostility to his teachings and in 622 CE, in what is known as the *Hijra*, Muhammad moved to Yathrib, later known as Al-Madinah an-Nabi (the City of the Prophet), then simply Madinah (Medina). However, in 630 he returned and conquered Makkah, which eventually became the main site of the *Hajj* (pilgrimage) which all Muslims are enjoined to undertake as one of the Five Pillars of Islam. The other four are the instruction to pray five times a day in the direction (qibla) of the *Ka'aba* in Makkah, almsgiving, fasting during the lunar month of Ramadan and the repetition of *La Ilaha illa Allah: Muhammad rasul Allah* (there is no god but Allah and Muhammad is his prophet).

Apart from his revelations, Muhammad had another extraordinary experience, that of the 'Night Journey'. On a steed named al-Buraq and accompanied by the Angel Jibril, he went to the Temple Mount in Jerusalem and prayed in the company of Abraham and Moses. He then ascended to the seventh heaven, where teachings were given to him. On the way home he saw a caravan approaching the city, and was able to substantiate the events of the night by announcing their arrival in advance in order to silence his critics.

After a long and successful life, Muhammad died in 632 CE. He was succeeded by four early followers Abu Bakr, Umar, Uthman and Ali but there was argument about the leadership and the Muslims split into Sunnis, the majority, who initiated a caliphate and upheld *Shari'a* law, and the Shi'as, who were led by Imams, thought to be infallible in their interpretation of the *Qur'an*. In the eighth century the mystic Sufi movements began and despite some hostility are now a part of both Sunni and Shi'a life. However, controversy still surrounds Sufi movements which are banned in Saudi Arabia.

Sikhism

The first of the ten gurus of the Sikhs, was Guru Nanak. He lived from 1469 to 1539 in Lahore, in the Punjab. He declined a life in business, instead pursuing an interest in the Hindu and Muslim religions. While bathing in the river, he had a revelatory experience and subsequently went missing for three days. On his return he proclaimed 'There is no Hindu, there is no Mussulman', meaning that in God's eyes such categories are unimportant. Guru Nanak practised bhakti or loving devotion to one God, *Waheguru* – True Guru, and adhered to a strict moral code. He enjoined his followers, known as 'Sikhs' which means 'learners', to recite the name of the Lord, to work honestly and to share their food with others. He was a bridge between the Hindu and Muslim communities, attempting to avoid ritualism and intolerance by offering a new spiritual vision.

After his death nine other gurus followed until the last, Guru Gobind Singh (1666 – 1708) announced the end of the line and established the order of the Khalsa. Since that time, Sikh authority is believed to reside in the *Adi Granth*, the holy scripture, called the *Guru Granth Sahib*. This was compiled by Guru Arjan (1563–1606) who also built the Harimandir or Golden Temple at Amritsar.

Sikhs keep the 5 Ks: *Kesh* – long, uncut hair; *Kangha* – comb to tend the hair; *Kara* – iron bangle, a reminder of the unbroken circle of truth; *Kaccha* – shorts for chastity; *Kirpan* – sword for defending freedom from oppression. Sikhs freely share food with others of any social position or religion by means of the '*Langar*' or community kitchen, which was a concept established by Guru Nanak and endures to this day. At the 2004 Parliament of the World's Religions in Barcelona a huge tent became the Langar, where free food was served to hundreds of delegates of all faiths and none.

5. Experiences of the Founders/Messengers of Less Well-Known Religious Traditions

Brahma Kumaris

This is a predominantly female movement – the name means the pure daughters of Brahma. It was, however, initiated by a man, Dada Lekhraj (1876–1969) who became known as Brahma Baba. He was brought up a Hindu and made his fortune as a jeweller. It was not until he was 60 years old, that his spiritual revelations began, in the form of visions of Shiva which occurred over a period of several months. He gained an insight into the divine which led to him giving up the business and founding a movement of Raja Yoga, which emphasized meditation and aimed at purity of body and soul, with members dressing symbolically in white. Brahma Baba lived until the age of 93.

He was succeeded by Dadi Prakashmani (1923–2007) as Chief Administrative Head (Dadi means elder sister). Born in Hyderabad, Sind, Dadi Prakashmani's childhood name was Rama. Her father was a renowned astrologer and foresaw his daughter's destiny to lead a spiritual life in the service of humanity that would span eight decades and reach across all continents. When she was only 14 years old, Rama became one of the Brahma Kumaris trustees, all of whom were women, and she took the name 'Prakashmani' ('Jewel of Light'). The course of her life was set and she went on to lead the movement, later joined by Dadi Janki (born 1916), as from its inception, the movement was led by women.

In 1984 Dadi Prakashmani was awarded the Peace Medal and she gave the presidential address at the Parliament of the Worlds' Religions Centenary in Chicago in 1993. The Brahma Kumaris World Spiritual University (BKWSU) now has centres worldwide and is increasingly socially engaged. In 1980 became a UN Non-Governmental Organization.

Brahmo Samaj

Rammohun Roy (1772–1833), son of a Brahmin, was a well-educated free-thinker who studied various religious traditions and disagreed with any form of what he considered idolatry, whether in Hinduism, Buddhism, Christianity or Islam. Seeing himself as a Hindu Unitarian, finding a monotheistic purity in the Vedas, he eventually founded the Brahmo Samaj in 1828 as a group of people committed to the worship of One God. He campaigned, ultimately successfully, against the practice of Sati (suttee).

The movement was subsequently led by Debendranath Tagore (1817–1905), the eldest son of Prince Dwarkanath Tagore. He had experiences of the immanence of God in all things, which moved him to turn his back on the luxurious life he could have led. Tagore disseminated the views of the movement, gained a large following and initiated services of worship. He compiled the *Brahmo Dharma* from passages in the *Upanishads* and established and a forest ashram in Bengal named Shantiniketan – the abode of peace. The movement expanded and spread, but ultimately split in 1866, when the Brahmo Samaj of India was formed. Tagore's son, Rabindranath, became a Nobel Prize-winning poet.

Baha'i

Baha'u'llah (1817–1892) which means 'The Glory of God' in Arabic, was the name taken by Mirza Husayn Ali when he assumed leadership of a group who thus became known as the Baha'is. A well-educated nobleman, married with three children, Husayn Ali, instead of following a political career, devoted himself to good works. This earned him the nickname 'Father of the Poor'. He was a follower of the Bab (meaning 'the gate') who led a religious movement, which aroused the ire of the Islamic clergy and led to the Bab's execution in 1850 and subsequently to Husayn Ali's arrest. Husayn Ali was spared death but imprisoned for four months in the 'Black Pit', a notorious dungeon in Tehran. It was there that he had a revelation that God sent manifestations to humanity from time to time, such as Zarathushtra, the Buddha, Jesus and the Bab.

> During the days I lay in the prison of Tihran, though the galling weight of the chains and the stench-filled air allowed Me but little sleep, still in those infrequent moments of slumber I felt as if something flowed from the crown of My head over My breast, even as a mighty torrent that precipitateth itself upon the earth from the summit of a lofty mountain. Every limb of My body would, as a result, be set afire. At such moments My tongue recited what no man could bear to hear.[33]

On release, he was banished but was accompanied by loyal followers who accepted that he was the next manifestation of the divine, as foretold by the Bab. A prolific writer, he wrote letters to world leaders including Queen Victoria, urging cooperation on an international level to bring about world peace. It was in exile in Akka (Acre) in Palestine, where he spent the last 24 years of his life, that he wrote the Kitab-i-Aqdas (the Most Holy Book). His teachings emphasize the oneness of God, religion and humanity.

Quakers

George Fox (1624–1691) having become disillusioned with formal creeds, decided to leave the Church of England to seek a more direct spiritual response to God. He led a solitary life, travelling widely throughout the country, and was known for his strong egalitarianism, epitomized by his refusal to doff his hat to anyone.

He had an extraordinary experience which he recorded in the first chapter of his diary,

> then, oh, then, I heard a voice which said, 'There is one, even Christ Jesus, that can speak to thy condition'; and when I heard it, my heart did leap for joy.[34]

He found comfort in a close relationship with Jesus Christ through the guidance of his own 'Inner Light' and spirit. He travelled around the country, spreading his message to groups of friends. Although welcomed by some, he endured harsh conditions and no little opposition as he spoke to crowds of people in towns and market places. He occasionally interrupted church services, to proclaim 'the truth', and was imprisoned eight times. Such was his faith that he did whatever he felt God told him, however strange. One day he felt compelled to leave his shoes with shepherds outside the city of Lichfield and to go through the streets crying 'Woe to the bloody city of Lichfield' during which he had a vision of blood running through the town and the market place. It was not until some time later that he learned of events many years before, which had led to a great number of Christians having been martyred there.

His spiritual experiences led George Fox to set up The Religious Society of Friends (of the Truth). They also became known as Quakers. It is said that this was as a result of Fox, when up before a judge on a charge of blasphemy, telling his honour to 'Tremble at the word of the Lord'. It is also perhaps an allusion to their actual trembling in meetings.

They eschew hierarchy, liturgy and any of the trappings of formal worship, and rely solely on the prompting of the spirit. Fox's movement grew and is still strong today, although more open-minded theologically. Friends are notable for their pacifism and their simple lifestyle, living according to the guidance of the spirit, seeing 'that of God' in everyone.

Christian Science

Mary Baker Eddy (1821–1910) was born into a devout, Puritan family in New Hampshire, USA in 1821. Finding the doctrine of predestination abhorrent, Mary argued with her father until she became feverish. Her mother suggested that she should pray for God's guidance over the matter. This she did, and was immediately healed. She continued her spiritual searching even after being tragically widowed after only 7 months of marriage and despite her own frail health. She investigated homeopathy, came under the influence of the magnetic healer, Phineas Quimby, and eventually concluded that it was faith in the drugs rather than their actual content, which cured.

After a serious fall, Mary had a vision of Life in and of the Spirit as the sole reality. This vision of the Absolute brought her immediate healing. Her further reflections on the event and subsequent study of the Bible led her to see mind as overcoming matter and to view God as the ultimate Mind. Healing was to take place without recourse to medical intervention, but through focus on the Spirit. She became the Discoverer and Founder of Christian Science and the author of *Science and Health*, the textbook of the movement.

Church of Scientology

L. Ron Hubbard (1911–1986) was a precocious child and an early seeker for meaning in life. He travelled the world exploring different regions, cultures and religions looking for an answer to the suffering of humanity. He became disillusioned with the thought of both East and the West and eventually abandoned academic study for life as a writer of thrillers. Yet his searching continued as he studied cell function and the link between mind and body. After being injured in World War II, he was able to complement those studies with practical experiments on his fellow patients, observing their reactions to medication.

He concluded that mind ruled matter and the thesis of *Dianetics* was born. Initially his teaching spread through word of mouth and many people were healed through his approach. He eventually wrote various books on the subject, notably the best-selling *Dianetics: The Modern Science of Mental Health*. He continued to explore the world and different levels of awareness, lecturing widely on Scientology. He attracted many followers, who eventually established the Church.

There is some controversy surrounding Hubbard and the movement, with prominent Hollywood figures speaking up both for and against. The most famous member is Tom Cruise, who extols the virtues of his beliefs, particularly on TV. It is said that Hubbard once declared that the best way to make millions would be to start a religion.

Mormons

The Mormon Church or the Church of Jesus Christ of Latter Day Saints, was founded by Joseph Smith (1805–1844). His experiences indicated that he was to restore the 'latter days' of the apostolic period, in line with the true teachings of Jesus which had been lost over the years. Mormons believe that the angel of the prophet Moroni informed Joseph Smith of the existence of buried records, mentioned in the Bible, which he found and published as *The Book of Mormon*. This told of a link between American Indians and the Lost Tribes of Israel. He formed and led a tight-knit community, but hostility from outsiders resulted in them moving several times. Joseph Smith was later imprisoned and ultimately murdered. Nonetheless, the movement continues to thrive, with its headquarters in Salt Lake City, Utah in the USA.

Theosophists

This movement was founded in 1875 in the USA by the Russian Helena Blavatsky (1831–1891) and the American Henry Steel Olcott (1832–1907). Helena Blavatsky was born in Southern Russia, the daughter of a German, Colonel Peter von Hahn, who had settled in Russia and Helena de Fadeyev, a renowned novelist. Her mother died when Helena was 11 years old and she was brought up by her maternal grandparents. She was an exceptional if unruly child, given to sleepwalking and endowed with psychic powers. Her sister wrote of her,

> For her all nature seemed animated with a mysterious life of its own. She heard the voice of every object and form, whether organic or

inorganic; and claimed consciousness and being, not only for some mysterious powers visible and audible for herself alone in what was to every one else empty space, but even for visible but inanimate things such as pebbles, mounds, and pieces of decaying phosphorescent timber.[35]

When almost eighteen, she married the middle-aged Nikifor V. Blavatsky, Vice-Governor of the Province of Yerivan, but she very soon left him and travelled widely. In 1851 in London, she saw Mahatma Morya or M. whom she recognized from childhood dreams. He became her teacher. She later spent time in Tibet learning from masters there. Eventually she met the American Colonel Henry Olcott, who had been interested in psychic phenomena from an early age and had investigated the spiritualist events at Eddy Farm in 1874. In 1875 Olcott and Blavatsky, along with William Quan Judge, set up the Theosophical Society – to promulgate the Wisdom concerning the Divine, which stemmed from Gnosticism and the ancient mystery schools.

Headquarters were soon established in India to continue the exploration of the spiritual realm underlying everyday reality. Their ideas included elements of Hinduism, Buddhism and Christianity. The Society for Psychical Research investigated Mme Blavatsky and Hodgson pronounced her a fraud, in a report which has since been challenged. Mme Blavatsky wrote first *Isis Unveiled* and later *The Secret Doctrine*.

Later theosophical luminaries included C. W. Leadbeater (1854–1934) and Annie Besant (1847–1933). When Annie rejected Christianity, she also left her clergyman husband. She joined the Theosophical Society and went to live in India. There she became politically active and the first woman President of the Indian Congress Party. She proclaimed Jiddhu Krishnamurti (1895–1986) a Theosophical World Teacher, but in 1929, aged 34, he renounced his role.

Anthroposophists

From his early childhood, Rudolf Steiner (1861–1925) had been aware of a world other than the everyday. This made for a lonely life, as others were unable to understand or believe in the spiritual world of which he was constantly aware.

> Spirit and nature were present before my soul in their absolute contrast. There existed, for me, a world of spiritual beings. That the

ego, which itself is spirit, lives in a world of spirits was for me a matter of direct perception.[36]

His own explorations led him to the Rosicrucians and to the German Theosophical Society, of which he became head. He had a powerful spiritual experience of the passion, death and resurrection of Christ, in which he was brought to

Stand before the Mystery of Golgotha in a solemn festival of knowledge.[37]

After this he moved away from the Theosophists to found the movement of Anthroposophy, or Spiritual Science. At its heart was Steiner's vision

of the free man, of the unity of the physical and spiritual aspects of reality, and of the evolutionary principle.[38]

The movement advocated close links to science while retaining an emphasis on inner spirituality. His teachings are followed in the Christian Community, and Waldorf or Steiner schools give a holistic education in line with Steiner's principles.

Unitarians

In sixteenth-century Poland and Transylvania, a liberal movement of Christians was formed. They stressed the oneness of God, rejecting the doctrine of the Trinity, hence the name Unitarian. Now self-governing communities of varying size gather in churches or people's homes in various countries around the world. Although rooted in Christianity, Unitarians' primary focus is a search for truth. In their services, some of which follow a Protestant pattern, readings from all the major traditions are included, as all are considered to be worshipping the same ultimate reality. Their symbol is a flaming chalice, the cup to share and the ever-changing flame, which requires fuel (the material level), heat (the spark of life and warmth of community) and air (the spirit).

Alister Hardy was a Unitarian,

My heart is in the Church of England, with all its beauty and deep sense of holiness, but not my mind which is repelled by its unreal dogmatic doctrines. . . . I am a Unitarian, . . .[39]

Gurus

The Hindu tradition of the *guru* (teacher) guiding a student through his or her spiritual development has led to many different groups. Some gurus have established *ashrams* (retreat centres). Below are some well-known gurus who have inspired movements loosely connected to Hinduism. While many are deeply revered, Gurus are particularly susceptible to scrutiny and there has been much disparagement of some of them, especially if they are considered to have enriched themselves at the expense of their followers.

Sai Baba (1835–1918)

He was revered as an avatar of Shiva, mainly among Gujeratis. Having been abandoned by his parents, brought up by a Muslim couple and later handed over to a spiritual master by name Gopalrao Deshmukh (also known as Venkusa), Baba made his way to Shirdi. He eventually settled there for the rest of his life, becoming known as Shirdi Baba. There he taught and performed miracles, such as lighting lamps with water instead of oil, stopping a storm and saving a girl from drowning in the well. Pilgrims were drawn to him and gave him gifts and 'Dakshina' money. He redistributed everything to those in need and ended each day as poor as he had begun it. Before his death, Shirdi Baba told some of His devotees that He would reappear in the Madras Presidency in eight years' time.

Satya Sai Baba

Satya Sai Baba was born in South India near Puttaparthi in 1926, eight years after the death of Shirdi Baba. As a child, he was exceptionally spiritual, full of compassion and different from the other children. In 1940, at the age of 14, he announced that he was a reincarnation of Sai Baba of Shirdi, and an avatar (incarnation of the divine).

Nowadays devotees flock to his ashram at Prasanthi Nilayam, near Puttaparthi, where he teaches and performs miracles. When asked about his identity, he explains that he is God, as is everyone else, for we all are embodiments of the Divine Atma, but he also explains that in a previous body he was Shirdi Baba. He does not require renunciation of other spiritual paths, aiming to make the Christian a better Christian, the Muslim a better Muslim and the Hindu a better Hindu through his teaching of love, universal brotherhood and the five-fold path of Sathya (Truth), Dharma

(Righteousness), Shanthi (Peace), Prema (Love) and Ahimsa (Non-Violence). It is believed that there will be a third incarnation as Prema Sai.

Ramana Maharshi (1879–1950)

It was an adolescent experience of the reality of death which triggered Ramana Maharshi's spiritual awakening. He felt convinced that he was about to die, lay down and seemed to undergo an experience of being dead. The continuation of his consciousness during this event led him to the understanding that he was eternal spirit in a body which dies. Leaving home soon afterwards, he settled near Mount Arunachala, which is deeply revered by Hindus, and there, in Tiruvannamalai, he set up his ashram.

He dealt with the question of the self, explaining that the sense of individuality arises with the body but is not bound by it. He taught release from the individual self by surrender to the Self, ultimate reality – the doctrine of *advaita* or non-duality.

Maharishi Mahesh Yogi (1911–2008)

It was the Maharishi who brought the technique of Transcendental Meditation to the West and founded the TM movement. His technique was based on Hindu practice, repeating a *mantra* (sacred word(s) or sound) to still the mind and attain tranquillity and enhanced creativity. He advocated that two twenty-minute periods of meditation should be undertaken daily, bringing increased health, calm and relaxation, as the metabolic rate during meditation falls to below that of the level of sleep.

The TM method is expensive to learn, which has led to criticism. However, it survives, and in 2008 film director David Lynch and folk singer Donovan toured Britain to drum up enthusiasm for TM in schools and universities as a method of inculcating calm and focus in young people.

Lord Sri Caitanya Mahaprabhu (1486–1533)

Visvambhar was born in West Bengal on a night of a full moon and lunar eclipse. Legend has it that as he was born to the sound of chanting of the holy name of Krishna, this continued to soothe him as a baby. Later in life too, although a renowned scholar, he became a devotee of Krishna and took the name of Krishna Caitanya. He travelled all over India popularizing the chant of the holy name. Eventually he became worshipped as an avatar of Krishna. He left eight verses of instruction as a basis for the movement of Gaudiya Vaishnavism, devotion to Vishnu and Krishna.

Prabhupada (1896–1977)

A. C. Bhaktivedanta Swami Srila Prabhupada followed in Caitanya's line. He renounced married life to become a sannyasin, studying and writing prolifically on Vedic scriptures. His English translation of the Gita, the *Bhagavad-gita As It Is* contains his own helpful commentary. In 1965 he left India to take the teachings of Vaishnavism to the West and although he arrived in America without resources, he founded the International Society for Krishna Consciousness (ISKCON) a year later. Often known as the Hare Krishnas, devotees chant the holy name of Krishna in order to purify their minds – a form of bhakti or worship leading to *mukti* or liberation from endless reincarnation. George Harrison of the Beatles, popularized the chant in *My Sweet Lord*.

> By practical experience also, one can perceive that by chanting this *maha-mantra*, or the Great Chant for Deliverance, one at once feels transcendental ecstasy coming through from the spiritual stratum.[40]

Mother Meera (1960–)

Kamala, later to become known as Mother Meera, was born in 1960 in Southern India. She was aware of going towards lights at the age of three and attained the spiritual state of absorption of *Samadhi* aged 6. Her Uncle, Mr Reddy recognized her unique qualities and took her under his wing, staying at the ashram of Sri Aurobindo in Pondicherry. In 1981 they went to Germany and a year later Mother Meera married a German. She lives in Balduinstein, where she gives Darshan, a silent communication of light, to people who flock to her from all over the world.

She is seen as an avatar, a representative on earth, of the Divine Mother, the sacred feminine, also considered to have become manifest in other ages as the Hindu Goddess Kali and the Virgin Mary. Mother Meera's task on earth is neither to teach nor start a religion, but to call down the Paramatman Light, meaning the light of the supreme being, to humanity.

> Paramatman is in everything, in all creation – earth, water, fire, sky, animals – at all times. But we can see the Light only sometimes. The Light has the quality of love, grace, power, bliss, jnana. . . . It is the

49

effect that matters: an unmistakable and extraordinary lightness and happiness and peace.[41]

Alternative Paradigms

Neale Donald Walsch

Writers such as Neale Donald Walsch have bypassed formal, traditional religion for a direct way of understanding the human relationship to the divine and alternative ways of communicating with God. Walsch wrote a series of bestsellers called *Conversations with God* in three volumes, followed by *Friendship with God* and *Communion with God* depicting a growing awareness of the spiritual messages inherent in everyday life, if only we would recognize them as such. The books were triggered by Walsch writing a letter to God, and then being unable to stop writing, as he seemed to be receiving answers. Although at first he felt this was just for him, he later thought that his questions were universal and so he published the communications – and his sales reflect the response worldwide.

Eckhart Tolle

The Power of Now, followed by *Practising the Power of Now* and *Stillness Speaks* are popular volumes which have given people a guide to spiritual enlightenment outside the mainstream religions, although drawing on age-old wisdom. Eckhart Tolle uses the word 'Being' rather than God to describe the

> . . . eternal, ever-present One Life beyond the myriad forms of life that are subject to birth and death.[42]

He teaches that to reach this Being, beyond and also deep within, one needs to still the mind, to attain a state of 'feeling-realization' which is enlightenment. His latest work suggests that a change in consciousness in humanity would lead to *A New Earth*.

Fritjof Capra (1939–)

A physicist and systems analyst, Fritjof Capra brought modern physics and Eastern Mysticism together in his best-selling *The Tao of Physics* in

1976. This was written at a time when such ideas were considered a risk to his professional standing, but now they are increasingly accepted. The parallels can be drawn to Western Mysticism too and a new paradigm seems to be emerging, which can encompass mystical insights of interconnection and the latest developments in physics.

Capra's writing was triggered by a mystical experience, described at the beginning of *The Tao of Physics*.

> I was sitting by the ocean one late summer afternoon, watching the waves rolling in and feeling the rhythm of my breathing, when I suddenly became aware of my whole environment as being engaged in a gigantic cosmic dance. Being a physicist I knew that sand, rocks, water and air around me were made of vibrating molecules and atoms, and that these consisted of particles which interacted with one another by creating and destroying other particles. . . . All this was familiar to me from my research in high-energy physics, but until that moment I had only experienced it through graphs, diagrams and mathematical theories. As I sat on the beach, my former experiences came to life . . . I *knew* that this was the dance of Shiva, the Lord of the Dancers worshipped by the Hindus.[43]

Deepak Chopra (1946–)

In titles such as *The Path to Love, Ageless Body/Timeless Mind, Perfect Health* and *Unconditional Life*, Deepak Chopra points the way to self-awareness and self-help. This has brought him a wide following and he has become a modern kind of guru, although he does not like the term. In an age of scepticism, he offers a path of integration of mind, body and spirit attractive to those seeking a holistic way of living without the confines of traditional religion. A successful endocrinologist in the USA, Deepak Chopra was inspired by the teachings of Maharishi Mahesh Yogi to evolve a fusion of Western and Ayurvedic medicine.

He brings spirituality and modern physics together in *How to Know God*. He envisages three levels of experience: the material world, where the sceptics remain; the transition zone and the highest level, God. Humans have some insights and mystical experiences in the transitional level. In Chopra's view, mystics are able to remain in the transition state for longer than the rest of humanity, who may occasionally get a glimpse of God in a flash of ecstasy. There is a parallel scheme for physics: material reality or the visible universe; the quantum domain or mind, where energy turns to matter; and the virtual domain or spirit, which is beyond time and space. In this scenario, mystics are just better quantum navigators. Chopra explains the different stages to achieving the mystical level of existence.

These writers, and others like them such as Marianne Williamson and Oriah Mountain Dreamer, appeal to a vast number of people who are searching for an experience of spirituality. They are looking for a path of inner development to gain an insight into themselves, their motivation and behaviour. As they grow in understanding they begin to live more fully, and they frequently become more aware of others and their needs. This leads on to an awareness of a deeper dimension of life. It is often then that an exploration of the more established religious traditions is begun, with a greater appreciation of their richness.

6. Religious Triggers of Spiritual Experience

Many spiritual experiences, especially communal ones, are triggered during religious services, worship or festivals. Others are solitary, the result of meditation or prayer.

Worship

A recognition of the power of the divine moves many believers to a sense of humility and awe and thus to worship. Rituals have been performed over the centuries in all parts of the world. Statues have been raised, temples and places of worship built, works of art and music created, liturgies composed and devotion offered to the divine, however named. Throughout the ages, whether in great ceremonies of public worship or in solitary silence, communication from those below to whatever is conceived to be the ultimate perfection beyond this world, have formed part of the human experience. Metropolitan Anthony of Sourozh, head of the Russian Orthodox Patriarchal Church in Britain, goes to the heart of what it means to worship.

> Worship to me means a relationship. I used not to be a believer, then one day I discovered God and immediately he appeared to me to be the supreme value and the total meaning of life, but at the same time a person. I think that worship can mean nothing at all to someone for whom there is no object of worship. You cannot teach worship to someone who has not got a sense of the living God; you can teach him to act as if he believed, but it will not be the spontaneous attitude which is real worship.[44]

Worship takes many forms, from organized Christian Sunday services to Chinese shoppers popping into the temple to light incense sticks on their way home. The Hindu path of devotion or *bhakti* is described in the

Bhagavad Gita, part of the *Mahabharata*. The many gods and goddesses of Hinduism are seen as manifestations of the divine. Special ceremonies and rituals are performed at altars or shrines, adorned with brightly coloured figures and offerings of food and flowers. Buddhism, not usually associated with bhakti, in the Pure Land Buddhism of Japan does become a religion of worship. By calling on the name of Amida Buddha, to bring to an end the ceaseless round of rebirth, one may enter the Pure Land and from thence attain *Nirvana*. But this cannot be achieved through 'self-power' *(jiriki)* but only through 'other power' *(tariki)*.

Christian worship may vary from the impressive rituals of high church services in the great cathedrals to informal celebrations. Worship may involve song, dance, lighting candles, processions and special clothing for those leading the proceedings. Charismatic services in particular frequently lead to a feeling of uplift and communal spirit. At the heart of Christian worship is the Eucharist or Communion Service, where Christ's death and Resurrection are commemorated. This is the experience of a newly ordained woman priest.

> When I celebrated my first Eucharist last year, I was completely bowled over by the moment of the Fraction – which is when the priest breaks the bread. I broke the bread and then the choir started to sing the Agnus Dei – Lamb of God. As the music circled around me and I was breaking the bread into small pieces, it was as if all the suffering in the world was in the small plate at that moment and that it was both broken and transfigured with glory at the same time. The experience was of deep emotion to the extent that I felt close to beautiful tears. It was both pain and beauty simultaneously. [45]

What is important is the inner response of the faithful. One of the most beautiful pronouncements on worship comes from a Muslim woman, the mystic Rabi'a of Basra,

> O God! If I worship Thee in fear of Hell, burn me in Hell; and if I worship Thee in hope of Paradise, exclude me from Paradise; but if I worship Thee for Thine own sake, withhold not Thine everlasting beauty.[46]

Festivals and Religious Ceremonies

Festivals are held to celebrate specific events in the religious calendar and are an outward form of worship which often involves the whole community. Christmas is not only observed by devout Christians but has become an annual celebration for many. In multi-religious, multicultural lands the year is punctuated by the different festivals for the different religions. In Singapore, for example, there is never a time of year when some festival is not either being planned or celebrated, from Chinese New Year to the Hindu Thaipusam (when bodies are pierced and structures called *kavadis* are carried in honour of Lord Murugan, son of Shiva and Parvati), Muslim Hari Raya Puasa (Eid-al-Fitr, the end of the month of the Ramadan fast), Buddhist Vesak Day (celebrating the Buddha's birth, Enlightenment and death) and ending with Christmas (marking the birth of Christ). Whether members of the traditions or not, all can enjoy the festivities, and also learn about the religion involved.

Jews celebrate many festivals within the family at home. Shabbat (the Sabbath) is kept holy in Jewish families. Preparations are made the day before so that no work is done on the Saturday in remembrance that after the Creation, God rested on the seventh day. As a Jewish woman explains,

> On the Shabbat I feel a different person. I feel more alive, more bright, more cheerful, the house seems to be a different place. In fact when one keeps the laws according to the Shabbat, it is like being in a different world. . . . On Shabbat we sing, on Shabbat we dance, on Shabbat we have time to study without any interruption. We have time to pray.[47]

At times of national importance leaders of different faiths join in worship, reflecting different approaches to the divine in mutual respect. Many festivals these days may be shared by members of different faiths. Here a Christian, enjoying a Shinto Waterfall ceremony in Japan in 1993 had a wonderful experience,

> We were celebrating the Year of Interreligious Understanding and came to Japan from Bangalore before going on to Chicago. We visited the Tsubaki Grand Shrine and joined in some Shinto ceremonies. We took part in the Purification by Waterfall ceremony (misogi)
>
> It was late at night and we dressed all in white in kimonos and headbands, and prepared ourselves with prayers, mine were more Christian than Shinto. We also clapped and shook ourselves to become more aware of the presence of the soul. Under the cold waterfall I experienced a complete oneness with nature and could not tell the difference between me and the waterfall. It was a peaceful, exhilarating feeling of complete peace and joy with the universe. [005437]

Religious and Spiritual Experience

All over the world, different ceremonies take place, often to mark rites of passage, birth, marriage and death.

Prayer

Communication with God, the divine or ultimate reality is at the heart of religious practice. Prayer may be formal, regular or an ongoing, informal communication. Some prayer is specific, involving gratitude, penitence or petition, while for some takes place in silence, as listening to God is as important as speaking. Just how far God might intervene in the day-to-day affairs of people remains a matter for debate, as does the question of just how right it might be to pray for selfish ends. But there is no doubt that for many people, prayer is at the heart of religious practice, it is what underpins a life of faith. This account is of an unusually powerful time of prayer.

> My experience happened some years ago . . . it happened during a period of prayer that I found myself going through a tense physical struggle somewhat similar to childbirth. I became suddenly aware of light rays about me. It frightened me, thinking that I had entered a forbidden realm by mistake. But what happened to me was most wonderful. I actually felt that I was in tune with the entire universe. I became imbued with a feeling of unity toward all mankind. That feeling to a certain extent has stayed with me. It was a startling experience and I honestly felt that I had made a new discovery . . . there is no doubt in my mind that God is a reality. [0673]

Here is an account of answered prayer.

> I suffer from endogenous depression which occasionally is so acute as to make me suicidally inclined. One of these attacks occurred in 1964 when I was in New Zealand. Being a Londoner and a newcomer, with very few friends in Wellington, I wrote for help to the vicar of my former parish in England. The feeling of despair left me suddenly some days later. When his reply arrived, I learned that as soon as he received my letter he had gone into his church to pray for me, and he mentioned the date and the time. Calculations, allowance for the time difference and so on, showed that this was the moment of my release. I am quite convinced that the prayers of this good man were in some way instrumental in bringing the power of God to bear on my desperate situation. . . . The Christian faith is important to me and were it not for the

support and comfort I derive from it I should probably have put my head in the gas oven long ago! [000642]

Some times of prayer are taken up with formal prayers and require dedication, even when the mind seems to wander. Such set prayers can often be helpful, particularly for people new to a faith. However, many people do find it quite easy to pray in a completely natural, informal way,

> I talk to God like I'm talking to you. I can be struggling on the car in an awkward position doing a job, and I get a bit frustrated at times, and I'll just say, 'Come on, God, you can see me struggling, get your finger out, you can see what I'm trying to do – come on.' Just like that. I find it very easy to talk to God. I really do believe that God is listening to me any time I wish to talk to him.[48]

Although such communication is easy for some, others find it difficult, so for them petitionary prayer is a way of bringing the person prayed for and their need into one's deepest awareness, as a Quaker put it,

> It is impossible to write about religious experience without saying something about prayer and the way in which the life of the spirit is sustained. Prayer is such a personal activity that I can only write about it from my own experience. . . . . I know many Friends who are able to engage in a kind of dialogue with God, and who are sustained by a sense of spiritual presence in their regular quiet times. While I respect their sincerity, and recognise the validity of their experience, I have come to realise that this way is not for me.

The writer and his wife then had a visit from a friend in trouble, and after she had left, they continued to discuss her predicament, empathizing with her.

> We began to see life through her eyes and, to this extent, were sharing her burden, so that she was no longer alone with it. We knew we had experienced part of what people mean when they say they are praying for someone.[49]

If prayer is the act of aligning one's will with that of the higher power, God, Allah or whatever name one might use, then there will be comfort for the believer whatever the outcome of the matter in hand. Some people feel that handing their fate over to God, whether in the short or longer term, results in guidance and help. They feel that things happen which would not have been possible had they not taken this step.

Some people live their lives constantly aware of a divine presence, so examples cannot be given in isolated incidents, but should be considered in the context of a lifetime. Prayer changes over time as one matures and may evolve from set prayers into wordless meditation. In 1989 *The Friends' Quarterly* published *A Journey in Prayer*, by Anita Billington, who recounted her life in the perspective of prayer and spiritual exploration.

> When I was a child the language of prayer came easily to me. My father was a Methodist minister, and during my happy childhood the day often started with family prayers. Loving my father as I did, it was easy for me to imagine a Heavenly Father who not only created the natural world to which I felt so close, but also cared for me. . . .
>
> As I grew up, prayer became a duty, and I felt guilty if I forgot. . . .
>
> When I was twenty-two, I went to the Bahama Islands . . . I was given a little anthology of prayers. It is worn with use. I treasure it still as I remember the comfort and strength I found within its pages.
>
> It was when I was thirty-three that I found myself in a situation where I did not know what to pray. After a long struggle against ill health, my husband was dying of a tumour in the gland beneath his brain and was rushed to hospital in Bristol. . . . At the hospital, the specialist could offer me little hope. There would first be an operation to put tubes through his brain. If he survived he might be paralysed and blind . . . . I walked out into the dark November night, not knowing what to do, and followed a sign that said 'Chapel'. . . .
>
> [I] went up to the communion rail, kneeling to pray. What could I say? My husband had suffered so much. How could I ask for him to live if it would mean more suffering? How could I know what would be best for him? I thought of our little family and our deep love for each other. Then I put us one by one into the palm of my hand and, lifting us high, handed us over to God.
>
> Words are inadequate to truly share what I experienced as I waited alone in the chapel that night. It was my Whitsuntide. Light surrounded me. Joy and peace filled my heart. The figure of Jesus was with me, looking at me with such love and calling me little sister. I touched a deep level of understanding and all was made clear to me. I knew, without any doubt at all, that whether my husband lived or died did not really matter to him. It would just be another step on his journey. Nothing could really separate us. If he died, it would, in truth, be just a little while before we were together again. When I finally left the

chapel, it was as though my feet hardly touched the ground. As I sat beside him, in the weeks that followed, I could feel a powerful stream of energy flowing from me to him. For days after his first operation, his mind was affected and everything he said was nonsense. I thought we would never communicate again. Then one day he turned to me and said, 'I can feel a power bringing me back to life'. . . .

The experience I had in the chapel at Bristol totally changed my perception of God and my attitude to prayer. No longer could I cope with church services to a God outside me. I had found my treasure, my pearl of great price. I had found it at the time of my greatest need. I had found it as I sat in silence, and I had found it within me. . . .

In the years that followed I made a conscious effort to bring all of my life into the presence of God. I would ask for guidance in every area of my life and this was very painful, for it meant honestly facing up to myself as I was. Amongst Quakers I found real Friends . . .

My life became an exploration of ways of keeping in touch with my God centre, the true source of my being. I discovered that I had reached the state of Living in the Presence. No longer did I have to offer up my needs and deep concerns. My needs were known. . . .

If the presence of God is within me, it is within everyone – within every single human being. If I reject anyone I cut myself off from the Presence. I can have no enemies. If I live in the thought of love towards all, my life will become one continuous prayer – a constant going forth from God the father of all, to all.

Dwell in the place of love and you are one with God. You are part of God's expression on earth.

This is the true reality.

This is true prayer.[50]

Experiments have been undertaken to establish whether prayers for healing are effective, and the results, reported in various medical journals, seem to indicate that such prayer is indeed effective. To the astonishment of many scientists, the results seem to indicate that people like Dr. Deepak Chopra may be correct in saying that there are healing forces in nature, which science is only just beginning to understand. In *How to Know God* he reported the results of the Duke project, formally known as the Monitoring and Actualization of Noetic Training, which presented its findings in 1998 to the American Heart Association.

The researchers took into account all manner of variables, including heart rate, blood pressure and clinical outcomes; 150 patients who had undergone invasive cardiac procedures were studied, but none of them knew they were being prayed for. Seven religious groups around the world were asked to pray. These included Buddhists in Nepal, Carmelite nuns in Baltimore, and Virtual Jerusalem, an organization that grants E-mail requests for prayers to be written down and inserted into the Wailing Wall. Researchers found that surgical patients' recovery could be from 50 to 100 percent better if someone prayed for them.[51]

Chopra explains that although the researchers found the results 'highly intriguing', what is really in evidence is a journey in consciousness, joining the persons praying and prayed for beyond time and space in what is in fact 'a quantum event carried out in the brain'.

There are rituals involved in prayer, with different religions having different requirements. Some religions require regular, formal prayer and many faiths have prayer beads to aid concentration. It is quite usual to kneel or prostrate as a sign of humility. Here just three traditions are considered in more detail.

Jewish practice requires a devout Jew to pray three times a day, often wearing the *tallit*, or prayer shawl, and perhaps two phylacteries, known as *tefillin*, which are little black boxes containing verses of the Torah, worn on the arm, near the heart and forehead, close to the mind. For Jews, prayer was established by Abraham, Isaac and Jacob and is viewed as a continuation of the tradition of temple sacrifice, in that it establishes communication between earth and heaven. An emptying of the mind should precede prayer, enabling concentration on the Divine. The prayers include avowals of God's unity and the relationship to his followers and also the hope of the advent of the Messiah who will unite God and man.

The *Shema*, meaning 'hear' refers to the first prayer Jews learn:

> Hear, O Israel, the Lord our God, the Lord is one, and you shall love the Lord your God with all your heart, and with all your soul, and with all your might. And these words which I command you shall be upon your heart.

Muslims are required to pray five times a day in the direction of the Ka'aba in Makkah (qibla) and in hotel rooms all over the world the correct direction is indicated for the faithful. Prayer rooms are becoming more widespread in public places to enable Muslims to obey the tenets of their faith in this way. The mosque (from Arabic masjid, meaning to prostrate) is of course the primary location for prayer. After removing their shoes and performing the correct washing procedures and covering their heads, male and female Muslims separate but perform the same ritual prayers. The majority of women pray regularly but at home.

Here is an extraordinary experience recounted to Prof. Dr. Cafer Yaran of Istanbul University, when he undertook a survey of religious experience in Turkey,

> When I was fifteen I wanted to learn the Qur'an very much but my father did not allow me to go and learn. We lived in a village and my father thought that my age is too old to do this as a girl and it would be better for our family if I spent the time with helping village businesses rather than learning the Qur'an. However, my desire has never ended and I strived to learn it insistently. My father hit me several times for this. At the end I lost my hope and started to pray only. One night after everybody went to sleep, I saw a light like a signboard on the wall. It was something framed luminously. There was nothing hanged there in normal case. When I looked carefully I saw letters on it . . . . That is, I saw the Qur'anic alfabet. My Lord had heard me and gifted me with such an extra-ordinary way to learn the Qur'an.
>
> Every night I waited everybody go to bed as early as possible. When the lights off, the signboard appeared, the luminous letters came out and I read them surprisingly. After 14 days, I thought 'I wonder if I read them right or wrong' and finding an old Qur'an I tried to read. I read for a while and that night I could not see the signboard at all. That is to say, I had learnt to read the Qur'an and there was not the signboard anymore.[52]

Christian church services include prayers of penitence, intercession for others and 'The Lord's Prayer' taught to his disciples by Jesus. Different denominations have different ways of praying, some with more formal prayers, some with none. Private prayer also varies in the same way.

Teresa of Avila (1515–1582) writes of different types of prayer, such as recollective prayer, in which God, and only God, is sought, but nothing else asked for. Teresa sees contemplative prayer as mystical, for it can only be initiated by God. In *The Interior Castle*, where the soul is likened to a castle with different mansions or rooms, she describes different levels of prayer. There is the Prayer of Quiet, in which thought is stilled, which ultimately leads on to the Prayer of Union in the seventh mansion. This is ecstatic prayer or rapture when the individual is no longer aware of individuality, but is caught up into a spiritual union with the divine.

Contemplatives and meditators try to quieten their minds, shutting out the everyday world and in that inner silence, they may touch a greater reality. A Catholic nun might say she had communed with the Holy Spirit or been with Jesus. A Tibetan Buddhist like the Dalai Lama would say that he had stilled his mind and achieved calm abiding.

Contemplation

Many mystics of the Middle Ages followed the path of contemplation, notably the anonymous author of *The Cloud of Unknowing*, who also wrote *The Book of Privy Counselling* and translated *Mystical Theology* by Dionysius the Areopagite. He was probably a member of a religious order, and his work gives guidance in spiritual development on the way to God through love. At the heart of the author's teaching is the way of love, the focus in love on God, to the exclusion of all else. It is necessary to learn to ignore detractors and the initial frustrations even though at first one will feel,

> nothing but a kind of darkness about your mind; or as it were, a *cloud of unknowing*. You will seem to know nothing and to feel nothing except a naked intent toward God in the depths of your being. Try as you might, this darkness and this cloud will remain between you and your God. You will feel frustrated, for your mind will be unable to grasp him, and your heart will not relish the delight of his love. But learn to be at home in this darkness. Return to it as often as you can, letting your spirit cry out to him whom you love. For if, in this life, you hope to feel and see God as he is in himself it must be within this darkness and this cloud. But if you strive to fix your love on him forgetting all else, which is the work of contemplation I have urged you to begin, I am confident that God in his goodness will bring you to a deep experience of himself.[53]

This summarizes the method of contemplation advocated by the author at the outset, and he explains just what is meant by the cloud of unknowing. He stresses that this is no literal cloud of darkness, but darkness in the sense of being in the dark about some matter, the absence of knowledge. It is this darkness of unknowing which separates man from God. Thinking is not the solution to this problem, it must be experienced,

> For the intellect of both men and angels is too small to comprehend God as he is in himself.
> Try to understand this point. Rational creatures such as men and angels possess two principal faculties, a knowing power and a loving

power. No one can fully comprehend the uncreated God with his knowledge; but each one in a different way, can grasp him fully through love.[54]

Meditation

Meditation is seen as allowing deep relaxation while maintaining awareness. The aim is to clear the mind of its incessant chatter and restlessness – in Buddhist parlance to silence the monkey mind or to bind the monkey – allowing what is real to emerge. There are various techniques of meditation, such as focusing on the breath, contemplating an object or pattern such as a mandala, or being guided into a visionary reality. Some people meditate on texts or repeat mantras to absorb the inner meaning. These are ways into the inmost heart or soul, sometimes named as the 'Christ within' or 'Buddha nature'.

Meditation is most often associated with Buddhists, for whom it is at the heart of their practice. It was through meditation that Gautama became Buddha, the Enlightened One. The Dalai Lama has written books which appeal to readers, Buddhist and non-Buddhist, the world over. In *How to Practise, the Way to a Meaningful Life* His Holiness explains three fundamental steps to happiness based on the Buddhist path: Morality, Concentrated Meditation and Wisdom, which lead from one to the other. First, self-awareness and compassion for all sentient beings is learned, then various types of meditation, the aim of which is calm abiding are explained. A summary for daily practice is given,

1. Choose an object of meditation and focus on it, trying to achieve and maintain stability, clarity and intensity. Avoid laxity and excitement.
2. Alternatively, identify the fundamental state of the mind, unsullied by thought, in its own state – mere luminosity, the knowing nature of the mind. With mindfulness and introspection remain in that state. If a thought arises, just look into the very nature of that thought; this will cause it to lose its power and dissolve of its own accord.[55]

The following accounts describe the experiences of a Christian who had taken up Buddhist meditation,

In silent prayer the experience of the presence of God is more frequent and expected. His presence is associated with a definite act of the will to place myself in the presence, and is accompanied by feelings of joy and peace. I practise a Buddhist form of meditation for 20 minutes each day, in which the mind is stilled by maintaining awareness of the abdominal movements in breathing. During this exercise I feel that on occasion I am aware of a presence in the stillness, but not nearly as frequently as in Orthodox Christian prayer.

In the summer of 1969 I began the practice of Buddhist Meditation described above. One afternoon about three weeks after I had started the daily practice, my whole being seemed struck down by a blinding flash of light. I was completely overwhelmed by the experience, which occurred shortly after I had begun the day's stint of meditation. My feelings were a combination of ecstasy, terror and awe. The experience came utterly unexpectedly and I felt that God had given me a vision of his power. For two days afterwards everything I did, even what would normally be boring drudgery, filled me with the greatest delight. I felt it didn't matter what happened to me; everything was very good. [from 003519]

Here is an experience recounted by a Christian philosopher of religion, Revd Professor John Hick,

I have been practising meditation, in a faltering sort of way, for some years, using the mindfulness method that I learned from the Sri Lankan Buddhist monk Nyanaponika Mahathera . . . The one moment of breakthrough that I have experienced so far was only a few months ago. In normal consciousness I am here and the world is there, apart from me, surrounding me and so to speak hemming me in, and arousing all sorts of hopes and fears. But as I opened my eyes after perhaps ten minutes of meditating I was suddenly vividly aware of being an integral part of the world, not separate from it, and that that of which I am a part is a friendly universe, so that there could not possibly be anything to fear or worry about. It was the same world, and yet totally transformed, and for a short time – only one or two minutes – I was completely free and completely happy. I was by myself at the time; but if this new consciousness had continued into daily life I believe that my attitude to others would have been a liberation from self-concern making possible love and compassion for everyone I had to deal with.[56]

Within the Christian tradition, meditation was revived for Christians by Dom John Main, who was instructed in meditation in what was then Malaya (now Malaysia) by a Hindu monk. When John Main became a Benedictine monk, he was instructed to give up the practice. But through

Religious Triggers

his reading he discovered the forgotten form of prayer of the Desert Fathers and Mothers and of the Conferences of John Cassian and instigated a Christian form of meditation using the mantra 'Maranatha', meaning 'Come Lord'. Dom Laurence Freeman has taken over the mantle of leading the World Community for Christian Meditation, www.wccm.org.

Some Christians, particularly the Eastern Orthodox, use the Jesus Prayer,

Lord Jesus Christ, Son of God, have mercy on me, a sinner.

It is repeated over and over again like a mantra, responding to the idea that one should 'pray without ceasing'. In this account, the practice brought great comfort at a difficult time,

During October of 1972 my father was dying after a long and painful illness. Towards the end, my mother was finding the strain very trying so I volunteered to sleep in the bedroom with my father. In fact he was in considerable pain, had lost the power of speech and every few minutes during the night he attempted to get out of bed. The whole experience of trying to make him as comfortable as possible during the night was like a nightmare to me. I found myself repeating the Jesus Prayer, 'Lord Jesus Christ, Son of God, have mercy on me a sinner'. As I continued to repeat the words silently, I began to feel wonderfully happy, and for the rest of the night what had been a terrible experience became a delight. I felt that my father and I cemented a bond which had been broken between us for many years. [from 003519]

Here is an experience based on this prayer, using a technique known as *sanyama*, which brings together concentration, meditation and Samadhi – meditative absorption.

I found the Jesus Prayer . . . in Metropolitan Anthony's book *Living Prayer*. I had already been taught the technique of *Sanyama* as described in Patanjali's *Yoga Sutras*. It is a most delicate process that requires deep inner silence. Patanjali lists various concepts and objects and tells you what will happen if you perform *sanyama* on them: for example, if you perform *sanyama* on the Pole Star, you will cognize the structure of the universe. (A simplistic analogy would be that the sutra or concept is like a computer program, and *sanyama* is the process of inserting it into the Cosmic Mind – and, as when you run a program, something happens – you get a result.)

So I performed *sanyama* on the Jesus Prayer. Instantly, my awareness was filled with a vision of a rose against a dark background. The rose was perpetually burning – but was never consumed. I remained rapt for I don't know how long.

When I re-emerged, deeply moved, into 'normal', waking state consciousness, the mind resumed its customary analytical interpretation: yes, the rose is a universal symbol in the west (the eastern version is the lotus); yes, I was reminded of the Cosmic Rose described by Dante at the end of *Il Paradiso*; yes, there was the burning bush in the Bible. I suppose the vision could be seen as a symbol of Divine Love – forever burning but never consumed or exhausted. I concluded that I had been privileged to experience a Platonic Form. I had put in the program and the Universal Computer had responded. [57]

Various religions include meditation as part of their practice, a good experience for members of different traditions to share. Here is the experience of a Christian among the Brahma Kumaris,

We were in Mount Abu in India at the H.Q. of the Brahma Kumaris. We were about 50 people all meditating with a leader and encouraged to do this with our eyes open. I was very deep in meditation when all around me the bodies of the others seemed to disappear and all I could see was a wonderful light around each person which would, I suppose, be their aura. I kept opening and shutting my eyes to make sure I was not dreaming. Afterwards I described this to the senior Dadi who smiled and said I had been blessed but should never try and seek such an experience again. I felt I had been made aware of another dimension to life which was very powerful and outside normal consciousness. (005443)

Blessing

The laying on of hands can be a powerful experience.

I and my family were staying with college friends in their family home. We had known them for 15 years or so, firstly as fellow students and later Dave became ordained in C of E and we were staying at their Vicarage in Hull. I was asked if I would like a blessing and I said I would. I was sitting with my head bowed. David stretched out his hands so that they were about 6 inches from my head. I felt an incredible warmth, as if my head was wrapped in cotton wool. It was a very pleasant experience, I felt held (I later asked if Dave had touched my head and he said that he had not.)

Religious Triggers

> I found myself going along a very dark tunnel – but I was not afraid – I could see a circle of bright light ahead. When I reached the bright light – I was in a beautiful garden. It was bathed in golden light and I felt such peace, happiness and tranquillity that I have never known before or since. There was no sense of time. I was not on my own – the Virgin Mary with baby Jesus on her knee in front of me. We made no contact – we were just being.
>
> Then all at once I was back in the sitting room in the Vicarage in Hull, just left with a wish to go back.
> I think it had all lasted a few minutes. (005439)

Silence

In the Daode Jing (Book of the Dao) it is said

> Those who know do not talk.
> Those who talk do not know.[58]

When members of different faiths come together, true communion is often best experienced in silence.

Mother Meera, an Avatar, an incarnation of the Divine Mother, explains the practice of Darshan in which she imparts the divine light of Paramatman to those who come to her in Germany, where she now lives. This takes place in complete silence.

> People are too active and rarely sit quietly. In silence one can receive more because all one's activities become concentrated at one point. My teaching is to give only the essence, the Divine, that which is necessary. I give exactly what is needed by each person.
>
> Paramatman is silent. God is silent. Everything comes out of silence. In silence more work can be done. The true experience of bliss is without words.[59]

Darshan

Here is an experience of Darshan with Mother Meera,

> I first attended Darshan with Mother Meera in April, 1993. At that time, it was possible to stay for ten days and go to eight Darshans – for me, this was a very good foundation. There were about 150 of us in the

room and we sat in silence for about two hours. One by one, each person went up and knelt in front of Mother. Before I got used to the process, I felt some anxiety about waiting, queuing and choosing the right moment to approach. I got down on my knees, bent forward and Mother took my head in her hands for a few moments. I did not feel anything special at first but when I went back to my seat, I became aware that something momentous had happened. It was as though she had taken me by the scruff of the neck (metaphorically) and had shaken a lot of fear out of me. The feeling that blockages and limitations had been removed and that new possibilities could now open up was strengthened in the subsequent Darshans. Important changes did indeed take place. I returned a number of times and I feel this has speeded up my inner progress. On one occasion, I was in the middle of a spiritual crisis, and while sitting quietly in the Darshan hall, important advice – loving but firm – came into my mind and this helped to resolve the situation.[60]

Renunciation

Many Hindus followed the path through life set out for man, with the stage of student followed by that of the married householder and then when his work was done, he would often retreat to the forest to meditate on spiritual matters. Ultimately he might renounce the world in pursuit of spiritual enlightenment or *moksha,* through living as a *sannyasin*, described below.

> He needs no house or furniture. He may live in a cave or take shelter beside a temple or on the veranda of a house. For clothing he needs only two pieces of cloth – which should not be stitched – one to wear round the waist and another to cover the shoulders or the head. There are even some *sannyasis* who renounce all clothing and are said to be 'clothed with the sky'. For food he needs only one meal a day, which he gets by begging or, more often, which a householder will offer him unasked. He can thus reduce his life to an absolute simplicity. He is totally detached from the world, depending on divine providence for his bare needs of food, shelter and clothing.[61]

It is in renunciation that one finds, according to William James,

> . . . the way to success [. . .] is by 'surrender', passivity, not activity; relaxation, not intentness, should now be the rule. Give up the feeling of responsibility, let go your hold, resign the care of your destiny to

higher powers, be genuinely indifferent as to what becomes of it all, and you will find not only that you gain a perfect inward relief, but often also, in addition, the particular goods you sincerely thought you were renouncing. . . . It is but giving your little private convulsive self a rest, and finding that a greater Self is there. [62]

Sacred places

Throughout the ages, there have been places revered as sacred: mountains such as Uluru (Ayers Rock) in Australia, Mount Sinai in Egypt, Mount Kailas in the Himalayas, Fuji-San (Mount Fuji) in Japan and Chomolungma or Sagarmatha (Everest); caves such as the Psychro Cave and other Minoan caves on Crete, and the Mayan caves in the Yukatan. Ancient man-made constructions such as the stone circles at Stonehenge and Avebury, huge pyramids in Egypt and of the Mayans and Aztecs are great wonders of the world. Humans have interacted with nature in diverse ways throughout the ages and some places are said to have special power. There are ley lines or leys, marked or unmarked lines connecting sacred places, nowadays often the sites of churches.

Places of worship have an atmosphere of sanctity which is often tangible. The poet Eric Gladwin has written of this,

> Prayer in an Old Church
> (St Mary's Thame, Oxfordshire)
>
> Dear God, who, through the fabric of this place:
> Knew of praise and joy and longing in the minds
> Of generations quietly kneeling here . . .
> Please hear us, in our turn
> And know our thankfulness
> For confidence in Your Peace; eternity.
> Aware too after last Blessing by Christ's priest
> When the heavy doors swing open to the mundane street
> That we have left this little gift: ourselves . . .
> To strengthen this, Your sanctuary of Peace.
>
> NOTE:

When we visit a place we leave behind an 'imprint' of ourselves on departure. This ancient Principle is termed 'psychometry' or 'Morphic resonance' in modern terms. This gradually increases in all sacred buildings when correctly used, especially near the altar or parts dedicated: as to our Lady. The very fabric of the building is thus permeated and so gives back, as it were, in times of distress.[63]

Perhaps there are more places than we are aware of which are or can become sacred through a particular interaction with humanity. Perhaps we need to open ourselves to greater interaction and co-operation with the forces of nature.

Findhorn on the Moray Firth in Scotland is now a thriving community and eco-village. It was founded in the early 1960s by Peter and Eileen Caddy with Dorothy Maclean, in the most extraordinary circumstances. They felt led to each other and then to a wild place on the Scottish coast, which had been used as a rubbish dump. There they created the most beautiful, lush garden with fruit, flowers and vegetables, including a 40 pound cabbage, which baffled experienced gardeners and members of the Soil Association. Those involved in the creation of Findhorn put the success down to a close spiritual connection to the place as they followed guidance given by angels, earth spirits and 'Devas' (beings of light), with whom the community members co-operated to work the land, enabling it to produce almost miraculous growth. Dorothy had begun to receive messages during her periods of meditation and was initially hesitant to accept them.

> Although I had begun this experiment with a large measure of scepticism, no doubt influenced by limited conceptions of such beings as fairies, as the contact continued and proved valid in giving help with the growth of the garden I accepted the reality of such beings, and we followed out their instructions. This seemed to delight them, particularly our putting into action what they suggested. At first some of them felt very distant and rather unfriendly, which they said was due to the treatment man had given Nature through his greed, thoughtlessness, and misuse. But as they found us heeding what they said, they became more and more helpful and friendly and asked us to plant as many varieties of vegetables as possible.

Precise instructions came through as to when to plant what and how to tend the plants.

> ... people were beginning to come to see the garden, and after seeing it they told their friends about it. A steady stream of visitors began to pour in to see the amazing growth, greenness, and abundance which was being produced in the sandy patch. The garden was becoming a local showplace, and people who came found it hard to believe that the first seed had been sown just a few months previously.[64]

Pilgrimage

Journeys to sacred places, whether natural landmarks, man-made structures or places where specific religious events took place are undertaken by people of all faiths. In a pilgrimage, the journey, a round trip, is as important as the destination.

Most religions have special sacred places, where particular events took place, or revered holy people lived, and visits to these have always formed part of people's response. There are pilgrimage sites all over the world, from the Island of Shikodo in Japan, with its eighty-eight temples to Santiago de Compostela in Spain. Religious traditions all have principal places of pilgrimage as well as lesser shrines. Hindus head for the holy river, the Ganges at Banaras or Varanasi, where Shiva is believed to have lived; Buddhists go to Bodh Gaya, where the Buddha attained Enlightenment; Sikhs to Amritsar, to the Golden Temple; Jews to the Wailing Wall, all that remains of Solomon's Temple in Jerusalem. Christians go to Bethlehem and Jerusalem in the Holy Land of Israel, where Jesus was born, lived and died. In France, Lourdes is a destination for those who are ill, usually accompanied by helpers, the patients hope for a miracle cure at the grotto where Bernadette saw her visions of the Virgin Mary.

The best-known of all pilgrimages is the annual Hajj to Mecca. This is required of all Muslims who are able to manage it physically and financially as it is one of the Five Pillars of Islam. Undertaken in the twelfth lunar month, the pilgrimage has a set pattern. On each day a particular ritual is performed, linked to the faith. Initially there is purification and all the men dress in white, symbolizing their equality before Allah. One may then perform the *umra* or 'lesser Hajj' and then proceed to the main Hajj. Seven circumambulations of the Ka'aba, the holiest shrine in Islam is the main event for the pilgrims. The great black marble structure is said to date back to Abraham, where he showed his obedience to God by being prepared to sacrifice his son Ishmael. Other rituals such as a standing in prayer on Mount Arafat from noon to sundown and stoning three pillars which represent the devil follow on subsequent days. Return home is joyful and is marked by the pilgrim taking the title Hajji or Hajjah.

The BBC has set up a website for people to share their Hajj experiences, from which these are taken,

> I performed Hajj in 2001 (when I was 70 years of age) along with my wife. Before my Hajj I was lucky to perform Umrah a few times when I was younger and fit. When I went I was very unwell and it was

difficult for me to properly walk. Before boarding the plane I fell very sick with high fever and vomiting. At a point I was even thinking whether I should cancel the flight. I became very, very depressed and prayed to Allah that He in His mercy would allow me to perform the greatest of the pillars of my faith. By the grace of Allah from somewhere I got the confidence that Allah would answer my inner prayer. My son, daughter-in-law and daughter all encouraged me to under take the journey and by the grace of Allah We boarded the plane late in the evening. Throughout the flight I was in a sort of stupor. Early in the morning we arrived at Jeddah, drove to Mecca. I was amazed that after arrival at Mecca I started getting my strength back and I could perform Hajj without help.

As a new Muslim and as an American the Hajj was the greatest thing I have ever experienced. I know Islam is getting all this bad coverage in the media but I saw the true peaceful Islam in Hajj. There was over three million people there and I did not see one fight. I did not see one person being rude to the other even though they were from so many different countries and cultural backgrounds. It was truly beautiful, a life-changing experience.

Truly the most amazing experience. A place where race, colour or cast play no role. Where everyone is as one, all there for the same reason – to praise their God. Approaching the mosque raises every hair, brings tears to your eyes and warmth to your heart. The beautiful voice of the Imam reciting the Holy Quran is sure to move you. The atmosphere is incredible, and there is always a feeling of safety and belonging. Just thinking about it brings tears to my eyes. May we all be granted the opportunity to experience this spiritual journey.[65]

In *The Road to Canterbury, A Modern Pilgrimage* Shirley du Boulay describes her walk of 130 miles along the Pilgrim's Way from Winchester, the ancient capital of Wessex to Canterbury Cathedral and its shrine to the martyr St Thomas Becket. She reflects on medieval times and the changes evident in the route today, as well as on the concept of pilgrimage itself. This is how she ends her book,

. . . it was the journey itself that was the point. . . .
I had been changed by this pilgrimage, but I do not expect to know how for a long time. Though on this Sunday morning I knew the pilgrimage had reached some sort of completion, it had not ended. This

symbolic microcosm of the inner journey had to find its resonances with the longer, day-to-day, pilgrimage. Perhaps my inability to know when it ended was a precise reflection of its inner parallel. We were resuming our day-to-day lives, our journeys of perpetual pilgrimage. This pilgrimage from Winchester to Canterbury had not ended on arrival any more than life ends with death. But I did feel that I understood a little better where the sacred place is to be found.[66]

The central tenet of all pilgrimage is that it is the inner transformation which is most important. Without that, the physical journey is pointless. The Sikh Guru Nanak denounced pilgrimage as devoid of religious meaning unless that journey to truth was stressed.

Fasting

The practice of abstaining from eating for a period of time has long been part of religious practice, as purification of the body is thought to lead to clarity of mind and spirit. Frequently the practice involves sexual abstinence too. In shamanistic practice, fasting is often part of the preparation for rituals and the Gospels too recount that Jesus fasted. Lent, the period leading up to Easter, was traditionally a period of fasting and reflection, although nowadays it is more usually just a time when people give up something, like chocolate or alcohol perhaps. The underlying purpose is to concentrate on the spiritual rather than the material.

Muslims fast for a month each year, during Ramadan, eating and drinking only after sundown, a practice known as *sawm* in Arabic. This takes place in the ninth month of the year, when the Qur'an was given to Muhammad, celebrated on the 27th day, which commemorates the 'Night of Power'. It is a time for increased focus on faith, with more frequent attendance at the mosque, a special prayer added to the normal routine, and some Muslims praying throughout the night. The end of the fast is marked by the celebrations of Eid-al-Fitr.

This extract of a blog of an Egyptian Muslim gives an indication of the experience,

> **The thing I love the most about Ramadan:** the fantastic settings in Cairo's streets from lanterns, colored lights, free food outdoor tables (ma"det el-rahman) and the cozy culture from meeting friends after breaking the fast (Iftar) or big family gatherings.

The hardest/most annoying thing about Ramadan : the wrong perception of people about Ramadan, that it's just for upkeeping yourself from eating and drinking, and not understanding the true meaning of it, from self-disciplinary and training your will, to sharing the moments of other poor people all over the world. The second most annoying thing is, people giving an excuse of fasting to behave stupidly/weirdly.

What I want to get out of Ramadan this year : I would like to talk to more people to make them aware of the 'true' spirit of Ramadan, or at least how I see it, and for me to question the religion which will lead me either to strengthen my beliefs or change it. [67]

Chanting

A member of the International Society for Krishna Consciousness described the effect of chanting *Hare Krishna*, the name of the Lord.

> I had already found the philosophy brilliant but it was the *kirtan* that really convinced me. I saw how the devotees would chant on the street for five hours and then, at one festival I attended, when everyone was lying down in a tent waiting for food, tired after being on the street all those hours, a spontaneous kirtan began and lasted for more than another hour. There was no one around to see. It was just an expression of the devotees' love for God. This personal expression of feeling for God was the best I'd ever experienced. Everything else was forgotten. Only the name of the One we loved or aspired to love was repeated, over and over, creating a wonderful connection with God. Chanting alone can lead us to love of God.[68]

Yoga

Widely popular in the West nowadays, yoga is practised in various ways. Some schools of yoga are more, some less closely based on the original teachings in the Upanishads, where Shiva is seen as the god of *yogins* or ascetics. A classic work is *The Yoga Aphorisms of Patanjali* in which yoga is explained as 'union', or 'yoke', a method leading to union with ultimate reality through control of thought-waves of the mind. Commentators have used the image of a lake. When the surface is disturbed, full of waves, the bottom, the atman or soul, cannot be seen. The aim is the one-pointed mind, resulting in clarity and stillness.

Yoga does not merely involve exercise, as is so often the case in Western classes, but is a holistic system including disciplined conduct and meditation as well as breathing techniques.

Here is an account of the effect of yoga.

> Over the past fifteen years some of the most exciting openings have come to me through the practice of yoga and the study of yoga philosophy. Through the practice of the physical postures of yoga I not only made my body supple and balanced, but found a way of bringing my awareness into the present moment, so that without any great effort I could touch the experience of life in the NOW. Through the practice of concentration and meditation I began to take charge of my mind so that I could at times prevent my mental energy from diffusing in all directions and could conserve my inner power, or direct it like a beam in the direction of my choice. Through Yoga Nidra I learned a technique in which my body, mind and emotions experience complete relaxation, while my consciousness, fully aware, touched the deep dimensions of power within me. Through chanting a mantra I can still the mind, or use the sound like a booster rocket to take my consciousness to higher dimensions of my being. By practising breath control I have discovered ways of linking body, mind and soul, touching the deep levels of peace within me.[69]

Interfaith

Interfaith encounters involve being open to new ideas, which may challenge our own deeply held beliefs, but are also profoundly enriching, as in the case of this Muslim,

> My faith, however, has become anything but quiet; it is turbulent, wild, rampant and unruly . . . . Learning about Buddhism makes me rethink Islamic Sufism; reading Judaism I find myself making analogies with Islamic Law; listening to a lecture about Christianity I instantly revisit all that I have known about revelation in Islam; and making acquaintance with Hinduism I startle from the flow of questions, which could never come to my mind earlier . . . . You keep knowing God and you thrill with the experience of this most of your time. You welcome what others dismiss as doubt because it has become the source of your joy and ecstasy.[70]

Search

In Asia the Ten Ox-herding Pictures are well known. They depict a man's spiritual search for his true self, the ox. He tracks, finds and tames the ox but the ox then disappears as the self searched for and found is transcended. Then the searcher also disappears and an empty circle is shown as the individual has lost importance and merged with the whole. That is not the end, however, as the last picture shows the man back where he started. He is back in the world, but now he is no longer of it, he has found the wisdom which will enable him to serve his fellows with compassion.

People are often led to faith or to a vocation after a search which can take years and many different twists and turns of fate.

> In my early years I had contact with the Church through Sunday school, singing in a choir and later church going, though my parents were not regular church-goers. I had some contact with a Christian group and church when I was at university. The period that I spent in the army was unsettling; I drifted away from the Church and I suppose that I would have classed myself as an agnostic as far as belief in God and Christ was concerned.
>
> After demobilization and resumption of university career, I continued the search for a satisfying philosophy and faith. I met and talked to several people who probably influenced me without my knowing it, but the turning point came at the time when I became emotionally involved with a female student who had recently become a Christian and to whom this experience meant a great deal.
>
> During this emotional upheaval I returned to my digs one evening and as I sat resting after the evening meal on my own in my room I saw a vision of myself wearing a clerical collar and in a pulpit in the act of preaching. As the vision faded I was rather disturbed at such an unusual and unexpected event, though, as I have explained, the incident took place when I was already in a charged emotional state. I went on to play badminton to try to take my mind off what I could not understand.
>
> Shortly after, I borrowed a new translation of the Bible from the library and as I was reading a passage from it one night I felt for the first time that God was speaking to me in the words that I was reading.
>
> Following closely after I had further mystical/spiritual experiences which made me strongly aware of the presence of God, once at an

uncle's wedding where I was best man and also during Holy Communion services. It would be impossible to describe these experiences in words but they were connected with, and deepened, the setting where they occurred.

At one stage I felt consciously that a kind of integration was taking place within me and that, as it were, I was being made to face in a particular direction.

At the same time as this vision occurred, I forgot to mention that I was made aware that I should go far afield with this message.

At Epiphany (I was immediately back in church), which followed soon afterwards, the conviction that I should go overseas was strongly reinforced by the service and the sermon.

Among the changes that took place in my life the greatest was the confidence I now felt to face new challenges, though I was well aware that I was being given help from outside to meet them also.

I was seconded from my teaching post for a year to train for the ministry. I was ordained deacon and served as a part-time curate as well as returning to my teaching post. I was ordained priest and went to South India to lecture in English and to be the chaplain to the church of South India students. In this way my vision came true.

What I consider particularly remarkable is that I had never intended to enter the ministry and certainly never thought that I should return to India (where I spent nine months during my time in the army) as a missionary. I now felt my life had far greater purpose and meaning, and looking for guidance has remained a constant attitude. [4107] [71]

Here a wide range of religious triggers of spiritual experience has been shown to produce many different experiences, often to the surprise of the experient.

7. Non-Religious Triggers of Spiritual Experience

Many spiritual experiences are not related to any kind of religious practice, but are triggered by glorious music, the beauty of nature or absorption in creativity. If there is any common factor, perhaps it is a shift of focus from the concerns of the everyday world, away from more self-centred pursuits, leading to an openness to another dimension. It is however the case that the triggers are more often less pleasant – illness, stress and depression frequently result in a change of direction, and are in retrospect seen as a challenge or wake-up call. Often the comfort felt at such times has a profound effect.

Place

> ... London's Charing Cross Station. For me it has become like a small Underground sacrament.
>
> The last time I passed through it, on the Bakerloo Line, was just after Easter Sunday when the imagination is sensitised to the nearness of mystery. I have always associated the place with Francis Thompson's poem 'The Kingdom of God', picturing angels ascending and descending between heaven and Platform 3. Synchronically, almost scarily, this is what happened to me as the train drew into the station. While only half aware of the sea of different faces and garments, and half listening to the lilt and timbre of many accents, I began to perceive in a more focused way the colours and textures, shapes and sounds flowing from the human panoply around me.
>
> In the sudden spring warmth they seemed to shimmer with divinity. It was one of those moments of disclosure that many people experience a few times in their lives, when, caught off guard, time stands still, and a deeper awareness breaks through. It was a gift of grace, when God's presence seemed to be pressing in on me more intensely than usual. It was all so mysterious, yet so intimate and energising.

I still remember my delight at the realisation that the power within Creation, the author of all the beauty I was just then experiencing, was, in fact, personally involved with me, utterly satisfying and fulfilling. There was also a strong sense of the part I played in this whole panorama. A line from de Chardin came to me: 'What I call my body is not part of the universe which I possess totally; it is the whole universe which I possess partly.'

Even though my experience was profound, it did not last long – just for a brief space between the opening and closing of those sliding doors at Charing Cross station. In one sense the unsolicited epiphany changed nothing; in another sense it changed everything.[72]

Illness and Prospect of Death

It is said that nothing concentrates the mind like the prospect of dying. Here, however, the result of a terminal diagnosis was rather unexpected.

15 years ago I had all the signs and symptoms of cancer of the colon. I spent half a Friday in St. Mary's and the specialist said 'It is difficult to think of any other possible diagnosis which fits the facts.' There was to be a final test on the Monday. I left St. Mary's and took a walk to Marble Arch and along Oxford Street. I was startled by the brilliance of the colours of the street. Several people looked at me and smiled (They saw the deep peace on my face). I spent a weekend of deepest happiness. All my worries disappeared. – 'I should be dead in 6 months.' I truly for once took no anxious thought. On the Monday the test proved that I had nothing seriously wrong and by the end of the week my brow was furrowed again. [569][73]

In this experience, illness was feared,

I am 41 now, yet I have never forgotten the experience I had when I was about 18. It is in many ways intangible because after all it was only a 'feeling' and yet it was very real to me then, and still fills me with a sense of wonder. A friend of mine had been suspected of contracting T.B. and I was dreadfully worried that I too may have caught it. So worried in fact that it was constantly in my mind. I was not religious in the sense that I went to church, but from childhood I suppose I have always been a 'believer' so I kept praying that I hadn't caught this disease. Many times I asked God to 'please let me be free of it', 'please don't let me catch it'.

It was Christmas and on Boxing Day I went by myself to the local cinema and even on the way and while I was there I was still sending up my little prayers. Then suddenly, during the film, and completely without warning, relief 'flooded through me'. Tears of joy came into my eyes because I knew, without a shadow of a doubt that I would be alright. This time my prayers were thanks and I walked home from that film as though I were treading on air, and I never worried a single moment more.

It is against my nature to set this down coldly in print for I feel that I haven't the ability to adequately describe something which had such a profound effect on me, but I have never been able to explain why worry should have turned to relief and joy with no 'outside' influence to cause it. I am a married woman, housewife and Civil Servant (no children) of British nationality and little or no religious upbringing, although my parents (and I) claim to be Church of England. [001709]

Accident

This experience changed the person's life completely and set her on a path of spiritual searching and development which continues.

It was a beautiful August evening, around 6:00pm. Clear skies, smooth flight.... I have never particularly enjoyed flying, so was aware of feeling anxious as I climbed on board the aircraft. But this anxiety increased dramatically when I 'heard' a voice inside my head saying 'don't get on the plane'. I immediately dismissed this as me being silly....

I also remember being about to confess to my friend about my 'silly' thought-warning, when the propeller coughed and stopped. We were flying at 1,500 feet.

My immediate thought was my friend was trying to scare me as a joke. But when I saw the blood drain from his face, I knew this was it. He valiantly tried to re-start the engine. It spluttered and died again. And then he went into hyper-mode – sending out mayday calls and jettisoning the fuel. I became paralysed, as he banked the plane, trying to find some where to land. The only place possible was a small field surrounded by high trees. He headed the plane for it. I can remember thinking 'this is it. I'm going to die'. But with that realisation came a flood of relief. Although I had never told anyone about it, I was going through a dark suicidal depression. I had made a series of disastrous life-choices which resulted in being semi-estranged from my children, my business partner walking out on me leaving me with a £30,000 debt, and my flat was in danger of being repossessed. A dear friend had also been murdered by a bomb-blast in Namibia. In strange sensation that dying in a plane crash would be a heroine's death, and perhaps make up for the mess I had made of my life.

I remember calling out in my head to 'my guides' to help me. I can't say I felt any presence, but it helped to focus on something beyond myself as I watched the ground coming nearer. I can remember facing a line of trees, and saying to the pilot 'we're going to make it'. He answered, 'no we're not. Get ready'. At that moment we hit the trees. I can't remember anything until the plane smashed into the ground causing the glass from the windows to blow into my lap. I can remember being thrown back into my seat, and thinking, my god, I'm still alive. Shit. And then the pilot screaming – get out the plane's going to blow up. That was the worst thing for me. I can remember throwing myself out of the door and running away from the plane. . . .

I remember sinking down onto the grass beside the plane, shaking. And then I remember as if the protective bubble I had surrounded myself with to shield myself from the awfulness of what life meant to me had been ripped apart. Metaphorically, it felt as if my skin had been torn away leaving my inside raw and exposed. I have never felt so lost, alone or frightened in my life.

. . . My recovery was very slow and painful – I felt desperately depressed and unable to work for weeks. It was during a bout of extreme despair, again lying on the sofa, that I had an extraordinary experience which changed everything.

It felt as if a sentence 'dropped' into my head, which said 'you will become a bereavement counsellor'. In that instant everything began to make sense, and I knew what I had to do I literally bounced off the sofa, and back into feeling more alive than I had for a long time. . . . someone else introduced me Elizabeth Kubler Ross's work, and I was back on a plane . . . this time to the West Coast of the US to start training as a Life, Death and Transition facilitator. This led to fifteen years of 'getting my self well'. . . .

In short, I divide my life into 'before the crash and after the crash'. I look back on the me who was before the crash and can't believe I was that mad hedonistic, crazy drug-taking party girl who had completely lost the plot and was heading fast towards melt-down. It catapulted me into a profound healing journey which led me to study with mystical teachers from around the world. I suppose one could say I embraced a shamanic journey. . . . [100051]

Despair

Sometimes it is in the depths of life, when there seems to be no hope, no light at the end of the tunnel that something happens which turns everything around.

> In utter disillusionment with self and church, I came to the 'end of my tether'. In a state of intense, inner wretchedness, of such intensity, that my mind seemed on the point of breaking, I got up at 4am and began wandering aimlessly in the wooded hillside. This went on for some time until, unexpectedly, the words of Psalm 130 sounded clearly in my mind . . . 'And plenteous redemption is ever found in Him; and, all his iniquities, He Israel shall redeem.' With those words light seemed to envelop me, and there flowed into my desolate heart such a flood of Love and compassion that I was overwhelmed by the weight of it. It was stricken by such wonder and amazement that I burst into tears of joy; it seemed to flow through my whole being with a cleansing and healing virtue. From that moment I knew that Love was the nature of reality. I was fit and well again. The experience is as real today as it was then . . . The awareness of Love fills one's being with tremendous strength. One is weak but at the same time very strong. It is a very unusual feeling. [0227]

In 1986 the journalist John McCarthy was kidnapped and taken hostage in Beirut. He was eventually held captive for 5 years. This happened early in his incarceration.

> I was to be in this solitary cell for les than three months, but after the first two or three weeks it felt as if I had slipped into a different timescale. Days passed without any variation. The food-and-bathroom run and then nothing. I read and re-read everything available. I relived much of my life and made endless plans for the future. But after two months with not the slightest hint that I might be released I got more frightened. So many of my reflections had me feeling quite inadequate that I really began to doubt that I could cope alone.
> One morning these fears became unbearable. I stood in the cell sinking into despair. I felt that I was literally sinking, being sucked into a whirlpool. I was on my knees, gasping for air, drowning in hopelessness and helplessness. I thought that I was passing out. I could only think of one thing to say – 'Help me please, oh God, help me.' The next instant I was standing up, surrounded by a warm, bright light. I was

dancing, full of joy. In the space of a minute, despair had vanished, replaced by boundless optimism.

What had happened? I had never had any great faith, despite a Church of England upbringing. But I felt that I had to give thanks. But to what? Unsure of the nature of the experience, I felt most comfortable acknowledging the Good Spirit which seemed to have rescued me.

It gave me great strength to carry on and, more importantly, a huge renewal of hope – I was going to survive. Throughout my captivity, I would take comfort from this experience, drawing on it whenever optimism and determination flagged. In the euphoria of the next few days I felt completely confident. But soon I found myself wondering how, even with the support of a Good Spirit, I was going to manage alone.[74]

Depression

The writer Eckhart Tolle explains at the beginning of his first book how his writing was triggered by an experience which he recounts at the beginning of *The Power of Now*.

> Until my thirtieth year, I lived in a state of almost continuous anxiety interspersed with periods of suicidal depression....
>
> One night not long after my twenty-ninth birthday, I woke up in the early hours with a feeling of absolute dread. I had woken up with such a feeling many times before, but this time it was more intense than it had ever been....
>
> 'I cannot live with myself any longer.' This was the thought that kept repeating itself in my mind. Then suddenly I became aware of what a peculiar thought it was. 'Am I one or two? If I cannot live with myself, there must be two of me: the "I" and the "self" that "I" cannot live with.' 'Maybe', I thought, 'only one of them is real'.
>
> I was so stunned by this strange realization that my mind stopped. I was fully conscious, but there were no more thoughts. Then I felt drawn into what seemed like a vortex of energy. It was a slow movement at first and then accelerated. I was gripped by an intense fear, and my body began to shake. I heard the words 'resist nothing', as if spoken inside my chest. I could feel myself being sucked into a void. It felt as if the void was inside myself rather than outside. Suddenly, there was no more fear, and I let myself fall into that void. I have no recollection what happened after that.

> I was awakened by the chirping of a bird outside the window. I had never heard such a sound before. My eyes were still closed, and I saw the image of a precious diamond. Yes, if a diamond could make a sound, this is what it would be like. I opened my eyes. The first light of dawn was filtering through the curtains. Without any thought, I felt, I knew, that there is infinitely more to light than we realize. That soft luminosity filtering through the curtains was love itself. Tears came into my eyes. I got up and walked around the room. I recognized the room, and yet I knew I had never truly seen it before. . . .
>
> That day I walked around the city in utter amazement at the miracle of life on earth, as if I had just been born into this world.[75]

Tolle lived in a state of bliss for several months afterwards, but still did not understand what had happened to him. It was the beginning of a spiritual journey which eventually enabled him to interpret his experience. He realized that the intensity of his suffering had enabled him to split from his unhappy ego and to discover his true nature, his pure consciousness. He learned to repeat the experience and eventually became a spiritual teacher.

This experience of love, triggered by long-standing depression, was sent in when the experient was aged 77.

> I will send you an experience which befell me in 1926, when I was like you aged 30. It has governed my outlook on life ever since. . . .
>
> After a serious abdominal operation in Spring 1925, while on leave in England from duty in Burma, I had been for about a year in a state of great depression, and had lost all belief in God. In spite of treatment by psychiatrists, both in and out of hospital, I had set out by sea on return to duty with the firm intention of taking my life during the journey. A book on theosophy which had been given to me before my departure, helped me to survive the journey and opened my mind to the possibility that a world existed beyond the reach of our physical senses. On reaching Burma, I got in touch with the local Theosophical lodge and for a few weeks found some peace of mind.
>
> Soon, however, the old depression returned until one day I was sitting on the slope of Mandalay Hill (very sacred to Buddhists), bemoaning my wretched state and wondering how I could carry on. Suddenly I experienced the most vivid sensation that I and all my surroundings were, so to speak, immersed in an ocean of love. I realised in a flash that there is indeed a spiritual world beyond the reach of our senses, and that the spirit of love, which many call God, permeates and

envelops our physical world. I was filled with intense relief and joy and the realisation that I must do all in my power to help establish God's kingdom of love upon earth. [003427]

Fear

Many people who do not normally pray, do so to ask for help in times of crisis. This experience, however, is recounted by a young woman Christian missionary. She had become a missionary as a result of this experience in childhood and linked the two events,

> Perhaps the following may not come under the heading 'Unusual Experience' to those who try to live out logically what they believe. To a great many people they would be unusual. The first experience was when I was ten. I attended a small country school. I had been accused of stealing. I hadn't done so but felt terribly ashamed that I had been accused. Later in the afternoon after school, I sat on a bank by the roadside and wished I could die. Before me was field of hay, not yet ripe and shimmering like brown-green velvet in the shadowy sunlight. It was beautiful and I thought, 'If I die I won't see that again'. Instantly on the thought came the knowledge that God knew I had not stolen and that nothing else mattered. The relief was tremendous. Two things resulted from that experience; I became a missionary and also realised more and more that inner integrity is an absolute for wholeness of personality. The second experience happened when I was a young woman.
>
> I was, perforce, travelling alone in the Kashmir Hills. It was near dusk. I had left the motorcar that brought me up the hill and, having been forbidden to take strenuous exercise, was being carried in a 'dandie' by four men for the rest of the way. A fifth, very unpleasant man insisted on coming with us. I saw this man eye my handbag and exchange a meaningful look with one of the men in the rear. I knew they meant to rob me, that there would probably be violence and I was terrified. Then it was as if a voice within me said, 'You say you have faith and this is how you react when it comes to the test'. I felt very ashamed, faith returned and I felt an extraordinary peace. I could even wonder what would happen, where it would happen (possibly in the belt of trees we were approaching,) and what I should do. One of the leading men turned. I smiled to him. As he was a Muslim (they all were), I asked him if he had ever been to Ajmer. Ajmer is the second Mecca to the Muslim. 'No', he replied and asked eagerly if I knew

Ajmer. I replied that I lived there. They all began to ask questions about the great mosque and I was able to answer their questions and even to tell them some things they hadn't known. I knew then that I was perfectly safe. We got lost on the hillside – my fault, not theirs – and I was nearly two hours late reaching my destination.

We parted, each praying a blessing on the other. The result of that experience was that during the Quit India months and during the troubled times at Partition I was able to travel anywhere in the country without fear. I am slight in build and timid by nature. [000005]

Anger

Neale Donald Walsch was so angry about the way things were in his life that he sat down and wrote a letter to God.

It was a spiteful, passionate letter, full of confusions, contortions and condemnations. And a *pile* of angry questions.

> Why wasn't my life working? What would it *take* to get it to work? Why could I not find happiness in relationships? . . . *What had I done to deserve a life of such continuing struggle?* [76]

When he had finished, Walsch found himself unable to toss his pen aside and was compelled to keep writing, and answers to his questions and frustrations seemed to come to him. He felt as if he were taking dictation and continued for some years until he had a series of *Conversations with God* eventually leading him to *Communion with God*.

Nature

The oral traditions are particularly sensitive to nature, with a focus on living in harmony with the earth and its energies. Black Elk (1863–1950) a Wichasha Wakau or Holy Man of the Oglala Lakota Oyate (Oglala Sioux Tribe) of North America describes this.

> Peace comes to the souls of men when they realise their relationship, their oneness, with the universe and all its powers, and when they realise that at the centre of the universe dwells Wakan Tanka, and that this centre is really everywhere, it is within each of us.[77]

The eighteenth-century Romantic poets and artists were particularly sensitive to the natural world and reflected nature in all its moods in their work. This is Jean-Jacques Rousseau (1712–1778) author of Le Contrat Social (The Social Contract),

> When evening drew near, I would go down from the peaks of the Isle and willingly sit by the lake on the shore, in some hidden retreat; there, the lapping of the waves and the agitation of the water would steady my senses and drive away any restlessness from my soul, plunging it into a delightful reverie during which night would often catch me by surprise, without my noticing it. The ebb and flow of the water, its continuous and at times surging sound would unceasingly strike my eyes and ears and replace the internal stirrings which the reverie was subduing inside me, and these were enough to make me revel in my existence without taking the trouble to think.
>
> . . .
>
> What does one enjoy in such a situation? Nothing outside one's self, nothing but one's self and one's own being; as long as this state lasts, one feels self-sufficient, like God.[78]

Artists are often particularly moved by nature, which leads them to a spiritual response,

> Sir William Rothenstein wrote in his recollections, *Men and Memories*, that 'one's very being seems to be absorbed in the fields, trees and the walls one is striving to paint' and believed the experience of painting out of doors gave him insight into the poetry of the great mystics, European and Eastern. 'At rare moments while painting,' he says, 'I have felt myself caught, as it were, in a kind of cosmic rhythm; but such experiences are usually all too brief.' Ben Nicholson is, perhaps saying the same thing more laconically when he is quoted in a monograph on his work as remarking, 'As I see it, painting and religious experience are the same thing.'[79]

The German Romantic painter Caspar David Friedrich (1774–1840) expresses the awesome, yet melancholy beauty of nature in his paintings. His figures usually have their backs to the viewer, and with them we gaze into the distance to the transcendent beyond. He said an artist needed to capture the natural scene as well as an inner response,

> . . . pure will . . . to represent Nature simply, nobly and greatly, as she truly is, if one has a mind, disposition and feeling to recognize and understand her.

The painter should not paint merely what he sees in front of him but also what he sees within him. If he sees nothing within himself, however, then he should refrain from painting what he sees in front of him.[80]

People have always felt an affinity with nature, yet aware of something 'other' within it. Here are two accounts sent to Alister Hardy,

As a child in the country, I wandered by myself sometimes but was rather afraid when I became conscious of solitude and silence. I became increasingly aware of a Presence which I associated with nature around me. In my adolescence I gave It the name 'God', and aimed at being alone to commune with It.

Natural beauty and vastness has always aroused an attitude of worship in me, at times in spite of myself. The words of Psalm 8 have often been in my mind: 'When I consider the heavens, the work of thy fingers, the moon and stars which thou hast ordained, what is man that thou art mindful of him, and the son of man that thou visitest him?' This attitude persists and is enhanced by the discoveries of the astronauts. [603]

Since adolescence, on many occasions, I have experienced the presence of God in nature. As far as I can recall this has usually been in times of fine weather and in pleasant surroundings, but not always. Frequently, as the feeling first appears, I notice a gentle breeze passing across my forehead. In fact as I wrote this I had the very same experience, and I take it as confirmation that allowing the record of the experience out of my hands is alright. The experiences of God in nature come unasked and cannot be predicted. [from 003519]

Music

Glorious music is often associated with spirituality as it is beyond words. At a recent conference on mysticism, many uplifting lectures took place, but the event most delegates remembered as most closely reflecting the subject, was a violin recital of Bach's Partita in D Minor on a solo violin, performed in a beautiful country village church. These two experiences express a similar feeling.

When I went to performance of Sir John Tavener's Beautiful Names in Westminster Cathedral last year, I had an experience that I regard as bliss. The setting of the piece in the cathedral, the subject of the piece (the 99 names of Allah in Islam) and the gongs and bells in particular of Sir John's orchestration all blended together so that these details no longer existed and the whole was fused so that I was caught up in the most amazing experience of being held and profoundly loved.

An experience similar to this was told to me by a student following her participation in the first performance of the piece that Sir John wrote for the Winchester University choir – Marienhymne (2004). She was singing in the echo choir in Winchester cathedral – out of sight of the other choir and the audience – in the retro-choir which has all the icons and many candles – the light is dim. She said 'I am a pagan and my goddess is Kali. In that piece, Kali took me in her arms and I never want her to let me go.'[81]

Music seems to reflect a deeper awareness of the universe and some people are particularly sensitive to this.

After conducting a concert with a large number of forces the music appears to linger in the universe for a long time afterwards – several hours. It happened first a long time ago when I conducted a performance of Handel's Messiah but has been repeated many times since. It is as if I hear the music of the universe, numerous angel choirs joining with the entire cosmos to make music. It is intensely uplifting and requires no effort on my part. It is as if the whole world is singing. When I am driving I often open the car windows to hear it more clearly.[82]

Sound

Drums are sometimes used in shamanic journeying to carry the experience along.

I regularly do shamanic drumming trips using the drum beat to travel on. These always produce insightful experiences. One experience will give you a flavour of them. I pass through a hole between the roots of a tree and down a series of tunnels under the earth which I associate with burrowing creatures such as badgers and rabbits. Sometimes I pass small animals huddled in corners on the way. In the end I come out into a bleakish desert place – a flat plain surrounded by tall snow-capped mountains. Into this landscape a unicorn appears – an amazingly beautiful creature – light blue with a glistening horn and a flowing mane. He asks me to ride on his back and I get the most amazing pertinence of strength flowing through my whole being and it is this strength that I take back when I return to the 'ordinary world' by the way of the dark underground tunnels and the tree root.[83]

Gongs can also be powerful, as this experience attests.

It resulted from an incident that happened during a music-making course, at which some tam-tams (a type of large gong) were used. Some of the participants, impressed by the quality and depth of sound created using the tam-tams, asked for the musician who was playing them to 'show us what they can really do', whereupon the musician began to build up the sound, layer upon layer, until the volume was so loud and the sound waves so dense that it completely took my breath away. I was standing probably 6 feet away at the time, and the sound waves hit me with the impact of a solid object, like a train hurtling towards me at 100mph. I couldn't move; I was rooted to the spot like a rabbit in the headlights of a car. Afterwards, my body trembled like a leaf for about an hour and I had the most awful sense that something dreadful had happened to me.

As the days passed, I gradually forgot about what occurred until one evening, about a week later, when I attended another music event. As I was listening to the music, my hearing suddenly became acutely sensitive and I had to run out of the hall as I couldn't stand the volume. This was the start of the delayed shock reaction that I was to suffer from for at least the next 5 years as it worked its way through my system and which soon catapulted me into my Near Death Experience.

Initially and for a few weeks after, not just my hearing, but all my senses became acutely hyper-sensitised. I couldn't eat (the plainest of rice tasted too strong), I couldn't bear the smell of food (not even cold food), I couldn't sleep, I couldn't bear any variation of light, I couldn't bear to be touched, I felt nauseous and dizzy all the time, my heart was constantly racing at two or three times its normal pace on account of the flood of adrenaline released into my system and I fell into a state of continual, abject terror – not of, or about, anything specific but simply as a physiological reaction to this physical event. My quality of life physically seemed unendurable, and psychologically, it was hell – I desperately longed to feel better, or to be out of my body so as not to suffer, but there was nothing I could do about it and I couldn't run away from it. Had I been courageous enough, I would have committed suicide many times over but, ironically, I was too scared to take this action in case I hurt myself further! I experienced a continual state of black despair and negativity so intense, and for so long, that

Non-Religious Triggers

I began to feel that I was carrying the sins of the world on my shoulders and that I was the unwilling, innocent conduit for the purging process. Maybe that's aggrandizing my role, perhaps I'm suffering delusions of grandeur, but it genuinely felt like I was symbolically somehow going through an 'Archtypal' human experience rather than something personal.
This triggered the following extraordinary experience of being somehow 'dead'.

During one of the nights when I couldn't sleep, I was lying in bed, experiencing what felt to me like a constant bombardment of electrical shocks shooting through my body from head to foot, as if I were plugged into an electrical socket and being mildly electrocuted. I was thinking how unbearable this sensation of 'fizzing' was, when I suddenly became aware that I had stopped breathing and, in fact, had not been breathing for a while. With this realisation came a reassuring sense that this was absolutely fine, that this was a state with which I was, in fact, far more familiar and 'at home' than when I was breathing – almost as if the living state was a temporary deviation from the norm. In an instant I both realised and accepted, quite matter-of-factly and with complete equanimity, that I was dead and no longer had a body. I had become simple awareness, with no form, and nothing around me, just a sort of grey nothingness. No sooner did this revelation occur (so it seemed) than I was once more back in my breathing body, shocked by this new experience. In hindsight, regardless of how it might be interpreted by others, for me it felt like an experience which had a quality of 'true reality' about it, as if – however briefly – I had instantaneously returned to my 'eternal form'.

During another night of 'fizzing', I experienced another interesting change of perspective on life. From out of nowhere, it seemed, I began asking myself 'Who am I?' I have no idea why I posed myself this question (other than as a distraction to the 'fizzing', but then, any number of more prosaic questions could have served just as well). I answered myself with my first name – but immediately shook my head. The answer was preposterous, ridiculous! So obviously Not True! So I asked again 'Who am I?' and answered myself by saying 'woman'. That answer seemed almost equally absurd. I posed the question a third time and answered with the word 'human' this time. It felt as though I was having a conversation with a part of myself that was patiently sighing 'try again – you're just not getting it, are you?' So, once more I asked 'Who am I?' and this time I finally answered to my own satisfaction – 'I Am'. I suddenly felt as though I had shot through a telescope from one end to the other, from the microscopic end to the macroscopic end, and briefly experienced the world from the macroscopic end, whilst being aware that both exist simultaneously.

Since that time, I have read books on spirituality and human consciousness etc and have come across the 'I Am' phrase to denote the 'Godly' or 'Divine' aspect of ourselves many times, but at the time of my own experience, I had had no prior knowledge or experience of this 'Am-ness' nor had come across those words in such a context. . . . [100054]

Whether pleasant or distressing, non-religious triggers have been shown to have far-reaching spiritual effects. It is particularly noteworthy that it seems to be at times of deepest despair that hope is given.

8. Types of Spiritual Experience

Some people, like William James, think of spiritual experience taking place in solitude, while others might think of shared worship or group activities such as dance or singing. Some practices, like prayer or meditation can be either solitary or communal. There is a vast range of experiences and they are impossible to categorize. In general one would probably think of a spiritual experience as a beneficial event, leading to an increase of goodness and love of one's fellow man. Yet things are not so simple. There are also negative accounts, visions of evil or even experiences of a hellish nature.

One feature which of many of these accounts have in common is the utter conviction of the experient that what took place is somehow very 'real' indeed, despite the unusual nature of the event.

> The specific occasions mentioned all had the quality of being more 'real' than 'ordinary' reality that is, that in them I had got nearer to an experience of the true state of affairs. In contrast to this, I have to state that in my more positivist moods, when reflecting on these experiences, I wonder if I am mad. My other self replies that I have in all cases been better able to operate in the everyday world, following the experience. [from 003519]

These experiences have not been fitted into any fixed categories but are simply listed under their principal features.

Spiritual Experience in Childhood

It has been found that children often seem to have a natural spiritual response which, due to lack of encouragement, withers as they grow up, often leading to denial of the spiritual impulse or dismissal of this side of their nature as childish. Often religion itself serves to put adolescents in particular off any kind of recognition of the spiritual side of life, as formal religion is dropped with relief as soon as possible, or completely ignored. However, the awareness of a greater reality often returns to the adult perhaps triggered by some kind of extreme state of mind, perhaps a wonderful sunset, great music or even a tragedy or period of depression. This is at times accompanied by a sense of something having been lost and then found again.

However, many experiences gathered by the RERC refer to events in childhood and research has been done on childhood spirituality by Edward Robinson in *The Original Vision* and David Hay with Rebecca Nye in *The Spirit of the Child*. Rebecca Nye interviewed children from two primary schools and concluded that their spirituality, which she elicited in individual conversations, was best described by 'relational consciousness' meaning a deep, reflective awareness of themselves in relation to their own selves, others, the world and God. Children were often conscious that their feelings and experiences were difficult to put into ordinary language, as they were different from everyday life, and many had recourse to religious language when describing their experiences.

> John (aged six) had been explaining his religious beliefs to me. These were clearly Christian and supported by his family, though neither they nor John attended church more than twice a year, at Christmas and Easter. I asked how he came to hold his beliefs. In his response he described a religious experience:
> 'I worked about it and I received . . . one day . . . I was with my mum and I begged her . . . um . . . for me to go to um . . . some church. And we did it and I prayed . . . and after praying . . . I knew that good was on my side. And I heard him in my mind say this: 'I am with you. Every step you go. The Lord is with you. May sins be forgiven.' [84]

> John had another experience, which he accepted as true despite his mother dismissing his interpretation of it.
> Well once I went um . . . in the night and I saw this bishopy kind of alien. I said, 'Who are you?' And he said, 'I am the Holy Spirit.' I did think he was the Holy Spirit.
> When in his shock, he called out to his mum and explained what had just happened, John was told that the Holy Spirit looks like a ball of fire, and his version of events was rejected. He seemed to accept his mother's authority concerning this sighting, though he added, 'But I often felt the Holy Spirit in me.'[85]

However, many children accepted spiritual aspects of life as quite normal, did not report special experiences and did not need to use religious language, although they were aware of a different level of perception in this area.

Types of Spiritual Experience

A survey of older children was undertaken by Dr Paul McQuillan, who looked at the spirituality of predominantly Catholic high school students in Australia, finding 76% of his sample of students reporting what he termed a limit experience. He used the term 'limit experience' to avoid reference to religion, but to focus on everyday experiences extended beyond the normal he used the Hardy Question and also Hay and Nye's concept of relational consciousness. His work is published in RERC Occasional Paper No. 34, *Encounters Beyond the Pond: The Limit Experience of Senior High School Students* from which the following three examples are taken.

Two experiences were described in fairly conventional religious terms:

> At times of great difficulty or danger in my life I have felt I could always pray to God and get help. One night we were in a traffic accident and I was very frightened, and I prayed. Somehow I knew there was someone else with us, a presence of some kind; and I escaped with just a few bruises. At other times too, when I have felt very depressed I have had this same feeling of being given strength and hope.

> It was about mid-morning, I came from the kitchen into the bedroom, sat at my dressing table, opened a drawer and began to do something quite ordinary, I can't remember what, when I was absolutely overwhelmed by the presence of God. I was absolutely astounded. I hadn't known there was a God at all.... I was pretty much an atheist or agnostic and had no interest in religion. I had no such thoughts at the time, however, I was just shattered, shaken to the roots of my being.[86]

The third reflected a more open view:

> [A]s I sat thinking, looking at the beauty of the valley below, I felt as if the whole scene became luminous, I was aware of the tremendous intensity of colour – I felt intensely happy, for no reason at all. I suddenly felt at one with the very life force of creation, whatever that is. I felt part of it. I felt caught up in a tremendous theme of praise ... the feeling of elation lasting for some time.[87]

The RERC has many records of experiences which took place in childhood.

> As far back as I can remember I have never had a sense of separation from the spiritual force I now chose to call God.... From the age of

about 6 to 12 in places of quiet and desolation this feeling of 'oneness' often passed to a state of 'listening'. I mean by 'listening' that I was suddenly alerted to something that was going to happen. What followed was a feeling of tremendous exaltation in which time stood still.[786]

When I was on holiday, aged about 17, I glanced down and watched an ant striving to drag a bit of twig through a patch of sun an a wall in the graveyard of a Greek church, while chanting came from within the white building. The feeling aroused in me was quite unanticipated, welling up from some great depth, and essentially timeless. The concentration of simplicity and innocence was intensely of some vital present. I've had similar experiences on buses, suddenly watching people and being aware how right everything essentially is. [680]

Many people have spiritual experiences in childhood, which are often not spoken about, yet have a lasting effect on their entire lives. Here is an example of two boyhood experiences, not obviously similar, but linked in the mind of the experient, which had remained unshared and unexplained until the grown man heard of the work of Alister Hardy. Now an active member of the Alister Hardy Society, he recounts the moments which had such a profound effect on his life.

The major incident in my life occurred in June 1949. It was a hot summer Sunday afternoon, I had gone out for a walk, and was lying on my back in a copse (on a knoll under a lime tree) lost in reverie. I was aware of the singing of birds, the buzzing of insects, the sound of bat against ball in the cricket nets near-by, aware of the scents of summer, and watching the flickering of the sun-light through the leaves of the lime tree. I was not really thinking of anything, and then my mind went a blank ... suddenly I found myself surrounded, embraced, by a white light, which seemed to both come from within me and from without, a very bright light but quite unlike any ordinary physical light. I was filled by an overwhelming sense of Love, of warmth, peace and joy - a Love far far greater than any human love could be – utterly accepting, giving, compassionate total Love. I seemed to sense a presence, but did not see anybody ... I had the feeling of being 'one' with everything, of total unity with all things, and 'knowing' everything – whatever I wanted to know, I 'knew', instantly and directly. And I had the sense of this being utter Reality, the real Real, far more 'real' and vivid than the ordinary every day 'reality' of the physical world. I do not know how long this lasted: it did not seem to be a *long* time in that dimension, and in this, a minute? a few seconds, a split second, I don't know. Back again in this world, lying under the lime tree, I felt thunderstruck. What was that?

What did it mean? I felt that it was of great importance and must have some tremendous meaning... but what? What was I supposed to do? Why me? Was I being 'called' for anything? Was I being called to be a priest (I was preparing for Confirmation at the time)? but that didn't seem right. I toyed with the idea of becoming a monk, but that didn't seem right, either. I remember at the time being puzzled that the experience did not seem to relate to the 'religion' I was being taught. and in which I had been brought up: saw none of the iconography of Christianity: I did not see Jesus, or 'saints', or 'angels', nor were received concepts of 'God' or 'Heaven' any part of this experience. I remember asking myself. Was that God? - but surely not: 'God' wouldn't come to me, an insignificant small boy!

But, whilst puzzling over this (and feeling intense chagrin that I was quite unable to remember anything of the wonderful 'knowledge' that I had then enjoyed) I was convinced, beyond all shadow of doubt, of the 'reality' of the experience, the Reality, the overwhelming Love, the 'Oneness' of all things – and this has lasted, despite all reasoning, later 'reductionism', and suggestions that this was just my 'imagination', or that I was 'dreaming', or 'hallucinating'. But, at the time, I could not 'ground' the experience, and I felt that I could not talk to anybody about it, so I locked it away, pondering over it - a very big, unexplained, question.

A month later, a second, different experience took place.

Again, it was a hot Sunday afternoon and I was in the Music School practicing a Mozart sonata on the piano. . . . suddenly, I felt an urge to go for a walk. I remember resisting this strongly, not wanting to go for a walk, but wanting to play the piano. But the urge to 'go for a walk' became too strong and, eventually, I had to put the music away. Going out of the Music School I thought that if I had to go for a walk I would go over to a high mound of land just outside the school bounds . . . But as soon as I set foot in that direction, I found I could not proceed – some 'force', exterior to my own will, prevented me, and so I had to take another direction! . . . again, starting to turn right, I found that I could not proceed: once more the 'force' stopped me. I tried again to go down to the village, but I couldn't. There was just nothing for it but to take the left turn. Walking down this road I came to four red-brick workers' cottages outside one of which a woman was clipping a high hedge. It was a very hot day, and it seemed only right and natural that I should offer to help. She looked at me quizzically, but gave me the shears and, after I had cut the hedge, she invited me in for a cup of tea.

... I subsequently often went there on Sunday afternoons for tea – and came to call her 'my second mother'. The 'force' never came back, and never again have I received such a direct physical or mental 'urge'. This experience was very different from the 'mystical' experience of a month earlier but, nevertheless, I felt that in some way the two were connected. I wondered at the time if this second episode was a 'guardian angel' or possibly the spirit of my Grandmother, who had died three years previously, looking after me? ...

This experience, coming so soon after the 'mystical' experience, therefore became linked with the other in my mind. Both, in their different ways, had overwhelmed and over-ridden 'my' consciousness and will-power. And the thought and remembrance of the two experiences affected in a very formative way my life subsequently. I have come to see that the form and nature of these two experiences was the best thing that could have happened to me, really opening me to the significance of the spiritual dimension. And the fact that I had to think about them so much was good: they left me with a questioning and 'open' mind, not locking me into any 'faith-system' – which enabled later developments, little by little, to widen my horizons, and 'perspective', more comprehensively. [Abridged from 004300]

Despite not clearly understanding the meaning of his experiences, he has never ceased to be aware of and receptive to a greater power directing his life.

Perhaps there is an openness in children, which is later reasoned away in adulthood, closing the mind to such messages, although some people, such as this person, are able to retain this.

I think from my childhood I have always had the feeling that the true reality is not to be found in the world as the average person sees it. There seems to be a constant force at work from the inside trying to push its way to the surface of consciousness. The mind is continually trying to create a symbol sufficiently comprehensive to contain it, but it always ends in failure. There are moments of pure joy with a heightened awareness of one's surroundings, as if a great truth had been passed across. [651]

Types of Spiritual Experience

Initiatory Experiences

For some people, an experience which seems of a religious nature can come as a surprise, and be taken as a wake-up call to question and search for the spiritual side of life.

Simone Weil (1909–1943) born in France to non-practising Jewish parents, was a brilliant scholar and later a teacher and writer of philosophy. She was a left-wing radical, nick-named the 'Red Virgin', who took her politics so seriously that she joined the anti-fascist cause in the Spanish Civil War and took a job in a factory for a time to understand what life was like for the workers. During World War II she became involved in the Resistance.

It was on a trip to Assisi that she suddenly felt compelled to sink to her knees in prayer, after which she began to explore Christianity. She began to have mystical experiences when she felt that Christ took possession of her. Weil's health was not good and she describes her experience during a retreat at a Benedictine monastery.

> I was suffering from splitting headaches; each sound hurt me like a blow; by an extreme effort of concentration I was able to rise above this wretched flesh, to leave it to suffer by itself, heaped up in a corner, and to find a pure and perfect joy in the unimaginable beauty of the chanting and the words. This experience enabled me by analogy to get a better understanding of the possibility of loving divine love in the midst of affliction.[88]

Eventually Weil embraced the faith and wrote about her beliefs and experiences, notably in *Gateway to God* and *Waiting on God*. However, she could never bring herself to be baptized or to join the church.

Conversion

Conversion may refer to the decisive change from unbelief to belief, from one religious tradition to another, or a more vague recognition of the right path in life. A change of state of mind is involved, often from confusion or discontent to clarity and happiness. This is often related to religion, and frequently includes feelings of awakened love for others and a new direction in life. Some religions are proselytizing, actively seeking converts, such as Christianity, while others, such as Buddhism discourage a change of faith from that into which one is born. The Dalai Lama takes

Religious and Spiritual Experience

this stance but whilst not aggressively evangelizing, Buddhism has spread its message widely.

Conversion is sometimes thought to occur more often during adolescence, a period of searching and unrest. Perhaps it is also a period of openness to the spiritual side of life. Often a life-long search is begun at this age, which may or may not lead to a settled acceptance of a particular tradition. The first major examination of conversion took place right at the outset of the study of spiritual experience, by Edwin Starbuck in *The Psychology of Religion*, published in 1899, in which he particularly examined the adolescent phenomenon of conversion, within and outside the context of formal religion. William James uses Starbuck's research and devotes two lectures in *The Varieties of Religious Experience* to the topic of conversion.

This is a classic 'born again' experience, written in the late 1960s.

I'm 17 years old, American girl, I live in Los Angeles, California. When I was 15 years old I was taking drugs, hanging around bands, such as the late Big Brother and the Holding Co., (Janis Joplin) Jefferson Airplane, Canned Meat, Mother of Inventions (Frank Zappa). I'm not trying to brag; I'm just letting you picture how, when your [sic] in that far and go places with them where they play, you get in very deep with sex perverts and drug users.

I always considered myself a Christian all my life, just as I considered myself an American. I never went to church. But when I was 15, during all the mess I was doing somehow Jesus reached for me and I accepted Him as my personal savior. That is simply stating in a prayer to Jesus that you are a sinner and want him to lead your life. When I said this I really didn't understand it, but just wanted it. No great change came with me as it did with people I know. But gradually I began realizing this great force covering me inside and out with love. I stopped taking drugs for good. Jesus made me start meeting Christian friends. I left my old ones, starting reading the Bible and going to church. I even was a counsellor at the Billy Graham Crusade last summer here.

Since I accepted Jesus I have seen things no non-Christian could imagine; yes, miracles so many it would take a book to explain. I suppose you would say I was a 'hippie', but I still am. I dress the way I like and go to a church of about 200 or more ex-hippies and drug addicts. The guys still wear their hair long, but we're all like children when we talk about Jesus. We love him so much! I'm not scared of anything, I look forward to death if that is what my Lord wants. There's a love in me that is super-natural. I never could love people as I do now with Jesus in my heart.

So many people think that teenagers today are hopeless. Well I'll tell you when I go to a Luv-in to witness about Christ I run into so many other 'reborn' Christians. The kids are finding Jesus and man there's going to be a revolution about him. You can't imagine until you accept him how he can change your life. When I walk down the street, he's next to me and I know that. Everywhere I go he's there. He answers my wishes and saves my life constantly. I truly am infinite with him and I feel love and pity for the people I know who laugh at me. Their eyes are closed like mine were but they can't even imagine the spirit world that true Christians know of. Demons, angels. Man if you think there aren't demons, wow I've seen them. This is getting too long. I'm sorry it can't be longer, but when I talk about the life given, the eternal trip, I never stop talking. [000059]

This is an account of a conversion from one tradition to another, triggered by a vision. It took place when Hugh Montefiore, later Bishop of Birmingham, was a Jewish teenager at Rugby School.

Sitting alone in my study, I saw a figure in white approach me, and I heard in my mind's ear, the words 'Follow me'. I knew that this was Jesus. How did I know? I have not the slightest idea. I had no knowledge of Christianity whatsoever – it had intentionally been kept from me. My parents were both Jewish – my father was president of his synagogue. I had never been to a church service. I had never read the New Testament. I had never discussed Christianity with my friends. The only manifestation of Christianity that I had witnessed was that a few boys knelt beside their bed to say their prayers at night in the dormitory. (Jews do not kneel to pray.) Apart from school, all my friends and acquaintances were Jewish. I had been barmitzvahed in my synagogue, and at school I did not attend chapel or religious education lessons. Far from attending them, someone from outside the school came to give me lessons in Judaism. I had not been searching for a faith: indeed, I had even thought of becoming a rabbi. Yet I immediately recognized the figure I saw as Jesus. How I knew this, I have no idea. He was not a person who had crossed my conscious mind. (Naturally I do not know what happens in my unconscious, or it would not be unconscious.) In my vision, Jesus was clothed in white, although I cannot remember the nature of his clothes, nor yet his face, and I doubt if I ever knew them. I feel sure that if anyone had been present with a tape recorder or a camcorder, nothing would have registered.

> The experience filled me, as conversions often do, with a very deep and abiding sense of joy and happiness.
>
> I do not often speak of this experience, partly because it is a private matter and partly because I do not wish to claim any special standing by coming to Christianity in this way. Indeed, it is an easier way than most, because the decision was, as it were made for me. . . .
>
> I cannot account for my vision of Jesus by any of the psychological or neurophysiological explanations on offer. That does not of itself prove that it was of divine origin, but my experience over the last 60 years of Christian life confirms my belief that it was.[89]

Sometimes, however hard someone has been searching for the truth, recognition comes with reluctance. A well-known description of conversion is given by C. S. Lewis at the end of his autobiographical *Surprised by Joy*, which makes it clear that many a convert is half-hearted or even unwilling to acknowledge the change of heart and mind, which eventually becomes unavoidable.

> You must picture me alone in that room in Magdalen, night after night, feeling, whenever my mind lifted even for a second from my work, the steady, unrelenting approach of Him whom I so earnestly desired not to meet. That which I greatly feared had at last come upon me. In the Trinity Term of 1929 I gave in, and admitted that God was God, and knelt and prayed: perhaps, that night, the most dejected and reluctant convert in all England.[90]

Regenerative Experiences

People of faith at times experience a deepening of their beliefs or an increase in depth of awareness. This happened to Joseph Estlin Carpenter, who was the founding Vice-Principal and from 1914 to 1919 Principal of Manchester College, Oxford. Brought up as a Unitarian, and with a belief in Darwinism as the mechanism of a more profound Divine creation, he had no 'intellectual doubts', but 'no sense of personal relationship to God' either. This religious apathy was changed by his experience, which he describes in a letter to a friend.

> I went out one afternoon for a walk alone. . . . Suddenly I became conscious of the presence of someone else. I cannot describe it, but I felt that I had as direct a perception of the being of God all around me as I have of you when we are together. It was no longer a matter of

inference, it was an immediate act of spiritual (or whatever adjective you want to employ) apprehension. It came unsought, absolutely unexpectedly.... This experience did not last long. But it sufficed to change all my feeling. I had not found God because I had never looked for him. But he had found me; he had, I could not but believe, made himself personally known to me..... I could now not only believe in him with my mind, but love him with my heart.... This event has never happened to me again... it was not necessary. The sense of a direct relation to God then generated in my soul has become a part of my habitual thought and feeling.[91]

Healing

Healing is a way in which people experience help from beyond.

> Just a brief line to tell you of my experience of the nearness of God. I had pains in my leg for a few days, and this particular night it was worse when I got to bed. After turning from side to side and not being able to get to sleep, I suddenly said, 'Oh, God, *make* my leg better' and immediately I felt the pain being drawn out, and my leg was quite better. This made me realize how near God is to us and that he does answer prayer.[92]

Some people are able to heal through what feels like energy in their hands, with no need of medication or any physical techniques. They stress that they themselves are not responsible for this healing, but that they are merely serving as a conduit for a higher power. Those healed say that they felt the power or warmth or flow of energy, quite different from ordinary treatment:

> I was working as a woman doctor in a remote mission hospital in West Africa at the time. For a variety of reasons, one other MO and I were temporarily the only doctors in a 160 bed hospital with a large outpatient department.
> The other doctor suddenly became acutely ill and had to be off duty for 10 days.
> It looked an impossible situation but had to be faced. I prayed that I might somehow be made adequate. The thought came at once that, as it was manifestly impossible to examine the patients in the wards as one would normally do, at least I could touch each one with an unspoken prayer for healing. This I did, unobtrusively, in the guise

of feeling the pulse, made a snap diagnosis of the new patients and ordered treatments.

In the Outpatients department one of the sisters saw the old patients; I saw numerous new cases and dealt with emergency surgery. In this way we got through those 10 days without, as far as I was concerned, undue fatigue but with a real sense of peace.

That alone was remarkable, but what impressed me most was the extraordinary number of rapid and rather inexplicable recoveries that took place during those 10 days. It was so noticeable that the staff remarked upon it though no-one knew what was in my mind at the time. I had not myself expected it, rather the reverse, in view of the lack of normal medical procedures.

The experience was pin-pointed months after when one of the African nurses at the end of the morning round, asked me to go back and see one of my patients who was crying. When we asked her what was the matter, she said that she knew she would not get better because I had not 'touched' her. She said that people in her town who had recently been in the hospital had returned home 'cured' saying that it was because I 'touched' them.

This I know can be explained away easily, but there remains the fact that in normal examinations, such as I had already performed on the patient in question, I had certainly touched a good deal. I think I always had a basic prayerful longing for each patient's recovery, but in the crisis described above there was obviously something else at work.[93]

This account traces the development of a capacity to heal:

Some years ago I spent a day receiving my first 'attunement' for Reiki healing. This involved spending a lot of time just sitting quietly, 'meditating'.

While in this state of mind, my grandmother (whom I had loved most dearly as a child) 'came to' me – that is, she suddenly came into my mind for no apparent reason, very strongly.

In the few days that followed the attunement I felt very different. Looking back on it I suppose I might call it 'Love' but what it felt like was more an absence of anything that would stop me loving, like worry, anger, anxiety, insecurity.

I was omnipotent and omniscient, but only in what mattered (I wouldn't have attempted to jump off the roof, or known how to get to the moon, or how to get hold of a fortune.) And I never tested these powers. I didn't have to, I just 'knew'. My self-confidence was confidence not so much in myself, but in everything (in 'God' perhaps).

I no longer needed to worry about whether I was doing the right thing, doing right. There was no conflict between what I wanted to do and what was right to do. Being 'good' or 'nice to others' was not my loss, but my gain. This was a revelation. It felt wonderful; so easy, so perfect, so *right*. (I was reminded of a beautiful experience, many years before, due to smoking dope, when a door was opened, and I saw a similar chink of light – but the effect was not as lasting or as strong, as real, as this time. I remember walking along the street, meeting a friend who said, 'Hello, I've come to annoy you!', and I said 'you couldn't possibly annoy me now. Nothing could annoy me right now.' He grinned knowingly.)

I remember loving my houseplants, cyclamens, so that they also loved me. I felt a two-way love for our horse as well. I found it a lot easier to love people, too.

I think it might have been the first time I was really aware of love.

During the next days and weeks the door slowly closed again, (but not completely). During this time, for the first time in my life I think, I was aware that people came to me, liked being with me. On one particular day someone said 'thanks for the vibe', and another person said of me that day, that I was 'bloody *radiant*'.

The experience taught me about love, about being 'open', and how to see outside of myself – outside of my self.

Healing:

To do healing, I have to be open, calm, detached almost, non-emotional (though I sometimes sigh involuntarily). A bit like meditating, my mind as clear as possible.

It's not me doing the healing – there is something that comes from somewhere else, and goes through me. It feels good. I have to be 'clear' for it to go through me.

I think that when it's most successful, there is a feeling that all is well. That any pain or illness is not there, will not be there, or perhaps rather that it is in a different dimension or place and is not important. That all will be well, and all *is* well. It is (obviously) very difficult to describe. A lightness and detached selflessness.

Sometimes I feel the person's pain or 'dis-ease' in my hands or arms, as physical pain, but never as emotional pain.

I also do the healing for myself, as a kind of meditation, connection, tuning in. Sometimes I see a momentary deep blue flash of light or colour a little in front of my eyes (my eyes are closed, but I'm really seeing it - it's not 'in my mind's eye'). A friend (a priest and healer) said, 'that means there's healing going on'. Someone else said that blue is 'the colour of healing'. [005455]

The influence of saints may be associated with healing:

Five years ago I suffered an accident to my right leg and it was broken in many places. . . . I was told by the consultant that he did not know how I would eventually walk. However, I have the personality that conquers most things and I eventually started to walk again.

However, since that time I always suffered pain in my leg, usually about three o'clock in the afternoon until the end of the day, and I thought that it would be something that I would have to grit my teeth and bear.

Three years ago I was on holiday in France and I was with four friends. It was in the afternoon and we had been walking a lot and I was longing to sit down and rest my painful leg. However, I walked into the cathedral at S and, as I was looking round at the statues of the saints, I suddenly felt an intense warm feeling in my leg, just like someone was filling my leg up with warm liquid. All I know is the feeling was so very strong. I looked up at the statue facing me and it was of Saint Teresa. So overwhelmed at that moment, I remember emptying all the francs in my handbag and lighting the biggest candle I could see. Tears were streaming down my face and it was days before I could tell my friends what had happened.

Ever since that day I have not had any pain in my leg. [94]

Healing is sometimes performed by shamans in a trance state, and there has been a resurgence of interest in shamanic practice in recent times although belief in spirit possession is no longer prevalent. Japanese religion is particularly noted for healing practices, and the use of amulets is common. Many Hindus and some Christians buy little models of arms, legs or whatever part of the body is ailing to aid in supplication for healing.

A concern for holistic health has led to a new understanding of the connection between what one eats and what one is, reflected in a healthier, more balanced diet. Many young people want to avoid unnecessary slaughter of animals and have become vegetarian. Concern for all life-forms and respect for all creatures also leads to a vegetarian diet being chosen. Jains and Buddhists do not kill sentient beings and so most are also vegetarian. Positive thinking is also now considered part of the healing process, as we become more aware of the interconnectedness of mind and body.

Miracles

Many people are convinced that their prayers are answered in miraculous ways, often in an extreme situation. The following happened to a friend of mine many years ago:

> Barbara had lost her first son to leukaemia as a child, and when her second, Chris, raced across the road into the path of an oncoming car, she screamed, 'Lord, not again.' She saw the boy gathered up as the car screeched to a halt. Chris was standing at the roadside, while the driver was convinced that he was underneath the car. [005440]

Guidance

Some people are aware of a sense of being guided through life. Quakers, in particular live their lives open to such promptings.

Eileen Caddy, who co-founded the Findhorn Community in Scotland, which was a 'guided' venture, wrote,

> I am firmly convinced that everyone can hear 'the still small voice within' if they want to badly enough. It is the beginning of a working relationship with God.
>
> There are certain lessons that have to be learnt when one has chosen to listen to the voice within: discipline, faith and obedience.

She explains that one needs to make time to listen, then,

> there is a great need for and belief. You can only gain faith by putting what you receive to the test and seeing how beautifully it works.
>
> Then you need to obey.
>
> I have lived by God's voice over the years and I have proved that His words are not vain and empty words, that when they are followed to the letter, amazing things happen.[95]

This experience of guidance was triggered by doubt:

> I wanted direction in my life as I had no idea what to do. I had work of various kinds, but was not sure what I really wanted to do with my life. Always full of doubt, I just said, 'If you are there, DO something, please. You can have my life, I will go where you ask, but just show me what to do.' Within two weeks, my entire life had changed, as

opportunities I had never dreamed possible came my way and my path was set out. . . . I followed the path, even though at times unsure of where I was headed, but I knew that it was somehow deeply right. Many things have happened as a direct consequence of that 'handing over' and I feel that the process continues. [005450]

Solitary

William James concentrates on religious experience as taking place in solitude. His work looks at many different examples of such experiences, and the RERC archive too has many accounts of solitary experiences. Many people find that the spiritual is more easily experienced in solitude, as there is then an opening to what is beyond the everyday bustle of life, to silence and reflection and the silence beyond thought.

Here is the experience of Debendranath Tagore (1817–1905), the eldest son of Prince Dwarkanath Tagor.

> The silent observation of the stars one night on the bank of Ganges beside his grandmother's death bed filled his mind with wonder and the thought dawned on him that the grand universe that he saw before him could not have proceeded from any finite being. One day in a state of extreme misery, while pacing up and down he noticed a stray leaf of a book flying past him. It was written in Sanskrit and those that knew better told him it was a page from the Upanishads. Ram Chandra Vidyabasgish who explained the meaning of the sloka to him. It was the opening verse of the Ishaponishad which said 'God is immanent in all things, in whatsoever lives and moves in the universe; enjoy therefore without being attached; covet not wealth belonging to the others.' From that day his course of life was changed forever.[96]

Debendranath's son Rabindranath Tagore (1861–1941) was the first Asian Nobel Prize winner, being awarded the Prize for Literature in 1913. He also received a knighthood in 1915, but later renounced it in protest against British colonial policy in India. Rabindranath's principal work was *Gitanjali*, a mystical work, and in his writing he felt that his intense perceptions of the beauty and complexity of the world around him were somehow given greater significance by divine guidance. Even as a child, Rabindranath was mesmerised by the beauty of the dawn and would leave his bed to watch night turn to day alone.

Types of Spiritual Experience

When at the end of the night, dawn makes its first stir, its flush appears like the weaving of an ornament. In remote corners of the sky, embracing the clouds here and there, colour breaks out in varied shades; the tops of the trees begin to glisten, the dew-drops on the grass start glittering – the whole incident has primarily the quality of decorativeness. . . . One realizes also that the deep, solitude-abiding tranquillity of the sleeping night has now come to an end and all the ache of awakening, striking a chord on the gamut of notes, will any moment burst forth with the vibration of a restless tune. Similarly the unfolding of the first religious-consciousness in me took rather a decorative form in my literary compositions. It broke out in various shades, colouring the peaks of my mental images and tinting the clouds of my fancy.

. . .

Day and night, life is renewed by death, the evil is outshone by good, the commonplace is being enriched by the unexpected. Whenever we are aware of it, we see the supernatural being manifested through forms, freedom being unfolded through bondage.

. . .

To realize the relationship of perfect love between the Supreme soul and the soul of all created beings is indeed true religious-sense – this love that holds duality on one side and non-duality on the other, union as well as separation, and bondage along with freedom. . ... It is the love that by acknowledging this world, truly transcends the world, and by acknowledging what is beyond the universe, accepts the universe in its true form. [97]

The following account by the disgraced government minister Jonathan Aitken, was recorded in his *Pride and Perjury*.

It happened on an early autumn walk along the beach at Sandwich Bay . . . there was not a cloud in the sky or a breath of wind on the sea . . . The beach was totally deserted and I was a good two miles from the nearest house, so I was able to drink in this beautiful moment of maritime solitude with deep contentment.
Suddenly, yet quietly, I became aware of someone else's presence on the beach. For a moment I thought I heard the crunch of footsteps on the shingle behind me, but when I turned round no one was there. But someone was – I sensed them, strongly at first, and then overwhelmingly. Again I looked around, particularly on my right, for the presence

felt as though it had drawn alongside me, but all I could see was the sun, whose rays seemed to be blazing even more intensely.

'Slow down', said a gentle voice somewhere inside my head. It was not an audible or even human voice, but I knew it was speaking to me. So I obeyed and slowed my pace.

The next extraordinary happening was that tears started to trickle down my cheeks for no reason at all except that I was feeling blissfully happy. Once again I felt overwhelmed by the invisible presence that was so close to me – in the sun, perhaps, or beside me, or inside me, but undoubtedly right there with me. And then amidst swelling feelings of joy, that gentle voice spoke again, saying words which were very close to this: 'Slow down. The road ahead of you is longer and harder than you think. But keep on it. Keep praying. Keep trying to find the way. Trust, believe, and you will discover the path. Do not worry about your problems. They will test you but I will guide you. I have work for you to do. I will show you the way. I love you.'

Then I shed a few more happy tears, feeling utterly insignificant yet totally protected and loved as this amazing presence gently faded away and I floated back to reality, wondering what on earth was going on.[98]

Communal

For many, spiritual experiences take place within a communal setting, often in situations of worship, such as church services, where they feel part of a community united in worship. In some services, experience is encouraged or even induced and there is often an uplifting experience triggered by singing, processions or communal prayer.

In Taizé, in France there is a community where the monks, Catholic and Protestant, welcome visitors, mainly youngsters, from all over the world. Gentle, repetitive chants, often in Latin, are sung by candlelight and so many have found this a wonderful way of worship, that similar services are held all over the world, and the chants are frequently used in mainstream worship.

Something very interesting at Taizé is that this formula of calming repetition has been taken up in the liturgy, that is it is not only used in personal prayer, but also in prayer together or common prayer. Some young people who know almost nothing of mystery, are introduced to it here, and they begin to learn how to pray.[99]

Types of Spiritual Experience

The philosopher Paul Ricoeur described what happens there.

> What do I come looking for in Taizé? I would say to experience in some way what I believe most deeply, namely that what is generally called 'religion' has to do with goodness. . . . goodness is deeper than the deepest evil. We have to liberate that certainty, give it a language. And the language given here in Taizé is not the language of philosophy, not even of theology, but the language of the liturgy. And for me, the liturgy is not simply action; it is a form of thought. There is a hidden, discrete theology in the liturgy that can be summed up in the idea that 'the law of prayer is the law of faith.'[100]

The *Toronto Blessing*, which began through the preaching of Randy Clark, in 1994 at the Toronto Airport Vineyard Church is perhaps one of the most well-known communal religious phenomena in recent times. Also known as Holy Laughter, this phenomenon can be traced back to the preaching of Rodney Howard-Browne, who inspired Randy Clark. Effects such as hysterical laughter, dancing and even roaring occur regularly and are attributed to the effect of the Holy Spirit. Not everyone would be comfortable with this kind of experience, and of course there have been accusations of coercion and fraud. As usual, judgement has to be undertaken over time, looking at what the long-term effects of the experience produce.

Visions

Some people see visions of religious figures or of dead relatives. Just how physical the visions are remains unclear in many cases, but the effect is of having seen the person. This may take place at times of particular need or stress but not necessarily.

Visions of the Virgin Mary seem to take place fairly frequently and she often seems to appear to children. Celebrated cases include appearances in 1917 in Fatima, Portugal to three children and between 1981 and 1993 to six youngsters in Medjugorge, Bosnia-Herzegovina, some of whom continue to receive messages to this day.

Perhaps the best known of all is the case of the appearances in France to Marie Bernarde (Bernadette) Soubirous (1844–1879). In 1858, at the age of 14, near a cave at Massabielle near Lourdes, Bernadette witnessed the first of 18 apparitions of a Lady of incomparable beauty. Bernadette, a girl who all her life suffered from ill-health, was afraid, yet attracted by the figure. She took out her rosary and they prayed together, so she felt reassured. When Bernadette returned with other children, the vision reappeared, but was only visible to Bernadette, whose face became radiant. Despite worried parents and sceptical neighbours, Bernadette obeyed the Lady's request that she visit the grotto each day for the following fortnight. The police became involved and a local doctor checked Bernadette's pulse and breathing but could disprove nothing. No-one could shake Bernadette's devotion to her Lady and the visits to the grotto continued, soon accompanied by crowds of onlookers.

The message from the Lady was one of repentance and she asked that a church be built on the site. During one appearance, Bernadette was instructed to drink at a spring near the grotto. There was no sign of water there, but as Bernadette scratched the earth, a trickle which eventually became a stream appeared. Bernadette had been asked by the Lady to bring a candle on her visits, and that tradition continues to this day.

There was much speculation as to the identity of the vision and when Bernadette asked her who she was, the Lady gave what was for Bernadette the incomprehensible reply of 'the Immaculate Conception'. The words had to be explained to her by a priest. The final vision was more distant, and then the Lady came no more. But life could never be the same for Bernadette, who was now famous, or in the eyes of many, notorious. There was a thorough investigation of her case and eventually it was decided that the visions were indeed genuine. Her family had not profited from the situation and Bernadette was affected only in becoming more drawn towards the life of a nun. She ended her days at the convent of Saint-Gildard, mother house of the congregation of the Sisters of Charity of Nevers and was canonized in 1933.

The grotto became a centre of pilgrimage, the first of three churches built there was consecrated in 1866. As it is believed that the water of the spring has healing properties nowadays more than 6 million pilgrims visit the shrine each year and many cures have been recorded, deemed miraculous. There are strict guidelines for such claims, and in 1905, Pope Pius X asked that all cases of alleged miracles or cures recorded in Lourdes be analysed scientifically. There is an international committee of medical experts and patients have to satisfy criteria ruling out cures which are due to medication or natural causes. Cures are observed over several years and then the cases are submitted to the Catholic Church for verification. By 2004, 67 such cures had been accepted, although many medical practitioners contest the findings, citing cases of normal remission and selective monitoring of patients. Whatever the truth of such miraculous cures, it is certainly a fact that pilgrimages to Lourdes are found to be spiritually uplifting and healing in a deeper sense.

Types of Spiritual Experience

This is a Christian vision received by a Jewish woman:

> About ten years ago my husband and I went to Seefeldt [sic] in the Austrian Tyrol for a holiday. The hotel was comfortable, - furnished in the modern style, very bright and cheerful, and we felt at once that we were going to enjoy ourselves.
>
> As I shut my eyes for sleep that night, I saw, beneath my closed eyelids, the distinct form of a crucifix. It was a white cross, – not very bright – but glowing and quite clear in outline. I felt little surprise, and I admit, no real sensation of revelation or religious fervour. Just a vague feeling of comfort and satisfaction before I fell asleep. The cross appeared to me almost every night for the eleven days we were there.
>
> I cannot rationalize this incident away. The cross was there. But I was born Jewish. And though I believe unswervingly in the Almighty Spirit, I have no faith in organized religion, and have not practised my own since I was a girl. My belief – and I think I share this with a good many people, is that God makes Himself manifest in the wonders and beauty of nature.
>
> However, there is one thing that may have a bearing on this 'vision' – if you can call it that – two days before we left Seefeldt – we learned that the hotel was partly reconstructed from an old monastery.
>
> I have never told anyone of this experience before. Not even my husband. But it *was* real.

Light

Light has always been associated with perceptions of the divine in particular with regard to Jesus, from the star and angels in the birth stories to the accounts of his transfiguration. Holman Hunt painted Jesus as the Light of the World. The painting shows Jesus, holding a lantern, lighting up the dark night. He is standing at the door on which there is no handle as it can only be opened from within. First shown at the 1854 Summer Exhibition in the Royal Academy, the painting resonated with the public and became immensely popular and widely reproduced.

The Spanish mystic Teresa of Avila (1515–1582) had powerful visions of Christ and describes the light associated with this:

> It is not a radiance which dazzles, but a soft whiteness and an infused radiance which, without wearying the eyes, causes them the greatest

delight; nor are they wearied of the brightness which they see in seeing this Divine beauty. So different from any earthly light is the brightness and light now revealed to the eyes that, by comparison with it, the brightness of our sun seems quite dim and we should never want to open our eyes again for the purpose of seeing it . . . It is a light which never gives place to night, and being always light, is disturbed by nothing. It is of such a kind, indeed, that no one, however powerful his intellect, could, in the whole course of his life, imagine it as it is. [101]

Here is an experience recorded on the Alister Hardy Trust website:

In 1956 at the age of 23 my husband and I were walking the cliff path from St Ives in Cornwall to Zennot. It was a bright sunny day in September, bright but not a garish mid-summer sun. My husband was walking his usual 40 yards ahead and disappeared over the prow of an incline, so to all intents and purposes I was entirely alone. Although there was no mist the light seemed suddenly white and diffused and I experienced the most incredible sense of oneness and at the same time 'knew what it was all about' it being existence. Of course, seconds later I hadn't the faintest idea what it was all about. However it struck me that the oneness was in part explained by the sensation that the air and space and light was somehow tangible, one could almost grasp it, so that there was not a space which stopped because my human form was there but that my form was merely a continuity of the apparently solid space. The experience was unbelievably beautiful, and I will never forget the quality of that bright white light. It was awesome. [0322]

This is a most comforting experience of light:

My father had had a severe heart attack and I laid him down in bed, semiconscious. Then I put out the light and let him sleep. Suddenly he turned his head and looked over to the corner of the room. There was a bright light shining, which on looking at my father, was reflected in his eyes. 'I have seen the glory of God and I am not to die yet' he said. He lived and walked about for another year. I am 69 and can see that light in my memory as if it were yesterday. Never have I seen a light which could compare with it. [2031]

An extraordinary, life-changing experience of light happened to Christopher (Kik) Woods (1943–2008). Despite a pedigree of clerics, he had no interest in things spiritual. Born in New Zealand, he spent several

Types of Spiritual Experience

years of his youth in England, where his father was a vicar. As a young man, he enjoyed a life of hedonism and adventure, partying so hard that a scholarship to Dartmouth College, New Hampshire was summarily cancelled after five terms. Eventually he took to working in publishing. It was at the age of 31, when he was back in New Zealand, leading the life of a truck-driver, that everything changed. One day his cab suddenly became flooded with light and Kik was overwhelmed by the conviction that he should become a priest.

He stopped at his sister-in-law's and announced that he was to be ordained. Astonished, she asked him if he perhaps needed a drink. He took one, but despite having had no previous interest in religion and not having set foot in a church for years, Kik was obedient to the call. He went to the United Kingdom and trained in Birmingham. After ordination, he took over a tough parish in Liverpool, where he remained for a quarter of a century. He also taught at Risley Prison and became a Canon of Liverpool Cathedral, and in fact died of a massive stroke while conducting a service.[102]

The following experience of light encompasses a feeling of unity often found in mystical experiences:

> I was in my car travelling through the Usk Valley in Wales. It was a beautiful day – clear and sunny and it was about 10 in the morning. I was aware of the houses in the hills and the beautiful view they would have over the valley and wondering how it would be to have a house in those hills with a spacious room with huge windows. My imagination conjured a studio (I am a fabric artist) in the spacious room with a large table and lots of fabrics and never-ending inspiration from what would be an awe-inspiring vista.
>
> As I drove on thinking the above thoughts could never be I was suddenly surrounded by light that was far brighter than the prevalent sunlight. It was profound . . . I was aware of being in a silent place of pulsating energy and at the same time being at the source of the light and quiet energy. I had to stop the car as the experience was overwhelming – I was connected to a profound, huge Presence. I felt tears pouring down my cheeks and I also knew they were tears of joy at the experience of this connection.
>
> I knew deep in my soul that I was experiencing a feeling of wholeness, a feeling of rightness and of being held in pure light. I was aware of being part of the Universe in a way that I would never be alone again. [005438]

Experiences of light often seem to include a feeling of being loved.

I heard nothing, yet it was as if I were surrounded by a golden light and as if I only had to reach out my hand to touch God himself who was surrounding me with his compassion. [183]

This is another account of an experience of light and love:

I found myself floating in an ocean of golden light. From every thing within my vision this golden light radiated to every other thing, in continuous pulsating streams of living vibrations. These streams of living light were visibly flowing along pathways of lasting, dynamic movement, outflowing and inflowing from and into every thing within perception, connecting every thing to every other thing. And I, too, was the golden light, and I, too, pulsated with the streams of living energy that outflowed and inflowed, inflowed and outflowed. I was infused with an indescribably beautiful sense of tranquillity and well-being; a deeply felt state of connectedness and wonderment, and bliss, and above all, LOVE. Only it was a million times more powerful than any previous experience of love, because I AM love, and the golden light that unites everything IS love and everything that is, is love; living vibrating love; and love is a golden light that unites everything in existence in a never ending dance, a joyful interplay of bliss and union.

In physical reality I was sitting bolt upright in bed, having woken suddenly and unexpectedly from a deep sleep. During the weeks previous I had been moving increasingly to the edge of burn-out due to physical exhaustion and emotional pressures. To the eyes of the world, what I was going through would most likely be called a breakdown, only that could not be further from the truth of what I was experiencing. Never before had I felt so alive, so clear, so awake, so calm, so safe. The bliss I felt was not euphoria – there was no sense of the excitement and restlessness that accompanies euphoric states. I was not feeling *any* emotion; there was, and is, **only love**, and **I am love** and **everything is love** and nothing is separate.

I recognized all the objects in my room – books, pictures, the vase of roses, the lit candle on the dresser – but it was as if I was 'seeing' them all for the first time with a very deep knowingness, an indescribable clarity of understanding and appreciation. I was aware, also, of the world outside my window that was open to the summer night; the stars and the silent houses and the river and gardens: they too were golden, living, streaming light; and **everything is one**, near and far,

Types of Spiritual Experience

beyond the night sky and the stars and in the depths of the heart. Distances dissolved; space and time had ceased to exist.

How long in terms of physical (chronos) time, I remained before I 'saw' the vision I don't know. What happened is extraordinarily difficult to describe in words (as is all of this!) but it was in Blake's words: 'Too beautiful to be untrue.'

I turned my gaze towards the wall above the candle flame. A face appeared, head and shoulders only. Transfixed, I found myself gazing at an exquisitely beautiful countenance; beyond imagination and experience, beyond words ...

The head was that of a young man or woman (in retrospect perhaps more male than female), the head framed with soft curls. What emanated from the face was indescribable beauty, love, compassion, serenity ... A white-gold light (unlike any 'light' I'd ever before known) emanated from the beautiful countenance, and as I gazed the face slowly turned from side to side. As it turned the expressions changed in a continuum of gentle motion, first to one side, then the other, slowly back and forth. To the one side the expressions were varying, negative states of being; increasing in extremity and ending in utmost anguish, before slowly turning back through the same spectrum to the centre and continuing to move to the other side in ever changing expressions of positive states, again increasing in extremity and ending in utmost joy. The expressions covered seemed to include the entire span of possible human experience, from agony to ecstasy, and everything between, in perfect order – nothing was left out – insecurity, doubt, anxiety, jealousy, deceit, betrayal, isolation, loneliness, separation, aggression, fear, hatred, lust, revenge, cruelty, cowardice, remorse, guilt, grief, alienation, despair, anguish and so on ... and back to the light of awakening, insight, pity, willingness, creativity, honour, courage, humility, altruism, charm, playfulness, delight, truth, sincerity, honesty, integrity, mindfulness, self-awareness, self-knowledge, wisdom, joy, love ... and back again, in reverse order, from light to shadow and from shadow to light, back and forth ... and all the time underlying the constantly shifting expressions was the original beautiful countenance of peace and unbounded love.

I don't know how long the vision lasted, nor how many times the face turned from light to shadow and back again.

It has been difficult indeed to attempt to express in writing the experience that I can only describe as transcendent and sublime in its mystical beauty. The transcendent state of consciousness I had suddenly and unexpectedly been pitched into stayed with me for a long time – several weeks – and the sense of unity and connectedness, and perfect love, was so real and so powerful that I feel certain it was authentic.

The experience transformed my life in many ways. One of the first things I did was join the Alister Hardy Society, in order to make sense of the experience. [005454]

Love

Many people find a sense of overwhelming love the most powerful of all spiritual experiences and it certainly features large in the mystical literature.

> One night of, I should think, neurotic misery I suddenly had an experience as if I was buoyed up by waves and waves of utterly sustaining power and love. The only words which came near to describing it were 'underneath are the everlasting arms' though this sounds like a picture, and my experience was not a picture but a feeling, and there were the arms.. . . it came from outside unasked. No wishful thinking was involved, my unhappiness did not matter if the world was sustained by love in that way. [0356]

Familiar throughout the ages is spiritual searching, often triggered by a longing to believe, but the inability to do so. This experience, triggered by doubt, brought an intense awareness of love.

> Exasperated after years of being unable to believe in God, yet unable to accept an atheist way of life, I determined to force the issue. I had some days free and undertook a kind of solitary retreat, reading, thinking and attempting to pray – but the gist really was – 'If you are there, let me know'. My head began to ache terribly and this went on for some days. During that time I had to take my mother and a friend to a concert, over an hour's drive away. I did it all, but felt somehow distanced, as if my real self was somewhere else. All the time my headache continued. It was a strange, incessant pain.
>
> Eventually I gave in and accepted that there was indeed a transcendent reality, or God, whom I asked to take the headache away. Within half an hour, the headache had gone and I was flooded with an extraordinary feeling of total love. This encompassed absolutely everyone, all creatures and all life. Breaking my solitude, I went to the local shop and realized just how much I loved everyone there - I felt as if I would have given my life for them. It was a love beyond anything I had ever

imagined, and which I have since recognized in the writings of the mystics. That feeling lasted for several days and it was almost a relief as the intensity faded. [005449]

Here a similar experience of love for absolutely everyone is recounted by an Indian writer:

> There was a man in the village community whom I had come to regard as a consummate bore. From afar, if I spied him, I would grasp any means of escape. His absolute determination to buttonhole me and then to pin me to the wall with his face close to mine to pour out his inanities, was a frequent experience from which there seemed for me no escape. In this, my moment of sudden enlightenment, all parts and portions of creation seemed suddenly to be imbued with a new and absolute significance. For the moment, all nature, including my pet bore, seemed to fit naturally into one inclusive pattern of past, present and future. Every one and thing achieved a new and striking significance. I wanted to run out of the house as I saw from my window my pet bore approaching and to embrace him. I wanted to tell him that he too had a part, a significant part inside this great overall picture. [from 002417]

Simone Weil felt that God could not be loved directly but only implicitly, as she explained:

> The implicit love of God can have only three immediate objects, the only three things here below in which God is really though secretly present. These are religious ceremonies, the beauty of the world and our neighbour.[103]

Voices

The phenomenon of hearing a voice can be deeply comforting.

> About five years ago I went through a domestic crisis. I divorced my husband after much stress and soul searching. I prayed earnestly in church one Sunday evening during prayer time. To my amazement I received a direct answer to my question, quite definitely a voice which to me filled the Church where I knelt – a voice 'like a rushing mighty wind'. I looked up expecting everyone else to have heard and was surprised to find silence. The message I heard changed my life, and

was to me a profound and deeply moving experience, one I can never forget and strengthened my faith, and saved my sanity. [003375]

The voice in this case seemed to compel obedience and to lead the hearer in a new direction in life.

A widow was devastated at the loss of her husband after 42 years of marriage, and 49 years since first falling in love (marriage postponed because of the young man's consumption). Her experience took place after an exhausting time of nursing her sick husband and the subsequent hectic period over the funeral.

Then I was on my own with unending days ahead. Everyone expected me to need help – including myself – but that first day the words of Psalm 139 kept coming back to me 'Oh Lord, thou hast searched me and known me'. Then I was aware of a presence in the room and looked round for my husband (forgetting, as so often happened) he was not there. No-one was there, yet there *was* someone. A voice said clearly – I have work for you –

I sat and prayed and thought, doing nothing, not moving. Then suddenly I thought 'I'll go to the prayer meeting tonight' – I had not been for three years! No-one expected me and the leader was horrified, I found out afterwards, as the subject was the story of 'The widow's cruise of oil'. I came home still thinking 'I am empty, Lord fill me'. The presence was there again 'I have work for you to do'.

I went to Church on Sunday with my daughters. The passage was 1 Corinthians 12. I came home alone again. Again I was being told 'I have given you gifts. I have work for you.' On the Tuesday I decided to rejoin the women's meeting. The speaker chose Romans 12.6. 'Having gifts that differ according to the grace given to us, let us use them.'

The voice was confirmed as that of the Holy Spirit. I rang my minister and he came to see me. I told him all this and said 'What do I do? He said 'You are an answer to prayer – 'I have been praying for over a week for someone to help me.' He explained we had in the Church a number of new Christians (women) from a mission I had missed. They were 'problems'. Divorcees, unmarried mothers, various problems easier to talk about with another woman. Would I visit them? I did. I have never been so busy in all my busy life. I had the experience of the world and troubles to help, to listen and often to advise. I went to solicitors' offices, matrimonial courts, bad debt offices etc. with them and eventually sorted them out.

Types of Spiritual Experience

(This work led on to her being appointed to the Church as pastoral Worker and to leading worship once a month.)

I am indeed, once again, a person. Not in my own sight, but in God's. [004507]

There are times when what is heard or overheard strikes a deep chord, which seems to bring a message, which again seems to have authority and compel obedience. St Augustine famously heard a voice, which he obeyed. It happened at a time of his life when he was finding it difficult to overcome the 'desires of the flesh'. He it was who had said, 'Give me chastity and continence, but not yet.' Although Augustine had been wrestling with doubts about the Christian faith, he had overcome them. However, he was still living an unrighteous life when,

> there occurred a famous experience which brought about his conversion. While in a garden, he heard a child's voice from over the wall saying 'Tolle lege, tolle lege' – 'Take up and read, take up and read.' Seizing a copy of the Epistle of Paul which he had been reading, he opened it at random, at the passage in Romans which says, 'Let us walk honestly, as in the day; not in rioting and drunkenness, not in chambering and wantonness, not in strife and envying.' The suddenness of the voice, the appropriateness of the message – both these facts impressed themselves on Augustine's mind. He felt that it was surely a divine oracle. His doubts were resolved.
>
> After a period of seclusion and self-discipline, he was baptized, in 387, on the eve of Easter.[104]

Tongues

On New Year's Day 1901 in Topeka, Kansas, a young woman named Agnes Ozman, like Dorothy in *The Wizard of Oz*, was about to be transported to a strange and wondrous place – not by a tornado, but through a born-again experience. She asked her teacher, Charles Parnham, to lay his hands on her and pray, and when he did, she began to speak in a language no-one had ever heard before. Some of the Bible students thought she was babbling, and others thought she was speaking Chinese, but they all agreed that she had been touched by the Holy Spirit and given the gift of 'speaking in tongues'. On that day was born the Pentecostal movement, which would transform Christianity throughout the world.[105]

Religious and Spiritual Experience

The Pentecostals survive and glossolalia is a phenomenon also recognized in shamanic rituals. Studies have shown that no known language is being spoken, although some claim to be able to understand the communications. Most people to whom it happens do not know what they are saying as the language seems to be spoken through them, but they feel that they are blessed and encouraged in their work for God. This is often a group phenomenon, taking place in such Pentecostal services, and accompanied by singing and ecstatic behaviour. But a quieter form takes place during private prayer.

The following experience had no connection with the Pentecostals and was clearly evaluated and interpreted in a specifically Christian way:

> In February 1994, at the age of 58, I received the Gift of Tongues. I have been a Christian for many years, reading my Bible and praying daily, so I know that Tongues are among the gifts of the Holy Spirit. I had never met anyone whom I knew had the gift, but I had read various books about the Holy Spirit in which Tongues were mentioned. As a young Christian I had thought it was a special heavenly language in which praise is offered up to God, but now I realize that Tongues are modern everyday languages. After all that was the purpose of Tongues given to the Apostles in Acts chapter 2 – so that they could share their praises of God with all the foreign visitors who had come to Jerusalem for the Passover.
>
> I have no idea what language it is I speak in Tongues. One night I woke up and was unable to get back to sleep. I lay thinking about the events of the past day, but this word – something like 'vanda' or 'wanda' seemed to keep interrupting my thoughts. Next day I was doing some cleaning in my village church when this 'word' came into my head again. I spoke it out loud and immediately it was followed by several other 'words'. I had no idea what language they were and felt puzzled about it.
>
> Next day after my Bible study, I prayed. As always I began by praising God, and then all these 'words' came pouring out. Was this the gift of Tongues? I could think of no other explanation, but as I continued to speak in Tongues I was aware that I was praising God and felt a great sense of joy. I visited my Rector and told him what had happened. He was very supportive but could offer no other explanation, not having experienced Tongues himself. He did not know anyone who had the gift with whom I could have shared my experience.
>
> At first my vocabulary seemed limited, just as it would have been if I was learning a new language like Polish or German. As time passed, my vocabulary has widened and often seems to be in a verse with some

lines repeated. I have tried to speak Tongues quietly in my head, but it doesn't work – they have to be whispered, said or even sung aloud.

I have often thought about the timing of this wonderful gift. I the early 1990s the . . . Diocese began to encourage Churches to set up Local Ministry teams. These Teams were made up of lay members whose function was to work with the local vicar in planning services and doing pastoral work within the community. Our Church had just formed an LMT, and I was one of the people nominated by the congregation to be a member. We began our first session of the two year training course in February 1994, and it was soon after that I received the Tongues. When I had first been asked to be a member of the LMT, I had been rather hesitant in agreeing as I was not sure that I could offer much to such a group. Looking back now over a period of time, I feel that in giving me the gift at that time, God had encouraged me in my inclusion in the Team. It was some time before I shared my gift with the other members of the Team, and they seemed as puzzled as I had at first.

In one book that I read, the American author implied that unless a person could speak in Tongues he or she was not a real born-again Christian. I cannot agree with that statement. One cannot teach oneself to speak in Tongues. It is a gift of the Holy Spirit and to be valued as such.

People ask me if I can speak in Tongues whenever I want. I'm not sure that I can or even want to. I am moved by the Spirit to praise God in prayer when I see something beautiful – a seascape, a setting sun or even just a colourful butterfly. Then I marvel at God's creation and praise him in Tongues. It somehow seems that I can express my praises more freely in Tongues than in my own language.

After 13 years I now find that I speak in Tongues most days when saying my prayers, and each time I feel uplifted and so joyful that I can praise God in this way. [005435]

Angels

People quite often report angelic presences, sometimes the figures they see even have wings. At times, people find that they are helped by mysterious figures who then suddenly vanish. Many people, nurses in particular, have reported seeing angels at the side of patients, or at the point of death, as if the angel were coming to take the dying person away. In all cases, whether the patient died or not, great comfort was received through the angelic presence.

Religious and Spiritual Experience

Perhaps one of the most famous accounts of an angel is that of Teresa of Avila, commemorated in Bernini's sculpture of her ecstasy.

> It pleased the Lord that I should see this angel in the following way. He was not tall, but short, and very beautiful, his face so aflame that he appeared to be one of the highest types of angel who seem to be all afire . . . In his hands I saw a long golden spear and at the end of the iron tip I seemed to see a point of fire. With this he seemed to pierce my heart several times so that it penetrated to my entrails. When he drew it out, I thought he was drawing them out with it and he left me completely afire with a great love for God. The pain was so sharp that it made me utter several moans; and so excessive was the sweetness caused me by the intense pain that one can never wish to lose it, nor will one's soul be content with anything less than God.[106]

In *Seeing Angels* Emma Heathcote-James has collected experiences from a great number of people who believe that they have been helped by angels. Here is an unusual account from *Seeing Angels* in which the angel is seen by more than one person. The husband relates how he and his son were sitting at the bedside of his wife, who had just had an allergic reaction to the anaesthetic of a hysterectomy.

> Suddenly, through my tears, I saw what I thought to be a figure, an angel, behind the bed rails – I ignored it, thinking it was [brought about by] exhaustion and anxiety. A few minutes later I looked to see my son staring at the same spot – he turned to me and asked if I too could see the angel behind the bed. That moment the staff nurse was passing the foot of the bed and I turned and asked her if she could see anything other than us in the cubicle – the nurse smiled and told us not to presume it meant the worst. She acted as if this was a normal occurrence. I turned back to my wife and watched the figure melt away. Literally from that moment on my wife regained consciousness.[107]

Here is a case where reassurance was given at a time of uncertainty.

> I was in my seventies, facing a major life-changing decision and was unsure as to what to do for the best. In the past I had often thought that I would love to see an angel but was quite unprepared to open my eyes early one morning to see a huge figure in the corner of the room. He was almost higher than the room itself, dressed in beige robes and had beautiful wings. He was very bright and seemed to shine. I opened and closed my eyes several times to make sure that I wasn't dreaming.

The angel seemed to be telling me, without words, to be at peace. From then on I felt calm and reassured about the move abroad which my husband and I were to make, which subsequently turned out to have most definitely been the right decision. [005444]

Dreams

Thich Nhat Hanh is a well-known Vietnamese Zen Buddhist monk, who was a peace negotiator after the Vietnam War and nominated for the 1967 Nobel Peace Prize by Martin Luther King. Thich Nhat Hanh has written many books on spirituality and in *No Death, No Fear, Comforting Wisdom for Life* he recounted a dream which altered his perspective on the death of his mother.

The dream took place over a year after his much-loved mother had died, a time when he was still deeply mourning her. Thich Nhat Hanh was sleeping in the highlands of Vietnam when he had a powerful dream of spending time talking with his mother, who looked young and beautiful. When he awoke, Thich Nhat Hanh went outside into the moonlit night, feeling very strongly that his mother was still with him. He felt as if the moonlight was his mother's gentle caress. Looking down at his feet, he realized that his own body was a continuation of her and his father and grandfather, that they lived on in him. He realized that the loss of his mother was a false idea, and that she had not left him, but would always be with him.

Many people have comforting dreams after the loss of a loved-one.

Twelve years ago my husband died after a most distressing illness and many months of growing paralysis. Neighbours and friends were so kind, but somehow I seemed numb inside and couldn't forgive myself for not being with him at the end, and I slept badly.

However, the third night after, came my most wonderful dream – or, rather, I'm sure it was a vision, as ordinary dreams are so soon forgotten. I dreamed that I was in a large field and crowds of folks were coming towards and passing me . . . but amongst them I was searching for one face, my dear husband. Finally, in despair I gave up and went home, and in joy I cried 'Oh you're home!' and went to him, and I felt the gentle pressure as he put his arm round me (he was so weak).

How can I describe the wonder and glory of his face? The memory makes my heart beat so fast even as I write after all this time. His face was so young and smooth, and a wonderful radiance all about him – even his eyelashes seemed tipped with sparkles of gold. He gave me the sweetest smile, which filled me with the strangest sense of happiness, even elation, and then he turned and resumed the same attitude as when he died.

I awoke sobbing, but they were tears of happiness – he had come back to comfort me and I knew he was 'home' with joy and at peace with his Lord, who had surely made his face to shine upon him.

Since then, both dear parents and several loved-ones have passed on and, apart from a sense of deep loss, I have never really grieved, and even rejoiced knowing they were at peace in God's keeping. [abridged from 2604][108]

In the following experience the dreams were 'manipulated' to try to keep in contact with the deceased.

I had lost my father in September 1985, so almost three years before, and still missed him. I had taken to trying to go to see him in dreams. Every now and again, I would think intensely about him before going to sleep, willing myself to go to 'the other side' to talk with him. This resulted in some very clear dreams in which he would walk with me, often through lovely woodland, like near our home. We would talk about what it was like for him to be dead. I can't really remember the gist of the conversations, but I would wake comforted that he was not entirely beyond reach. He had been a deeply religious man, and had always disapproved of mediums, which is why I didn't try that.

In Tioman – a holiday resort island – I tried to dream again. I found myself in what seemed like a Middle-Eastern setting but no sign of Daddy. I asked a shadowy figure where he was and was told that he was sitting under a tree some way away. This communication was imparted somehow, words were not really the way it happened. I got the impression that I shouldn't try to see him. I wanted to know why the living couldn't talk to the dead, why those over there were not able to communicate with us. The figure said – or imparted – something about language, life and death, indicating that the way of communication was different. He began to rock rhythmically towards and away from me, seeming to say 'It's like this, like this' while moving forwards and backwards. I woke suddenly to my husband comforting me, asking if I had had a nightmare as I had been making the most awful moaning noises.

I subsequently stopped trying to contact my father that way and came to an acceptance of the separation of the living and the dead. [005448]

Types of Spiritual Experience

Dreams can sometimes give messages, and if one is open to that interpretation, a new turn of events can result from a dream.

> I was climbing a muddy steep cliff path. I kept slipping back, clutching tufts of slippery grass that came away in my hand. I could see the top of the cliff, but not what was beyond it, except white sky. I fell to the bottom of the path, and started up again, the same thing happened.
>
> On my left, I could see a sort of antechamber with white pillars, from which broad marble steps led upwards, parallel to the cliff path. There were people standing among the pillars. They seemed to be talking amiably, they were wearing robes, or flowing clothes of some sort. These did not have a formal or ritualistic look, they seemed to be quite informal and comfortably casual.
>
> No-one seemed aware of me, still struggling up my steep muddy path within a stone's throw. I went on trying, and failing, to reach the top.
>
> Eventually I gave up, and, wondering as I did so what would be the reaction of these clean, relaxed, sophisticated people if I approached them, I abandoned the cliff path and went into the marble hall. To my surprise and pleasure, I was able to wander around without causing dismay, I don't remember engaging in conversation, but I felt welcome, and even experienced a sense of familiarity in this place among these people.
>
> After a while I approached the staircase. 'So much easier, but am I allowed?' I thought. I began to mount the steps, and found I had someone on each side of me, amiably accompanying me. I woke before I reached the top....
>
> Two days later I ... enquired about the MA in Religious experience ... there was a residential the next week, and I should just come and join in. that's how I came to be an MA student, editor of De Numine, happily part of the life of TRS... feeling I have come home. The significance of the dream should be obvious, I'm just slightly disappointed in the Lampeter College dress code these days, and I haven't found the marble staircase. [100058]

Shamanic Journey

The term shaman originated in Siberia and the phenomenon spread through northern Europe, Africa and North America. Shamanic journeying is an inner experience but using the imagination. For example, shamans use rhythmic drumming and other devices to put themselves into an ASC (altered state of consciousness) and acquire knowledge for healing and other purposes. Jung rediscovered this technique and called it 'active imagination'. The portals into the mythic realms can be pictures like the tarot cards or sigils like the runes.

In this process you go through your chosen portal into a landscape that you start by imagining – but very soon the world you are in takes on a life of its own and moves out of your conscious control, as this experience of a Shamanic journey within the Nordic Tradition attests:

> I went on a course on STAV – the ancient Viking wisdom system as taught by a Norwegian nobleman in whose family the tradition had been handed down over 1,500 years. The whole system – cosmology, mythology, martial arts, exercise system, healing, divination, meditation and inner journeying methods and so forth – can be unpacked and recreated from the 16 runes of the younger futhark (the runic alphabet).
>
> The shamanic journeying technique in this tradition is called *utsæte*: you go out into the forest at night, sit against a tree, shut your eyes, imagine you are walking into a cave, see a door with one of the runes on it – and walk through it into a landscape that you imagine. (You have been through a carefully prepared induction session in which you may have discovered your animal guide.) Pretty soon, however, the figures and events escape your control and take on a life of their own!
>
> On this occasion, I found myself in quite a long chain of varied events, of which I select two episodes – commentary in square brackets:
>
> I was walking along in a forest and began to feel this was rather slow and tedious – so I summoned a horse. The animal appeared, and I mounted it. It started walking, then trotting, then galloping – and then it took off and started to fly through the air. At the same time, I became aware that it was in some way like a giant white spider – it had eight legs. (I knew at once that this was Sleipnir – the eight-legged horse of Odin; and I strongly suspected where we were going.) We were flying over a hilly, wooded landscape that seemed endless. Eventually, I could see ahead a tall, thin crag on top of which was perched a castle. We flew toward it (I should also say that I had no control whatsoever of where or how we flew – I was being taken there and was powerless to prevent it). We landed on a high stone platform at the side of the castle. I dismounted and the horse trotted away. Ahead of me was a great door, so I walked through it into the castle.
>
> The experience was initially very confusing. It was as though I had wandered into a multi-dimensional, utterly disorienting, MC Escher-style labyrinth of intricately fashioned woodwork; it was almost

impossible to discern what was up, what was down, what was ahead, what behind – particularly as I was floating through it without gravity. Eventually, I found myself in a room – not very large, lit only by a roaring fire. Opposite me, sitting in a high-backed chair, sat a long-haired, bearded, one-eyed figure clad in animal skins. Two ravens sat on top of the chairback behind him; at his feet lay two gigantic wolves. His single eye pierced into the depths of my being. He was inspecting me. . . . Finally, I said: 'What do I do now?' 'You get out!', he replied curtly. As I slipped away from the castle, the warriors' feast was starting in the great hall . . . [Valhall, Odin]

[Odin had advised me to visit Heimdahl]. I didn't have to keep trudging through the forest: I could do this more quickly. I materialized a door with the Heimdahl rune on it and stepped into Heimdahl's realm. It was dark and at first I could see nothing. Then I became aware of thousands of tiny pinpricks of light – and then I realized that these were *eyes*. I noticed that a number of bridges were curving down from different directions to meet in this arena. Heimdahl spoke to me – I never saw him, only heard him. He was welcoming and kind: he said: 'Come here whenever you want – you will be welcome.' [The experience left me with an enhanced understanding of the mythology: . . . Heimdahl is the watchman who guards the bridge Bifrost that leads into Valhalla and such is his alertness and sensitivity of perception that he can hear the sound of the wool growing on a sheep's back! But now I knew that bridges from all Nine Worlds converged on his home – this is reflected in his rune and he is much more than just a watchman: he represents an intense awareness at the centre of the universe.][109]

Shamanic Healing

As a result of practices of initiation, which often replicate death and resurrection, shamans gain extraordinary powers of healing and communication between the living and the dead. Although usually associated with primal cultures, the phenomenon has not disappeared as the following experience involving modern technology shows.

Soul Retrieval Via The Internet

One of the numerous roles that the shaman has always been required to perform, in both indigenous and now in neo-shamanism, is as the person who is called upon when emergency strikes – physical or spiritual. Indeed, certain alternative practitioners would even go so far as to suggest that the former is in any case nothing more than a symptom of the latter. Take the case of my partner, Keti, for example, a non-believer in shamanism and a devout Orthodox Christian, who had an aneurism while in transit at Vienna airport and who was rushed by ambulance to hospital. There she was operated on immediately and by the time I had flown in from London to be by her side, she had already been placed in an induced coma to protect her from any further complications and was lying in an intensive care unit. As for her chances of recovery, I was told by the surgeon who had operated on her that realistically they were extremely low.

. . . In desperation (and by e-mail as this was my only means of contacting him at the time), I turned to the shamanic practitioner (and my teacher) Jonathan Horwitz, who had never met Keti and who knew nothing about her except for the nature of her illness, and this was his response:

Dear Michael,
A very powerful helper has arrived at the scene. A Chestnut Mare. If it is possible for Ketevan to understand this beautiful mystic practise we call shamanism, please ask her to open herself up to this power of the Chestnut Mare. This Helper may even already have a meaning for her. Ask her to let the Chestnut Mare into her dreams. And keep me in touch.
Love to you both,
Jonathan

This was followed by Jonathan carrying out a soul retrieval for Keti despite the fact that he was in an extremely remote region of Sweden at the time. A copy of the e-mail he then sent me, summarising what he found, is presented below:

Dear Michael!
. . . I did a soul retrieval immediately after we talked. She was standing right next to her body and looked ready to leave. I pleaded with her to get back into her body and said that the situation would be different if she returned, and she wouldn't be feeling the need to leave. Finally she agreed to re-enter her body, but she didn't seem convinced, but she did it with sort of a 'Well, here goes . . .' feeling.

. . .

Much Love to you,
Jonathan

As for Keti, she woke up the very same day it was received. The 'outsider' could justifiably argue this was nothing more than a coincidence, though the 'insider' would clearly not share this view.

This account has not been presented though, to prove or disprove the power of shamanism. The reason for offering it to you is rather to show what a crucial role the shaman still has to play, even in the lives of sophisticated urbanites, and how the role has evolved to suit the times we are now living in – with soul retrievals even being carried out via the World Wide Web.

(Incidentally, to bring the story up to date, the doctors now say that given time Keti should make a full recovery). [Abridged from 005436]

Drugs and Trips

Aldous Huxley famously experimented with mescaline, taking four-tenths of a gram as part of a piece of research. He was looking at an ordinary vase containing a rose, a carnation and an iris.

> At breakfast that morning I had been struck by the lively dissonance of its colours. But that was no longer the point. I was not looking now at an unusual flower arrangement. I was seeing what Adam had seen on the morning of his creation – the miracle, moment by moment, of naked existence.
>
> 'Is it agreeable' somebody asked. . . .. Neither agreeable nor disagreeable,' I answered. 'It just *is*.'
>
> *Istigkeit* – wasn't that the word Meister Eckhart liked to use? 'Is-ness.' The Being of Platonic philosophy – except that Plato seems to have made the enormous, the grotesque mistake of separating Being from becoming, and identifying it with the mathematical abstraction of the Idea. . . .
>
> I continued to look at the flowers, and in their living light I seemed to detect the qualitative equivalent of breathing – but of a breathing without returns to a starting point, with no recurrent ebbs but only a repeated flow from beauty to heightened beauty, from deeper to ever deeper meaning. Words like Grace and Transfiguration came to my mind, and this of course was what, among other things, they stood for. My eyes travelled from the rose to the carnation, and from that feathery incandescence to the smooth scrolls of sentient amethyst which were the iris. The Beatific Vision, *Sat, Chit Ananda*, Being-Awareness-Bliss – for the first time I understood, not on the verbal level, not by inchoate hints or at a distance, but precisely and completely what those prodigious syllables referred to.

Huxley felt that he was beyond time and space and being given a sacramental vision of reality . . . where everything shone with an Inner Light, and was infinite in its significance.[110]

Drug-induced trips are not uncommon, but not often discussed. This, however, is an experience which was related to a drug but in an unusual way, as no substance was taken:

> In 1998: I attended a conference run by the Religious Studies Department of Newcastle University. One of the speakers was giving a talk on ayahuasca, a hallucinogen made from an Amazonian vine Banisteriopsis caapi. I sat listening at the back of the hall. I had never taken the drug, and didn't even drink alcohol, but while he spoke, I 'saw' the devic spirit of the vine rise in front of me in the hall. She smiled benignly, then faded away. An hour later I became aware that I'd spontaneously developed a heightened state of awareness, went back to my room, lay on my bed under the duvet for several hours, while streams of hallucinations ran through my mind, like a continuous film. Artefacts, sacred drawings, rituals, practices and paintings from all over the world streamed in front of my closed eyes. The stream of information was culture bound, depending on whether the 'channel' was on Africa, Central Europe, South America, or Siberia. This continued for several hours. I was aware of what was happening but couldn't stop it, so I just witnessed it. Later that evening, once it stopped, I talked to my colleagues: they suggested I'd had the 'gift' of the full stages of an ayahuasca 'trip' with none of the discomforts experienced by people who consume the actual substance. [100057]

An account of a real ayahusca trip is given by the Chilean novelist Isabel Allende in *The Sum of our Days*. She took the substance to deal with writer's block, and found herself reliving incidents from her childhood and then seemed to undergo death.

Synchronicity

C. G. Jung (1875–1961), the Swiss psychiatrist who initially worked with Freud is particularly known through *Memories, Dreams and Reflections*, which became central to the thinking of the counter-culture of the 1960s. He was interested in the workings of the unconscious and in the way events seemed linked in ways inexplicable by causality. He saw synchronicity as an acausal link between events, in other words, meaningful coincidences. Jung thought that part of the psyche was not subject to the laws of space and time and that synchronicity showed the inherent meaningfulness of the world. This way of looking at life has become quite widespread, with many people today maintaining that there is no such thing as a coincidence, everything is part of a pattern.

In his popular books beginning with *Conversations with God*, Neale Donald Walsch builds on this sense of presence, interpreting it as God's communication with us. We just need to recognize the way the communication takes place, enter into a conversation, move on to friendship and then communion. In the last in the series, Walsch writes:

> Each of us has the ability to access eternal wisdom. Indeed, I believe that God is inspiring all of us, all of the time. And while all of us have had this experience, some of us have chosen to call it something else:
>
> Serendipity.
> Coincidence.
> Luck.
> Accident.
> Freak experience.
> Chance encounter.
> Perhaps even Divine Intervention.[111]

Here is an event which meant a lot to a grieving son, which enhanced his respect for his mother's spirituality:

> When my mother, aged 83 was taken into hospital with pneumonia, I was sent for and got to her bedside about 7.00 pm. She was just able to talk, and the nurse said she might live for some time. My sister was visiting tomorrow so I decided to go home to my wife and children, but first I would go the Reception and leave a note for the chaplain asking him to give her Holy Communion. Walking down the long corridor in this huge hospital I saw a man in a clerical collar approaching. I asked him if he was the chaplain. He was. He gave her the sacrament at 9.00 pm. She died at about 4.00 am the next morning. What a Synchronicity between my thought and his appearance. [005452]

Sense of Presence

Some people have experiences of a presence, which they feel is giving them a message.

Religious and Spiritual Experience

In early 1960, before I became a Catholic, I was in a state of considerable unrest with regard to my religious opinions and as a result was undergoing quite a lot of mental anguish. One night I was lying in bed feeling very disturbed when suddenly I became aware of a presence in the room. There was nothing to be seen and no voice spoke, but I was aware that the visitor was Our Lady and that she was conveying to me that there was nothing to be worried about and everything would be all right. I found myself in tears of gratitude and happiness, and immediately felt at peace. Although I was received into the Catholic Church shortly after this incident, I have never consciously felt that this was what precipitated the move. It has always seemed like an isolated act of grace to me as an individual. [from 003519]

Other people live their lives with a constant awareness of a presence or power beyond them, which they may choose to call God and they find a guide and ever-present support throughout life. They pray when they need to connect to this power, in gratitude or supplication and feel their lives to be guided. They just follow the way that seems to be given to them, keeping in almost constant touch with this spiritual presence.

I have a growing sense of reality, and personal identity, which comes from being united to something more powerful than myself, something that is helping me to be what I want to be. [000843]

Recently I met someone who seemed to me an elderly, slightly disabled lady, but the more we spoke, the more I realized just how inaccurate that description was. Revd Audrey Day is one of the brightest, sparkiest people I have ever met. We discussed this book and she offered me accounts of her experiences. She sent me extracts of her unpublished autobiography, entitled *He Never Failed Me Yet*. I read her story, and there were so many experiences: of answer to prayer – receiving and being that answer; of calling to the ministry – she was among the first women to be ordained, after 36 years of active work in the church; of being healed through the laying on of hands. Unable to choose a single experience, I decided that she was a perfect example of a lifetime lived as a spiritual experience.

She has been aware of God since her childhood. This was not because it was easy. On the contrary, she was an extremely delicate child, suffering congestion of the lungs, pleurisy and slight rheumatic fever at the age of five, which left her with valvular heart disease, so that she was unable to start school until she was over seven, and then was frequently absent due to illness. Her body may have been weak, but her spirit was strong. Unable to do sport or swimming, she climbed trees instead.

Types of Spiritual Experience

Audrey was a religious child, confirmed at 12 and felt that had she been born a man, she would have trained for the priesthood. She trained in the Church Army instead but was ordained in the Church of England as soon as it was possible for women, which was not until many years later.

Here are a few extracts from a lifetime lived in a constant awareness of a sense of Presence, the first during her Church Army days:

> I have had many answers to prayer in my life; one that sticks out happened in Oswestry. In those days we were given a very small salary and although we were allowed to wear mufti on our days off, I did not possess a warm winter coat, so had to wear my grey uniform one. I brought my need to the Lord in prayer, and one day whilst visiting, a lady said 'I have bought a new winter coat and I don't like it, I wonder if you know anyone who could do with it?' I asked if I could try it on, it fitted perfectly, I then told her of my prayer and asked if she would mind if I had it. Needless to say, she was delighted.
>
> ... I took most of the services ... one day we were told the floor was unsafe and we would have to raise £40 for the repair. On the Sunday I asked the congregation to pray for the money; afterwards the treasurer said 'I could have laughed this morning when you said we need £40 for the floor repair. Let us pray – as if it was 40 pence.' When I got home there was a message from one of the parishioners who had been fund raising for us to say she had raised £41. I rang the treasurer and said, 'O ye of little faith wherefore didst thou doubt. We have the money and £1 over.'
>
> Despite the weakness and pain I was still able to do my work and God had much to teach me of Himself, as was shown very clearly one beautiful spring day as I cycled round the Parish taking bunches of daffodils to those who were sick. I was passing one house where an elderly man was ill, whom I had visited earlier in the day, when despite the fact that there was no one else in the street I heard a voice telling me to visit again. After an argument, I decided that I would call with a bunch of flowers. As I knocked at the door, it was opened by the man's daughter who said, 'Thank God you have come, I was just praying someone would come, my Father has collapsed and I cannot get him back into bed.'

Despite feeling that she should not pray for healing, rather for the courage to endure, a friend, Margaret, did lay hands on her for a very painful jaw condition, for which she had had several operations and which prevented her from eating properly:

> ... I awoke quite early, with NO pain in my jaw at all. I could hardly believe it; I decided to try some toast for breakfast and found I could

eat it, it tasted delicious. After three months on mashed up foods it was wonderful. I had always said grace before meals, but now it meant so much more. . . . I had to attend the hospital again . . . and they were most surprised when I told them my jaw was healed. They were very sceptical and made an appointment for 6 months time. This appointment was a waste of time.

. . . [Margaret] felt led to give me laying on of hands for my heart trouble. I had never experienced anything like it before. It was rather like an electric shock. It seemed that the laying on of hands gave me a certain strength . . .

Later her heart was so troublesome that she would wake dreading the day. At that point she felt that it was not wrong to ask for healing.

It was while we were praying that Margaret felt led to give me laying on of hands, as she did so. First of all it was so hot I felt I would be burned. Then it became ice cold; it was wonderful but rather frightening. Later that night I found the actual marks on my body. It was about this time I was given the text of Ezekiel 36:26 'A new heart also will I give you and a new spirit will I put within you.'

Comforting though this was, and followed about 12 days later by five glorious pain-free days, healing was not complete and a six month period of paid leave was arranged, during which time Audrey began to write this memoir. During that time, Audrey realised that she was holding back, that she herself needed to deal with some of her own feelings, of envy in particular. She did this in prayer and after the next laying on of hands, when again she received marks on her body and initially felt sore, she was finally pain-free and felt 'wonderfully well'.

Later Audrey herself laid hands on the suffering, whose healing followed. Although now retired from the ministry, her life continues in this vein. She still achieves so much, often in the face of adversity and pain, but as the chorus that inspired this says:

He never failed me yet, he never failed me yet, everywhere I go I want the world to know Jesus Christ never failed me yet.

The Numinous

It was Rudolf Otto in his *The Idea of the Holy*, published in Germany as *Das Heilige* in 1917, translated into English in 1923, who coined the term

Types of Spiritual Experience

'numinous'. Taken from the Latin 'numen', meaning holy power, Otto formed the word 'numinous' to express that which is beyond the everyday world, beyond the moral and rational aspects of holiness. He was referring to what he describes as the 'mysterium tremendum et fascinans', the awesome yet fascinating mystery of the divine. For him this power was wholly other, and filled him with fear and awe, and yet drew him constantly to itself.

He recognized the importance of the numinous at the heart of religion, indeed for Otto this numinous preceded formal religion. It was for him sui generis, unlike anything else, and in his view could not be taught. People may be led towards it, and then it may arise, awakened within consciousness. It comes from the spirit and may be manifest in many different ways, even in wild and non-rational ways. It is the mystery beyond human understanding, which generates feelings of awe and fear, and it is eternally fascinating to humanity.

The great physicist Albert Einstein who formulated the Theory of Relativity and fathomed the depths of time, space and the universe, felt this awe:

A spirit is manifest in the laws of the Universe – a spirit vastly superior to that of man, and one in the face of which we with our modest powers must feel humble.[112]

The Sufi poet and mystic, Mevlana Jalaluddin Rumi describes this awe:

Go and contemplate in God's wonders, become lost to yourselves from the majesty and awe of God. When the one who beholds the wonders of God abandons pride and egoism from contemplating God's work, that one will know his proper station and will be silent concerning the Maker. Such a person will only say from their soul, 'I cannot praise You properly,' because that declaration is beyond reckoning.[113]

Here is an account of an experience of the numinous.

A friend persuaded me to go to Ely Cathedral to hear a performance of Bach's minor B Mass. I had heard the work, indeed I knew Bach's choral works pretty well . . . The music thrilled me, until we got to the great Sanctus. I find this experience difficult to define. It was primarily a warning – I was frightened. I was trembling from head to foot and wanted to cry. Actually I think I did. I heard no 'voice' except the music; I saw nothing; but the warning was very definite. I was not able to interpret this experience satisfactorily until I read some months later Rudolph Otto's *Das Heilige*. Here I found it: the 'Numinous'. I was before the Judgement Seat. I was being weighed in the balance and found wanting.[114]

The Dark Night of the Soul

The expression used is a reference to a work of that name by St John of the Cross, in which he recounts his spiritual purgation. This experience was that of a prisoner (R).

> My time in HMP Woodhill saw the culmination of a lifetime of anger and hatred. Something was happening to my body/mind that was beyond my control – it felt like a poison coursing through me. I just felt dirty and corrupted internally. I had pains in my liver and kidneys. I had no appetite. I couldn't taste the food I ate.
>
> There was no joy in my life. I don't mean fun or happiness, but the contentment of just being. I knew that if I continued the way I was going I would do irreparable damage to myself.
>
> In Taoism they believe that the energy of the emotions is stored in the major organs: anger in the liver; hate & impatience in the heart; worry/anxiety in the spleen; sadness/depression in the lungs; ear/stress in the kidneys. Too much of the particular emotion can damage the related organ and since all organs are interdependent, the whole body eventually fails. But they say the organs can be restored by developing their opposite emotions.
>
> But if you have any dual concepts you will experience one or the other. I strove to attain a state of mind that transcended duality. I saw the 'Me,' the 'ego,' the 'images' that made up R as the cause.
>
> The belief systems, the concepts and word associations that I was attached to . . . I let it all go. I stopped believing in them. I wasn't born with them and I was determined not to die with them. I saw it all as 'worldly shit,' garbage that I'd collected and been conditioned to on the way.
>
> All of this just hit me whilst I was in this dark hole. The choice was quite simple: get myself out of it or stay in and probably die in it. All I know was that a stillness still existed within me, it was calling me somehow. I don't really know 'how' I managed to get back in touch with it. I ceased thinking – literally. I lost my psychological memory (not factual memory).

Types of Spiritual Experience

I went into a deep meditative state that lasted many months where I didn't know who I was. I had lost all concept of a past and future. Only a 'Now' existed. I can tune into the 'now' moment at will now, no matter what I'm doing. It's like I've got a switch in my head to 'tune out' anything I don't want in it.

I went through a period where I didn't seem to have enough 'energy' to think, let alone speak and I went on a number of silences, lasting three to four months. I see those periods now as a recuperation period. I had to make space in my mind in order to heal inwardly.

I threw out everything that was of no use to me. I went back to the 'Empty Box', the tabula rasa or the state of mind in Zen called mushin and I've been there ever since. The 'Empty Box' has grown in size since then and gets bigger every day. One day it will encompass the Universe. But 'acceptance' is the key, I feel, that gets the healing process going.

What was worse for me I think is that I should have known better. I'd been meditating for years beforehand reading about Buddhism and spiritual practices etc. and yet I'd turned my back on the path.

Most people walk down the path of self-destruction out of ignorance or habit, because they know no other way. But I'd chosen to self-destruct because I'd started to hate everyone and everything around me. Acceptance is the water that douses the flames.

I'm not sure it would have happened the way it did if I had not known about meditation. But I've always been strong willed, determined. Adversity has been my life.

There was no question of me giving up, even if it came to my very last breath. It's just something I have in me. It's not a conscious thing. I think once a person has re-discovered that 'sacred thread' no matter how much they get lost in darkness, they will never lose sight of that sacred thread. Because the sacred thread is a part of us whether we like it or not. We've just go to be still enough to notice it, feel it, become one with it.

I don't know what made me get the foothold on the path. Maybe my soul has been to the edge of insanity, and fell over into darkness, and it didn't like it there. But only after it had punished the body by making it burn so the message sunk home did it allow it to pick itself back up. St John of the Cross would call the experience I went through 'The Dark Night of the Soul' I suppose.[115]

The Dark Side – Negative Spiritual Experiences

There are experiences which indicate evil as well as good. Indications of a darker side to the spiritual have been investigated by Marete Jakobsen in her Occasional Paper *Negative Spiritual Experiences: Encounters with Evil*. She cites examples from the RERC archives of experiences of intense evil, which have terrified people. Many, even non-Christians, have found themselves making the sign of the cross or calling on God or Jesus to deliver them, which seems to have been effective in most cases.

> A year and a half ago I was asleep in the night, and woke very suddenly and felt quite alert. I felt surrounded and threatened by the most terrifying and powerful presence of Evil. It seemed to be localized within the room. It seemed almost physical and in a curious way it 'crackled', though not audibly. It was also extremely 'black' and I felt overwhelmed with terror. I stayed rigid in my bed for several minutes, wondering how to combat this blackness. I felt it was a manifestation directed very personally at me, by a Power of Darkness. I was overwhelmed by despair and a desire to go out and kill myself by jumping in the Thames nearby, but I knew that I must withstand this.
> (He gets a crucifix and commands it to go away. He is shaking with fear and calls a friend and leaves the building.)
> I hasten to say that although I am a sensitive and sometimes emotional person I am usually sceptical about abstract phenomena! I have not told many people of these experiences because of their 'melodramatic' sides. I have been as objective as I can in describing them. [003191].[116]

> I awoke in the night with a terrible feeling of oppression in the room and my heart seemed to stop beating when I saw hovering near the ceiling in a far corner a luminous, grinning gargoyle-like face, not static but pulsating. I was instantly wide awake and filed with terrible fear and anger that this thing should come and manifest itself to me. I remember picking up anything within reach and flinging it at the grinning evil face and like a flash it darted to within inches of my face. I was petrified and felt as if I was suffocating in a blanket of evil. I remember praying and saying aloud, 'God help me' and with this spoken word it vanished and a fresh ice cold air filled the room and it seemed sweet and pure. [002739][117]

Here an analysis turns into an experience:

> I then became increasingly aware of the two forces upon which our universe is based. The two forces which scientists call positive and negative, and which philosophers call good and evil. The feeling climaxed until for one split second I was aware of the meaning of the

universe with its many horrors and that I, as a human being, was totally at the mercy of the two universal powers. [002743][118]

This account shows how fear can be transformed:

I was living in an old Regency house divided into flats which felt very gloomy. An exorcist came and cleared it, and it then felt much better.

Before he came, I was in bed one night, and felt that there was a presence of some kind in or near the fireplace. It seemed unpleasant, threatening perhaps, and I was a little scared.
    After a while I found that I said to myself that if I wasn't frightened of it, it wouldn't harm me. I then stopped feeling scared, and it changed and became not exactly friendly, but no longer threatening – neutral.
    I realized that the fear was of my own making, that it was destructive, or rather that the opposite of fear gave me strength. It wasn't so much that I had found strength to overcome fear, but more that the realization that I didn't have to be afraid gave me a kind of strength, a good, calm feeling.
    I wish I could follow this advice more often. It was a revelation, though I didn't realize at the time how important it was. I have since realized that 'facing up to' fear is not fighting it, but rather overcoming it with something not quite opposite, but completely different – a kind of strong calmness. [005456]

People seem even more reluctant to admit to negative spiritual experiences than to positive, perhaps because of a feeling of having done something wrong to deserve such an event, or even of being an evil influence on others. However a small percentage of the accounts in the RERC archive do admit of such experiences.

Dangerous Aspects of Spiritual Movements

Spiritual leaders, often starting out as well-intentioned teachers, sometimes use the power which they accumulate to hold sway over their followers. While receiving good guidance from a spiritual teacher can be helpful, being in thrall to a guru or a particular community or church can be dangerous, as disciples take too much on trust and cease to exercise their own judgement. The issue raised here is just what kind of experiences are truly beneficial to spiritual progress.

The People's Temple

A case of a mass following leading to tragedy took place in Guyana in 1978. Jim Jones (1931–1978), a charismatic leader originally a minister of the Disciples of Christ, founded a community in the USA named the People's Temple. Originally based on Christian ideals of shared wealth and responsibility and aiming to care for the elderly and infirm, the community was forced to move several times due to controversy. This was linked to Jim Jones' increasing megalomania and control over his followers. There were cases of sexual abuse and faked healings.

Eventually the community moved to Guyana where Jonestown was built in the jungle. Congressman Leo Ryan, supported by friends and relatives of members of the community as well as disillusioned defectors began to investigate the cult. He and two of his colleagues were murdered on their visit to Jonestown. Jim Jones then ordered his followers to give their children poisoned juice. This was a ritual which they had rehearsed in the past. The adults were then instructed to commit suicide and in all more than nine hundred drank juice he had poisoned and died. Jones shot himself. What had begun as a well-intentioned venture had deteriorated into a crazy cult led by a drug addicted megalomaniac.

Branch Davidians

In 1993 David Koresh was the leader of a group of Branch Davidians, a sect with links to the Seventh-day Adventists. He believed that he was a prophet referred to in the Biblical Book of Revelation, and that this heralded the imminent end-time. His community settled at the Mount Carmel Centre near Waco. Koresh had begun to abuse his power by taking 'spiritual wives' and became increasingly fixated on the end of the world. He began to stock up on food and ammunition in preparation for the apocalypse. When the Bureau of Alcohol, Tobacco and Firearms attempted to raid where David and his followers had set up their community, they held out in a siege, which lasted for 51 days. During that time the media became interested. David broadcast his religious ideas while the world was becoming aware of the goings-on in Waco and learning that David had sexually abused many young women followers. It was eventually decided to send in the FBI in a CS gas attack, which led to a fire and the deaths of 74, many of them children.

There are many sects and movements in which individuals, often vulnerable, are held in thrall and even abused. As religion can operate on a deep level, at times taking absolute control over an individual, it is important to understand the difference between spiritual support and human power dynamics. In *Ungodly Fear, Fundamentalist Christianity and the Abuse of Power*, Stephen Parsons gives an overview of different kinds of abuse of vulnerable people.

> The story now to be recounted can be summarized in a few sentences. After eight years as members of a large, successful charismatic church in an English city, John and Rachel left to become members of a community church which was run by an American pastor and his wife. Within a short time they had handed over £78,000 to the church, the proceeds of the sale of their house, hoping in that way to become founding members of a group living in community. The reality was very different. After a couple of years they found their position so impossible that they left, even though in doing so they became temporarily homeless and penniless. John and Rachel are now members of no particular church, but they are able to look back over their experiences without bitterness, with their faith still intact.

John later analysed what had happened, giving an insight into that kind of situation.

> The church was creating dependency without responsibility. I was getting my identity from the church. I was fleeing from family responsibility by going to all these meetings. I shudder now to think of all the damage done. The status we had was from the organization, not one under God. We propped up the organization. We were being offered palliatives without ever being offered a path to responsibility. We both had low self-esteem. Give me more comfort was the message. You're sold the wrong stuff. We ended up worse off in the end.[119]

With difficulty John and Rachel left the first church. Only after another similar experience of authoritarian church communal life, entailing the loss of money and control over their lives, were they finally able to free themselves from a damaging cycle of dependence. Theirs was a tale of vulnerable people in thrall to a manipulative organization. In the end they had to take responsibility for themselves, rejecting institutions but maintaining their faith.

Irreligious Experiences or De-Conversion

People who reject religion often feel a euphoria similar to that of a religious convert. Richard Dawkins' website cites a number of such cases in

'Converts' Corner on Richarddawkins.net. Douglas Adams, author of *A Hitchhiker's Guide to the Galaxy* starts it off:

> And I thought and thought and thought. But I just didn't have enough to go on, so I didn't really come to any resolution. I was extremely doubtful about the idea of god, but I just didn't know enough about anything to have a good working model of any other explanation for, well, life, the universe, and everything to put in its place. But I kept at it, and I kept reading and I kept thinking. Sometime around my early thirties I stumbled upon evolutionary biology, particularly in the form of Richard Dawkins's books The Selfish Gene and then The Blind Watchmaker, and suddenly (on, I think the second reading of The Selfish Gene) it all fell into place. It was a concept of such stunning simplicity, but it gave rise, naturally, to all of the infinite and baffling complexity of life. The awe it inspired in me made the awe that people talk about in respect of religious experience seem, frankly, silly beside it. I'd take the awe of understanding over the awe of ignorance any day.
> Douglas Adams The Salmon of Doubt, p. 99.

> Douglas, I miss you. You are my cleverest, funniest, most open-minded, wittiest, tallest, and possibly only convert. I hope this book might have made you laugh – though not as much as you made me. . . Douglas's conversion by my earlier books which did not set out to convert anyone inspired me to dedicate to his memory this book which does!
> Richard Dawkins The God Delusion, p. 117

Is Douglas Adams Richard's only convert? Or is he just the first of many? Please write in to Converts' Corner if you have lost your religion (or have been encouraged to come out of the closet) as a result of reading The God Delusion or other Dawkins books.

The website continues with numerous responses, such as,

> At 52 I now have the absolute confidence to be an atheist and to tell anyone that cares to know. Since coming out, I have discovered that most of the people I know are either atheists or wavering agnostics! Thank you Prof Dawkins.

It is not just Christians, usually the target of Dawkins' criticism, who follow his lead.

> I was born and raised a Shiite Muslim. At the age of 17 years, I began taking religion seriously and was on the quest for the 'meaning of life'

and 'truth'. I read the Koran almost inside out (five different translations from the various Muslim sects plus their commentaries). I even learnt some Arabic and was reading the book from its original language.

At age 19, I left mainstream Shiite Islam and became a so called 'reformist Muslim' who forsook all the Islamic traditions but still considered the Koran to be divine in origin, and tried to interpret the Koran from a modern perspective. That led to various on the road to Agnosticism. That was when I was 21. At the same time, I started reading the Bible and the Hindu scripture the Bhagvad Gita. I then came across a book that changed my life. It was the late Carl Sagan's Cosmos (a book version of the famous television documentary series). I was an atheist.

These experiences are obviously very 'Dawkins-centred'. However, the feeling of relief which the deconverted often experience at being able to stop pretending to believe what they find unbelievable is palpable.

The range of spiritual experiences is vast, including positive and negative, but perhaps they are best evaluated over the course of time. Those with lasting effects may be valued more highly, and sometimes negative experiences lead to a positive evaluation overall.

9 Dying and Death

At the heart of religion is the understanding that our earthly life is part of a greater whole, a transient period in the context of eternity. In most religions death is not regarded as the final closing of consciousness. On the contrary, spiritual consciousness is seen as an indication of a greater reality, of which we are part. Some religions have a pattern of reincarnation, some of an eternal hell or paradise awaiting the deceased. Most envisage some kind of post-death judgement, whether this leads to rebirth or continued existence in either a favourable or tormented state. This affects the way religious persons live. An awareness of a moral order inherent in the universe, or emanating from God can put our lives into a moral context and so lead the believer to a better life.

> For those who seek to understand it, death is a highly creative force. The highest spiritual values of life can originate from the thought and study of death.[120]

Exploration of ancient burial sites all over the world seems to confirm that ancient peoples regarded death as a transition to another life. The pyramids in Egypt are the most spectacular examples of this, as the Pharaohs went to the next life with everything they could wish for, including servants. In Chinese temples, fake banknotes, known as 'hell money' are burned for the deceased, to ensure wealth in the next life, and frequently paper mansions, cars and all the necessary trappings of a comfortable existence as well.

Evidence for life after death comes through belief in what religions recount; through messages from the deceased, either through mediums or direct communication or dreams; through Near Death Experiences; death bed visions; hypnotic regression; instances of people seeming to remember past lives and purported evidence of reincarnation. Parapsychology studies such phenomena and continues to bring forward evidence and arguments for and against survival. In the USA Professor Ian Stevenson has studied children who seem to remember past lives, often with birthmarks indicating injuries received in one of those previous lives. In Buddhism the

Dying and Death

tradition of Lamas reincarnating, even leaving messages and clues, is widespread. A young boy able to recognize objects owned by the deceased lama is accepted as his reincarnation and subsequently trained in a monastery to fulfil his appointed reincarnated role.

Much debate as to whether the mind and body can function separately continues as a result of the controversy surrounding the subject of survival of death, with sceptics taking the view that without the brain and the senses there can be no consciousness, while others argue for a dualism of mind and brain, enabling the former to function without the latter.

Here is an account with subsequent detailed analysis, by someone who was given intimations of a previous life.

I had repeated recall, over years in my 20s and 30s, of someone in a concentration camp, and I 'received' a whole historical picture of that person's life and death. These 'past-life-type' images came 'whenever' and didn't arrive in sequence, but I knew where they fitted in the narrative. I could always tell which was common consensus reality, and which was part of this historical scenario. I prayed that the experiences would stop, and eventually they did.

This series of experiences of 'tuning into a concentration camp' informed me that there was more to life than the mundane reality, that human beings could perceive non-local realities, shifting in time and geographical space, spontaneously or at will. They made me feel:

- as if reincarnation was a certainty;
- that there was no point in suicide since one would be reborn with recall of same scenarios;
- that unexpected death, like murder, or an accident, can be remembered once one is reborn;
- that unresolved issues can also surface during the next life, in order to be addressed;
- that unless a person has a similar experience, they do not believe it;
- that I could better understand my mood swings as if I'd had Post Traumatic Stress Disorder (I'd had no trauma in this life, but had technicolour recall of torture in the life of a person who was killed seven years before I was born);
- that people who were considered by common consensus to be delusional or hallucinating, may not be. They may simply shift between different time and space realities, and not realize it;
- I was lucky. I always felt I knew which reality was common consensus, and which visionary.

I believe nothing caused me to have the experience. I believe I was born, like so many other people, with the ability to shift the focus of my attention to different historical and geographical locations. I believe this is a normal human faculty, which has been pathologized in white British, American and Australian societies. Or, it has been kept quiet by those many who have the skill and remain silent. Or it has been pathologized by those who get lost in it, and become anxious and confused. [100056]

Dying

Within religions, survival of death is accepted and so treated as something natural for which one could prepare. Dying well according to the guidance offered by special religious texts has long been accepted practice. The Egyptians had their *Pert em hru* and the Europeans their *Ars Moriendi*. Tibetan Buddhists have the *Bardo Thosgrol Chenmo*. The English title is *The Tibetan Book of the Dead*, the Tibetan *The Great Liberation by Hearing in the Intermediate States*. This has recently been translated into English in its entirety for the first time, under the auspices of the Dalai Lama, who has written a learned introduction. All these works give detailed advice on dying, which is also applicable to spiritual practice in life. Shamanic initiation draws on a viewing of death as a transition to new life, and many rites in tribal religions imitate the pattern of dying and rebirth. There are myths in most religious traditions which reflect this pattern, and it is also the core of the Christian religion, as in the words of the Apostles' Creed, Christ

> was crucified, died, and was buried;
> he descended to the dead.
> On the third day he rose again; he ascended into heaven.[121]

Some forms of Hinduism indicate that the ultimate fate of the individual is to merge with the absolute. In Buddhism all passions and trials disappear in the state of *Nirvana*. Christianity, Islam and Judaism believe in a judgement followed by sojourn in a place commensurate with what one is due, paradise or hell, although there is often a location where further development and purification can take place. Many people do indeed experience a dying and rebirth in their spiritual lives. Special practices and even drug-induced experiences can give rise to insights into the pattern of living, dying and being reborn.

Dramatic experiences are now being reported taking place when the brain has ceased to function, during accidents, operations or illness. As

Dying and Death

resuscitation techniques improve and people survive after longer periods of unconsciousness, there are more and more reports of Near Death experiences. These are often preceded by an Out of the Body experience. Are these spiritual experiences too and what might such experiences indicate as to the possible survival of death?

Spiritual experiences often give a new perspective to the age-old questions as to why we are here and whether there is any purpose in life beyond material wealth and professional success. They may throw light on the purpose and value of life. Whether one is sceptical or a believer, the question of human consciousness is of profound importance. Is the mind identical to the brain or can the two operate separately? Does anything of what we are survive our death?

Apart from the existential fear of death, there is the anxiety about dying, yet those who work with the dying, such as carers and nurses in hospitals and hospices often find the process a peaceful one. Nowadays pain can be managed and the end is generally calm. There have always been unexplained phenomena around the dying, and recently these have begun to be studied.

Here is an account of a recent event.

Leading up to my mother-in-law's death she had been ailing for some time, nothing specific, just her general health, she was 86 and getting weaker and weaker. My father-in-law was pretty much her full time carer for at least a year or so. She couldn't really do much, just sat in her chair and would seem to 'just not be there' at times. When I would visit she would say 'do you think I'm dying?' I felt embarrassed, it being a difficult question to answer, so just replied, 'I don't know'. To which she replied, 'Because if I am, it's wonderful!'

It was finally getting too much for my father-in-law to cope with and the day before she died she had been assessed for extra help or to see if she had to go into a care-home. She obviously didn't want to do that, and choose to slip away quietly instead.

The night she died, my father in-law washed her to make her more comfortable, starting with her feet – (not wanting to be too sentimental but when he told me this it made me think of Jesus washing the disciples feet, with such love). He was beside her all night long and her last words to him were 'I am at peace'. Apparently she looked younger and beautiful and it was a very peaceful passing.

Initially, I felt her presence with us very closely. Then I felt she was agitated with me and I wondered why, and if I had done something wrong to upset her. My father-in-law wanted help to sort through her clothes, it was too upsetting for him. I felt this was what she was asking me to do and once I had done so, the feeling of agitation left. My husband had a dream of her in her prime a day or so after she died.[122]

This is a premonition of death, which had a profound effect.

I was sitting on a train, when it felt as if curtains in my forehead parted. I was standing at the end of my life, aged 76, looking back over my shoulder in wonder at a broad stream of colour radiating away from me that had been my life. My life was lion-yellow in colour – with light and dark 'patches', and I knew I could dive into the colour at any stage to examine what had happened at that point in my life. At the same time, I was conscious of being surrounded by the most extraordinary love – it looked like sparkles set amongst 'darkish' infinity. I do not have adequate words to explain exactly what it was like, but the *feeling* coming from this infinity was one of unconditional love and acceptance of who I was, what I had done, and how I was in my life. I had never encountered such love during my life, nor have I since. While I was looking at my 'life' from over my shoulder, I was conscious of beginning to drift upwards and I knew I was dying. I then realized that my life was only an experience, but it was how I used the experience that mattered. It was a powerful realization that swept over me and I could feel myself changing my thought patterns. As soon as I understood the implications of this, the curtains in my forehead closed, and I was back on the train.

For days after I mourned the loss of that infinite love – still do, although a lesser extent. Yet I have tried all manner of ways to make my curtains open again, but have never been able to. Nonetheless, I am forever hopeful.

I suppose it is the same feeling that C. S. Lewis wrote about in the Narnia chronicles – the desire to return to Narnia, but unable to find the opening.

I began to look at life as just an experience – and became much more conscious that each life experience I was having was as an opportunity for growth. It helped me to become more in control of my feelings, and therefore to make informed choices about the way I wanted to live my life. It also confirmed my belief that there is more going on around me than just the physical/material world. Whether there is a God, I don't know. But I do believe love is a powerful force in the world and beyond, and there are many ways of experiencing it. I also believe that I will return to this experience of infinite love when I 'die', which will probably happen when I am 76. I have already started the process of spiritually preparing myself for my death. Part of this preparation includes choosing to do PhD research in end-of-life experiences to help improve spiritual end-of-life care for the dying, their relatives and carers.

I have no idea if there is a reincarnation process. It certainly did not feel like that while I was having my experience. It felt more as if I was drifting 'up' to a different level of consciousness, free from my body, which felt warm and inviting. However the experienced ended before I could grasp what was to come.

Due to the experience, I have no fear of dying – in fact I am really looking forward to it. However, I am aware I am fearful of the way in which I die, which I know is contradictory. But I guess that is the human part of me stepping in to protect me from ending my life before my time.

I think about my death on a daily basis – sometimes hourly. Not in a morbid way, but with great fascination of what is to come. I also often take myself to the point of my death in meditation, hoping (in vain) to feel that extraordinary love. I would like to think my later years will be spent closer to the mystical in time of reflection and spiritual retreat, so I can completely surrender into my dying process when my time comes.

I think the most important thing for me is that I KNOW it happened. And it happened TO me. It was not imagined, nor was it some kind of inner creative visualization. It was as real as I am sitting here writing about it. So, it gives me a feeling of warmth and comfort knowing that I encountered – and more importantly capable of experiencing – such a profoundly personal event. It also gives me comfort, knowing there is something 'tangible' awaiting me when I die.

At the time of the mystical experience, I had been going through a particularly hard time emotionally, and in retrospect it felt as if I 'was given' this experience to help me along my way.

Regarding the sceptics. I always wish a mystical experience upon them – and then we'll talk! [100052]

End of Life Experiences

Great comfort is often brought about by experiences around the dying. Nurses have often reported such events and an End of Life Experience (ELE) study is being undertaken under the direction of Dr Peter Fenwick. Hospice workers and home carers report that ELEs appear to be part of the dying process, which has profound spiritual and existential implications for those who have them, or witness them.

The study suggests that ELEs fall into two main categories:

1. 'Transpersonal ELEs' which possess otherworldly qualities helping the dying person to let go, such as deathbed visions of predeceased

loved ones, the ability to transit to and from other realities, change in room-temperatures around the time of death, the appearance of light and love around the body or in the room at the moment of death, and co-incidences which occur around the time of death. These co-incidences include reports of the dying person 'appearing' to a relative or close friend at the time of death, clocks stopping synchronistically or the appearance of significant birds, butterflies and/or animals at the time or death. However, because of their ethereal qualities, these ELEs cannot be easily tied into the pathological process of dying.

2. 'Final Meaning ELEs' which appear to have substantive qualities, firmly based in the near and now, which prompt the person to process unresolved business so they can die peacefully. For example, the desire to reconcile with estranged family members, or to put their affairs in order, previously confused or semi-unconscious people experiencing unexpected lucid moments that enable them to say farewell to loved ones, and the dying person, against all medical odds, hanging on to life until a special relative arrives.[123]

Sue Brayne, one of the researchers cited the following examples:

The manager of a counselling centre with which I am associated recounted a couple of days before her mother died that her mother repeatedly called out, 'I'm coming! I'm coming!' to a blank wall. At the time, the manager put it down to a lack of oxygen, but now thinks there may be more to it.

A more disturbing story I heard was about a young woman who was to be admitted to hospital for a routine operation. A couple of weeks before she went into hospital, she told her mother she had seen the 'Angel of Death'. Her mother thought she was making it up, so ignored it. The girl died on the operating table.

On the other hand, I was told this story by a friend. Her friend had a three-year-old daughter who was critically ill. The night before her daughter died, the mother saw an angel standing at the end of the child's bed. This soothed and reassured the mother, because she believed her daughter had been collected by the angel and was being cared for in death.[124]

Her colleague Hilary Lovelace quoted these:

A 38-year-old man was dying. Too young to die he thought, and he was resisting; he was denying. Then his mother and his own eight year-old son, both of whom were dead, appeared to him in a vision and after that he said to the nurses, 'Now I feel I can die with peace, because I know I'm going to join my loved ones.'

. . . a lady said to the chaplain of the hospice, and to her husband, 'I'm so scared that I'm going to go alone.' The husband said to her, 'Look, don't worry, ducky, I'll be with you; I'll hold your hand'. She said, 'Oh, no, I don't want *you*; I want someone to collect me from the other side!' When her husband and the chaplain were sitting with her at the moment of her death, in the middle of the night, the door of the room swung open, and nobody came in. They took notice of this and at that moment the lady's hand went into the air, as if grasping another offered hand, and then fell down as she died peacefully. The husband said, 'Gosh – it looks like she got what she wanted; it looks like someone came to meet her'. And he felt hugely comforted by this – though we shall never know whether *she* was comforted! [125]

This moving account is of an experience which gave a strong indication of the survival of a small child and brought great comfort to his mother.

The second of my three much-loved children was a little boy called Mark who died when he was 15 months old. Over the years I longed to know exactly where he was.

Then I heard that my father was dying. He had suffered for many years. By the time I reached the moorland farmhouse where he lived it was late. He was being nursed by my mother and brother in the familiar room with its homely wood fire and raftered ceiling. When I stooped to kiss the beloved face so deeply etched by suffering, his eyes were closed and sealed and he was too far gone to know I had come.

Suddenly his face was transformed by an expression of tender joy and delight as he struggled to sit up. He held out his arms for something, then cradled them as if holding a baby and rocked gently.

'Oh,' he said, 'oh, tell Rosemary, little Mark is here. He's here!' Then he fell back.

When Father died my brother stood up and with tears said, 'Thanks be to God.' Then the room filled with a warm, translucent light and we rested in its peace.

Next morning our neighbour called and said she had woken twice during the night and looked out. It was dark except for a beautiful light shining above our roof.[126]

Out of the Body Experiences

Some people have experiences of being outside their bodies. This may happen in times of stress or critical illness or even near death. The writer of the seminal work *On Death and Dying*, Elisabeth Kübler-Ross, had an Out of the Body experience but had no idea of what had happened. It was not until later in her life that she began her research into dying patients and then Near Death experiences.

> A few seconds later I was in a deep sleep. But instead of 'falling' asleep, I felt as if I was rising up out of my body, higher and higher, but without any control or fear. Once aloft, I perceived several beings take hold and carry me off to someplace where they fixed me up. It was like having several car mechanics work on me. Each had their own specialty – brakes, transmission and so on. In no time, they had replaced all the damaged parts with new ones and set me back in bed.
>
> In the morning, after just a few hours' sleep, I woke up feeling blissfully serene. The nurse was still in the room, so I told her what had happened. 'You obviously had an out-of-body experience,' she said. I gave her a puzzled look. After all, I did not meditate or eat tofu. Nor was I a Californian. Nor did I have a guru or a Baba. My point? That I had absolutely no idea what she was talking about when she said 'out-of-body experience.' But if they were anything like that, I was ready for another flight anytime.[127]

In a BBC Radio 4 series, *Devout Sceptics*, Bel Mooney interviewed well-known people about their views on faith and doubt. Certain interviews were then written up in a book of the same name. Melvyn Bragg was interviewed and asked about a personal article he had written earlier in which he had admitted to having had terrifying Out of Body experiences as a boy. He was then asked whether this led him to believe in the soul as distinct from the body. He replied:

> If I was asked on pain of life and death, I would say, yes, I do. It's an impossible question to answer, for obvious reasons, in that it doesn't stand up to any proof you can think of, but from the experiences I had it is possible for some essential thing in you, the thinking . . . to be removed from this corporeal frame, as it's been described, and exist somewhere else, in my case the corner of a room. After I'd written the article I got a great number of letters from people saying they had floated around the town where they were born, in cities, across the seas . . . One of the things which interests me about the description of

out-of-body experiences, where people have almost died and floated towards death and pulled back, is that they're always the same . . . Early Christian writing is full of such descriptions. So in terms of evidence, what does it add up to? It adds up to the possibility of continuity, the notion that there may be something so distinctive and extraordinary, something that does exist outside what we are, what we seem to be. If I had strong faith I'd say it is a fact. It's something that has to be grappled with, because if you're going to believe in a patterning and creative and religious universe then you have to believe in continuity and continuousness.[128]

Many OBEs are the first stage of a Near Death experience.

Near Death Experiences (NDE)

Some kind of survival of death seems to be indicated by the NDE. Modern resuscitation techniques have given many people the opportunity to 'return from the dead'. Accounts abound in the popular press and are investigated in television documentaries of people who have miraculously survived clinical death.

A typical NDE begins with an OBE, viewing one's own body from above, seeing and hearing what is going on, but being unable to communicate. Realization that one has died is followed by entry into a dark tunnel with a bright, welcoming light at the end. There the person seems to be met by a being of light and love, and often deceased relatives as well. As the person does not in fact die, it is often at this point that it is made clear that the time is not yet ripe, and a return to the body takes place, often against the person's will, and occasionally into pain. Some people however, go on to experience a life-review, where they themselves feel the suffering they have caused others, judging themselves and their behaviour. On their return to life on earth these people frequently live completely transformed lives. The NDE leads them to greater compassion for their fellows and a more spiritual, less materialistic attitude. Many change to more caring professions, some become religious, but almost all report that they no longer have any fear of death.

This is not merely a modern phenomenon, however. There are myths in different parts of the world, and reports across the centuries which have a similar pattern, including Plato's account of Er in *The Republic*. However, these days there is an increasing amount of reporting, recording and analysis of NDEs and they are no longer seen as something one does not mention. They are discussed openly and are frequently the subject of articles in the media. They give people hope of life after death and are often the cause of a change in attitudes and way of life. In their investigation of NDEs, in *The Truth in the Light*, Dr Peter Fenwick and Elizabeth Fenwick found that people were transformed in many ways after their NDE, primarily in their attitudes to death. 82% reported that they no longer feared death, for example:

> I suppose this experience moulded something in my life. I was only a child when it happened, only ten, but now, my entire life through, I am thoroughly convinced that there is life after death, without a shadow of a doubt, and I am not afraid to die. I am not. Some people I have known are so afraid, so scared. I always smile to myself when I hear people doubt that there is an afterlife, or say, 'When you're dead, you're gone.' I think to myself, 'They really don't know.'[129]

Another example of an NDE from the same book is that of Derek Skull, a retired Major, who described himself as a very down-to-earth sort of person. He would be the very last person to make up anything as strange as an NDE. In fact he had not been able to make sense of his experience and had told no-one, not even his wife about it. Some time later he heard a radio programme about NDEs and realized what had happened to him. At the time of his experience Major Skull was in intensive care after a heart attack. His room had windows too high for him to see out of and the door was closed.

> I was lying there feeling terrible – absolutely at my lowest point, I'd never felt so low. Then these women just descended on me like three witches. They had to insert a catheter. I'd never had anything done like that and they gave me no warning, nothing. I didn't know what they were up to. I can remember shouting, 'Who's that dreadful woman in the white coat?' and someone saying, 'That's the doctor.'
>
> I felt this enormous tension, as though I knew something was going to happen. Then I felt absolutely airy-fairy – as if I was levitating, quite serene, withdrawn from my body. I floated up into the top left-hand corner of the room. I looked back and saw my own body, lying there with its eyes closed. It didn't seem at all surprising for me to be up there. I could see through the windows at the top of the room to the reception area outside the ward. Suddenly I was conscious of my wife waiting at the reception desk, talking to someone who was sitting down behind the desk so I couldn't see them properly. She was wearing her red trouser suit. I thought, my God, what an inappropriate time to

arrive. It's not visiting hours, I haven't shaved, I'm looking dreadful, and anyway, I'm up here and she's down there, and here's the body. What's going to happen?

The next thing I was conscious of was being back in my bed, I opened my eyes and there sitting beside me was Joan in her red trouser suit. I wasn't a bit surprised, because I knew she's arrived, I'd already seen her.[130]

Derek Skull interpreted his experience to mean that something, a soul perhaps can become detached from the body and if that is what happens at death, he is no longer worried about it.

Mellen-Thomas Benedict refers to his death, rather than a NDE, which took place in 1982. He had inoperable cancer, knew there was no hope and had explored various spiritual teachings while preparing himself for death. One day he knew that he would die. He had arranged with his carer to leave his body unattended for six hours after his death, as he had read that this was a time when things might happen. He died for an hour and a half, during which time his heart was monitored and all the physical symptoms of death were apparent. His body had even begun to stiffen. Benedict recounts that his experience began with the usual NDE pattern of events, being outside his body. Then he met the Light.

As I began to move toward the Light, I knew intuitively that if I went to the Light, I would be dead. So as I was moving toward the Light I said, 'Please wait a minute, just hold on a second here. I want to think about this; I would like to talk to you before I go.' To my surprise, the entire experience halted at that point. You are indeed in control of your near-death experience. The Light kept changing into different figures, like Jesus, Buddha, Krishna, mandalas, archetypal images and signs. I asked the Light, 'What is going on here? Please Light, clarify yourself for me. I want to know the reality of the situation.' I cannot say the exact words, because it was a sort of telepathy. The Light responded. The information transferred to me was that your beliefs shape the kind of feedback you are getting before the Light. If you were a Buddhist or Catholic or Fundamentalist, you get a feedback loop of your own stuff. You have the chance to look at it and examine it, but most people do not. As the Light revealed itself to me, I became aware that what I was really seeing was our higher Self matrix. . . . I was not committed to one particular religion. So that was what was being fed back to me.

. . .

Then the Light turned into the most beautiful thing I have ever seen: a mandala of human souls on the planet. . . . . I said, 'Oh, God, I did not know how beautiful we are.'

He realized that the whole of humanity would be saved.

The Great Light spoke, saying, 'Remember this and never forget; you save, redeem and heal yourself. You always have. You always will. You were created with the power to do so from the beginning of the world.'[131]

Benedict then wanted to discover more about the universe and he was able to see a subtle energy around the earth, created by humans, a spiritual level. He travelled out beyond our universe, before the Big Bang and into the Void. This is full of an energy, which is also all around and within us as Absolute Consciousness.

I saw that the Big Bang is only one of an infinite number of Big Bangs creating Universes endlessly and simultaneously.

The Ancients knew of this. They say Godhead periodically created new Universes by breathing out, and de-created other Universes by breathing in. These epochs were called Yugas.

I discovered that creation is about Absolute Pure Consciousness, or God, coming into the Experience of Life as we know it.[132]

He understood that creation is God exploring God's self and the uniqueness of each person enhances this. Benedict found that there are many heavens (of different kinds, reflecting our own expectations) and that the end of all religions is the same God, but not God 'out there', God within everything.

I asked God, 'What is the best religion on the planet? Which one is right?' And Godhead said, with great love: 'I don't care.' That was incredible grace. . . . I immediately understood that it is for *us* to care about. It is important because we are the caring beings. . . . Each has a different view. And it all adds up to the big picture; it is all important.[133]

After his experience Benedict was completely cured and his insights have enabled him to contribute to research into cellular communication and quantum biology. He is able to access the Light through meditation and now works as a healer.

Black Elk, a Wichasha Wakau or Holy Man of the Oglala Lakota Oyate (Oglala Sioux Tribe) of North America shared his experiences with John Neihardt in *Black Elk Speaks*, perhaps because both men had had NDEs. Black Elk had gained healing powers and foresight through an extremely complex NDE at the age of nine, when he was unconscious for 12 days. It was eight years before he was able to come to terms with the experience, and then only with the help of a medicine man. In his NDE Black Elk was taken to six grandfathers, each of whom gave him particular powers.

> I saw more than I can tell and I understood more than I saw; for I was seeing in a sacred manner the shapes of all things in the spirit, and the shape of all shapes as they must live together like one being. [134]

Aged 26, Black Elk had another NDE, while in Europe with Buffalo Bill's travelling show. He fell ill and was presumed dead. In fact he felt that he was travelling on a cloud to his family back in South Dakota. He subsequently went back and saw everything exactly as in the vision and learned that his mother had dreamed of him visiting on a cloud at exactly that time.

This experience is that of a doctor, tempted to attribute it to the after-effects of anaesthesia. However, subsequent events made this an inadequate interpretation of the messages given during the NDE.

> In 1979 I was a part time GP, mother of two toddlers, and married to a solicitor in full time legal practice who was also an NSM (non-stipendiary minister) in the Anglican Church. An NSM has received part-time training, is an ordained priest and has a role in local ministry, but at that time there was no question of the priest taking on a full time job in the Church of England.
> Whilst in hospital, following the birth of my third child, and some hours after anaesthesia for a minor procedure, I had a strange but vivid experience.
> I felt myself floating in outer space, in deep black 'nothing' but with occasional stars. I became aware that someone, or something was communicating with me, but saw no face or source of this communication, it felt like it was God, or a being.

The message was clear and was in two parts:

1. That we (my husband and I) were to take on total care of souls
2. That I was to do something about the dignity of dying

It was a pleasant, comforting experience. As a doctor, I cast it aside considering that it was simply the result of anaesthesia, and it made no sense to me with the limitations of my husband's role as NSM, and my very part-time job in General Practice, with now three young and demanding children to care for. At the time there was political discussion about resuscitation in hospitals and the lack of dignity involved. How could I influence that?

I was embarrassed by the experience and did not tell my husband, but mentioned it laughingly on two occasions to trusted female friends when they came to visit.

The experience did not influence any decisions, nor did it change the way I lived my life, but my life changed.

Without any knowledge of my experience, some four months later, my husband told me that he wanted to cease his work as a solicitor, that he had discussed with the Bishop of Worcester the possibility of becoming a full-time priest.

Within a year, . . . we had sold our house and changed our lives as he became Priest-in-Charge of four country parishes. I continued with part time general practice alongside being a 'vicar's wife' and mother. We had total care of souls.

In . . . the Rectory kitchen, my husband showed me a piece in the local newspaper about a group of people who wanted to develop a Hospice at Home . . . . He said, 'You'd be good at that'.

We both knew that my life was far too busy to add anything else, but I was interested in what was going on, and went to a dedicated service . . . [and was] asked if I would be able to help in some way. My youngest was still only three, so I did not feel able to join in until she had started school. . . .

The story is long, but despite difficulties at home in freeing up time, and pulls in commitment between hospice, parish and family, I became more and more involved in the evolution of the Hospice, and later Palliative Care . . . . I became the first Macmillan Consultant in Palliative Medicine in [the area] and was responsible for developing services for the dying, as well as caring for dying patients and their families.

Dying and Death

> It seems that both commands made to me in that spiritual experience ... came to pass, but not by my will.
> I cannot laugh at that experience now. [100059]

Although most reported NDEs are positive, there are also negative experiences. Yet these too may give an indication of continuation of life after death and have a positive effect on life. Revd Martin Israel describes his negative NDE and the consequences in *Happiness That Lasts*. A steady decline in his health, including a form of epilepsy and Parkinson's disease, was suddenly exacerbated by what seemed like a complete shutdown of his system and he was almost completely unconscious for five weeks.

> During this time I felt that I seemed to descend into a vast pit of darkness where I could 'sense' the souls of a vast concourse of people who were unknown to me personally. I seemed to be in hell, and even now I believe it might be possible that this was literally true. There was despair, darkness and a lack of communication between the souls that were there. The gloom was appalling, and there seemed no hope anywhere. In fact, I believe there was a total dissociation between my rational mind, which was shattered, and my spiritual mind which was forlorn and lonely but entirely free.
>
> ...
>
> Despite this terrifying experience I thank God for the privilege of experiencing it, because it has taught me so much and radically altered my personality and outlook on life.
> I now know we are all immortal, not through our own deserts, but by the immeasurably great love of God. I had long believed this on a mental level through my mystical nature, yet I could never entirely feel it in the depth of my soul. After I recovered normal consciousness, coming as it were, back to myself once more, I knew that the supreme consciousness, which is one way of speaking of God, pervades all creation and loves it, whatever its nature and use may be. For us humans there is an individual as well as a collective destiny and the end is glorious, but this life is only one step towards that destiny, which no one alive can know with authority.
> Incarnate life, because the body is frail, is bound to be involved in suffering, and its intensity bears no relationship to the character of the person. But the way of suffering is an essential part of the progress of the person towards self-knowledge and the recognition of God ... But

as it was revealed to Julian of Norwich, all shall be well. The important duty in this life is that we should live as perfectly as we can in the present moment. [135]

These days as more people report NDEs and more is publicly known about such experiences, it is possible to study similarities in pattern and effects. Although these experiences do seem to indicate some kind of continuation of consciousness after death, there continues to be much debate. Scientists such as Dr Susan Blackmore, who has herself had an NDE, maintain that these experiences are due to the dying brain.

> Severe stress, extreme fear and cerebral anoxia all cause cortical disinhibition and uncontrolled brain activity ... Tunnels and lights are frequently caused by disinhibition in visual cortex, and similar noises occur during sleep paralysis. ... OBEs and life reviews can be induced by temporal lobe stimulation, and the positive emotions and lack of pain have been attributed to the action of endorphins and encephalins; endogenous opiates that are widely distributed in the limbic system and released under stress.[136]

Since Raymond Moody's bestselling *Life After Life,* published in 1975, brought such experiences to the world's attention, much research has been done. Kenneth Ring, a psychologist in Connecticut undertook scientific research into NDEs. Using carefully crafted statistical analyses, he concluded that Moody's initial findings were generally correct. In his first book, *Life at Death* (1980), Ring developed the Weighted Core Experience Index to measure the most frequently recurring elements in 102 cases, and found that the core NDE tends to fall into five stages. These were peace (60%); body separation (37%); entering the darkness (23%); seeing the light (16%); entering the light (10%). Bruce Greyson, a psychiatrist then at the University of Connecticut, proposed a fourfold typology of NDEs: cognitive, affective, paranormal and transcendental.

George Gallup studied the phenomenon statistically, and reported in 1982 that 'about 15 percent of all adult Americans, or about 23 million people, said they had a close brush with death' involving an unusual experience, roughly one in twenty Americans.

Various other studies have been undertaken on NDEs, notably by the Dutchman Pim van Lommel, who led a 13-year study of 344 cardiac arrest patients in 10 hospitals, of whom 41 reported NDEs. The study also had an 8-year follow-up. The results were published in *The Lancet* in 2001. These were his findings:

- Awareness of being dead: 50%
- Positive emotions: 56%
- OBE   24%
- Moving through a tunnel   31%
- Communication with the light   23%
- Observation of colours   23%
- Observation of celestial landscape   29%
- Meeting with deceased persons   32%
- Life review   13%
- Presence of border   8%

Peter and Elizabeth Fenwick investigated over 300 NDEs in *The Truth in the Light*. In *Religion, Spirituality and the Near-Death Experience*, Dr Mark Fox gives a considered appraisal of various responses, scientific and theological, to the NDE and includes a study of the RERC archive accounts.

Professor Paul Badham's Occasional Paper *Religious and Near-Death Experience in Relation to Belief in a Future Life* gives an overview of NDEs from sources as varied as St Paul, Tibetan Buddhism and A. J. Ayer and discusses what these experiences might mean. He draws attention to the various interpretations of the Being of Light.

> Concerning the Being of Light which contemporary experiencers see and name in accordance with their own tradition, this also is in accord with the *Tibetan Book of the Dead* where we read, 'The *Dharmakaya* (deity) of clear light will appear in what ever shape will benefit all beings.' Commenting on this verse for his English translation Lama Kazi Dawa-Samdup says, 'To appeal to a Shaivite devotee, the form of Shiva is assumed; to a Buddhist the form of the Buddha... to a Christian, the form of Jesus; to a Muslim the form of the Prophet; and so for other religious devotees; and for all manner and conditions of mankind a form appropriate to the occasion.'[137]

As many NDEs occurred during a heart attack this has made such cases valuable for further research as patients were in a similar physiological state, many in Intensive Therapy Units. Penny Sartori, an ITU nurse researching NDEs obtained her PhD in the subject with Peter Fenwick and Paul Badham. Although she had placed pictures up on top of cupboards in wards, in the hope that during the OBE stage, they would be seen, none were. However, patients reporting NDEs were able to describe correctly the procedures which had been undertaken during resuscitation attempts, while those without NDEs had no idea what had happened and were unable to guess correctly. Penny found that about 25% of her patients reported NDEs.[138]

Most people who have had such an experience are convinced of continuation.

> I have never really feared death since. It opens up marvellous possibilities! If this life were all we had, I should think it most illogical and rather a poor deal for many. As it is, my experience suggests there may be something much more meaningful hereafter. I hope so.[139]

Others, like the well-known atheist philosopher A. J. Ayer, ultimately return to their long-held view that death will be the end for them, even if they have been temporarily shaken out of this assumption:

> His first response was to think that, 'on the face of it, these experiences are rather strong evidence that death does not put an end to consciousness.' However after rehearsing some of the philosophical problems associated with life after death, his conclusion was more modest: namely that 'my recent experiences have slightly weakened my conviction that my genuine death, which is due fairly soon, will be the end of me, though I continue to hope it will.'[140]

However they are interpreted, these fascinating experiences are now far more widely reported, and due to advances in resuscitation techniques, are on the increase, and so are set to continue to provide a valuable source of material for study. Their similarities and differences to religious expectation make them of particular interest for the study of religious experience.

Post-Death Experiences

People who have been bereaved often find comfort in intimations of continued contact with the lost loved-one and some of the most common spiritual experiences are those of widows and widowers sensing the continued presence of their deceased spouse. This may be a feeling of their presence, or hearing their voice, or signals by means of lights going on and off or some other phenomena. Sometimes there is practical communication, help in finding important items or documents, while others experience

Dying and Death

comforting dreams of the deceased. Emma Heathcote-James collected many such experiences in *After Death Communication*.

This account comes from a friend, who was bereaved in 2006, and is particularly interesting as so many people became aware of the scent of roses, and the later synchronicity with the poem chosen for her Memorial Service.

> It was Monday 11th December, my wife Liz had died on 20th November. My daughters had flown out to Cyprus with me to help and to attend the Memorial Service to be held on Friday 15th December.
>
> It was noon on a beautiful sunny December day. I was working in my study with the sliding doors of the sitting room open. My daughter, Rebecca, was writing a Eulogy for the forthcoming Memorial Service. She spotted a white feather on the lawn – fascinated – she brought the feather into my office and said that she had heard that a white feather was sometime a sign of Angels. I said that I wasn't aware of such a claim, but took the feather anyway, and placed it in front of a picture of Liz on my desk.
>
> Rebecca continued writing, but after a few minutes, she asked 'Dad can you smell roses?' Indeed the scent of roses was starting to fill my study. Perplexed I went into the sitting room which was also filled with the scent. (The house had only recently been completed and the garden not even begun, so there were no flowers at all there and no cut flowers in the house.) The scent was in the sitting room – even stronger in my study, then up the stairs and in the master bedroom. (There was no scent in any other rooms in the house.)
>
> I then called my mother and my other daughter Hannah to the sitting room – who immediately identified the scent as roses. Of course we soon realized that Liz was visiting us – and were all so happy and felt very, very comforted. The scent lasted for about half an hour. After the excitement and the scent had gone, I went to look for the white feather – it was nowhere to be found.
>
> The previous evening Rebecca had asked me what my favourite flower was and I had replied, roses. A few hours prior to this experience I had ordered bunches of lilies for the Memorial Service. Liz was for sure telling me to change to roses – which I did.
>
> I had asked some close friends to pay a Tribute to Liz at the Memorial Service and I went to visit them shortly after our experience. Before I said anything about the roses, David read me the poem he intended to quote at the service. It was 'The Scent of Roses' by Thomas Moore which had long been a favourite of his. The last line is, 'But the scent of the roses will hang around still.'

Another friend told me four days after Liz died – that on the night she died Liz had appeared to her in a dream, to assure her that she was fine and not to worry. [005441]

At the time of that dream, her friend had not yet known that Liz had died. These events brought comfort to Liz's widower, and to her family and friends.

Here is another account, this one involving experiences of the widower and bereaved son who were about 8,000 miles apart.

Singapore, March 1985.
Some weeks after my mother died in England in January 1985 I had a very powerful dream in which she came to see me, smartly (and uncharacteristically) dressed in a tweed suit, and clearly ready to embark on a journey. I have no recollection of any conversation we held, but I have an abiding memory of being actually with her.
I was awakened from this experience by the alarming sound of our three normally docile dogs howling and barking frenziedly outside the bedroom window. I got out of bed, together with my wife and we went outside to see what the fuss was, and I seemed to hear singing, and also my mother's voice. The house and garden outside were bathed in the light of a brilliant full moon, while the dogs kept up their clamour. I calmed them down, and as there seemed to be nothing else the matter, we went back to bed. It was 4 am.
The following evening I telephoned my father to see how he was getting on (this had become a regular thing since our loss). He told me that the previous night he had carried out the melancholy task of scattering my mother's ashes in his garden, carrying out a pact agreed between the two of them and not divulged to anyone else, that this should be done in the light of a full moon.
Bearing in mind the 8-hour time difference between England and Singapore I asked him: 'would that have been about 8 pm?' and he said 'Yes, why do you ask?'.
I then told him what had been happening in our house and garden 8,000 miles away at that very moment. [005451]

Dr Penny Sartori, who has herself been involved in NDE research, reported a strange sighting at the seventh Ecumenical Conference on Christian Parapsychology, jointly sponsored by the Churches' Fellowship for Psychical and Spiritual Studies and the Alister Hardy Society and

Dying and Death

Religious Experience Research Centre, held at St Luke's Campus, University of Exeter in 2006.

At the conference, Penny gave a talk on NDEs, after which Diana Fynn, author of *On the Turn of the Tide* briefly spoke to her. Penny had bought the book at the conference, and she read it immediately following the event. Her experience was so unusual, that she wrote the following to Diana:

> When I first got home, I flicked through the book and looked at the photographs. I immediately recognized you and I also recognized the man in the photograph above yours on the last page – James Smeall. This part may sound ridiculous to you but he was at the conference. Before I presented my paper I saw him in front of me walking alone amongst other conference attendees then I saw him alone again after I had presented my paper and was walking to the coffee room. I looked at him nodded in acknowledgement, smiled at him and said 'Hi' and he smiled back and nodded. He looked quite normal and was wearing light coloured trousers and a white shirt and maybe a beige or white coloured jacket and his shoulders were hunched as in the photograph. I had no idea that he had died until I got to that chapter in your book. I looked at his photograph again to make sure I hadn't mistaken him for someone else.
>
> I discussed this with my husband who immediately thought that I had seen someone who looked like James at the conference and not James himself. Does James have a brother or maybe a son who was in attendance at the conference? Did you see anyone else who closely resembled James? I have begun to doubt myself now but I know that when I first saw his photograph in your book I immediately said to myself 'Oh, that man was at the conference too' and wished that I had spoken to him when we had acknowledged each other.
>
> I hope you don't mind me telling you this but nothing quite so unusual has happened to me before. Maybe there is a perfectly rational explanation for this and I merely saw someone who closely resembled James. I just find it mystifying as to why I immediately recognized James's photograph and thought nothing unusual of it until I read the chapters about him in your book which told me that he died in 1999.

Diana replied, and her letter, including Penny's experience was published in The Christian Parapsychologist in December 2006.

Penny found my address and wrote to me that week. I phoned her to tell her that James had no brothers or sons, but that he had been the

Head of St Luke's College for many years from 1945 and was deeply attached to the place, where there is now a building named after him. I was not really very surprised that that he was there and that she had seen him, but sad that I had not. Recently I had been aware of the fact that he had said at our last meeting, through a medium six years ago, that we would meet again, and had wondered whether I ought to arrange another meeting with a different medium so that he could come if he wished to. I am not a medium myself but have been involved in many meetings of this sort over the years.

Later that week I spoke to Crawford Knox who was also a speaker at the meeting and who knew James Smeall and also knew many of those who were at the meeting. I asked him if he could recall anyone who might have been mistaken for James, but he could not, and felt it was very unlikely.

It strikes me that the meeting between Penny and James was quite possible even though it mystified her. At the time of his death James appeared to another friend in a dream in a place which I recognized from her description as the Hospice ward in which he was dying. The friend did not know that he was ill or where he was, but felt she had to ring me to find out. As I have already mentioned above, he returned at a meeting I had with a medium some months after his death and spoke at length on matters of great interest to me, all of which I have included in *On the Turn of the Tide*.

A member of the Alister Hardy Society published an account in the society's journal *De Numine* No. 35 in 2004, from which the following is taken:

My wife Sally died of cancer . . . aged 59. . . . We had been married for 30 years, and had always felt ourselves to be exceptionally close at a deep level. . . . As Sally approached death, we agreed to try and tune in to each other afterwards at 10 every Sunday evening. This never succeeded.

Within hours of Sally's passing there began a display of psychic phenomena in the lights of our house and other places that continues to this day. This account is of something different and, to me, more precious: her interactions with me and a friend in the four months after her death, which have not come again, but which were very wonderful.

. . . Three months after Sally died, I was with a walking group in Southern Italy. . . . enjoying a mountain walk through a large glade, my mind was almost forcibly drawn back to her, against my inclination. Focusing intently, I saw her lovely smile, with a flash of the high cheek-bones and long hair of our early married days, and sensed her cheerful and loving presence. Then she appeared in front of me as a fairy, small with fluttering wings. I didn't much like this image, as I preferred to think of her with more power. This fairy then nestled with great tenderness in my heart (the bottom left corner), with her smiling head to one side resting on folded hands.

There was a short pause, and then I had words given to me. I heard and saw nothing: it was like a date-stamp being imprinted on my brain, a kind of thought transference. They were *I will always be with you*. It took another short pause before the significance hit me. This was what Sally had said to me at Easter-time, when we knew the battle for life was lost, and repeated once or twice before she died. . . . I felt I had received a clear message that Sally was closer than I could have dreamt, and that she was lodged in my heart. I wept with joy as I walked, and was deeply comforted. That the sense of comfort has remained may be due in some degree to her continuing visitations in the lights, to which her message may partly refer.

It struck me that Sally came through to me only when my mind had stopped churning and was relatively at peace. The same circumstance accompanied her second visit a month later in which, rather than being a passive recipient, I found myself an active participant. I was at home . . . and had just gone through three days of extreme upset at some things I found she had done. This may not have merited such anger, but in my vulnerable state I felt for a while that the world had fallen in.

I had at last calmed down, and was lying in bed gazing abstractly at my dressing-gown on the door. It was there that I seemed to see Sally: as in Italy, not to imagine that she was actually in the room, but presented with a vision of her in symbolic form, with enough of her features to make no mistake about her identity. I saw her head, from above, but in the guise of Mary Magdalene who, as a seeker and a passionate and misunderstood woman, had long held a special place in Sally's inner life. She was distraught, and in an echo of the Gospels was washing my feet with her hair and her tears. This had an extraordinarily powerful effect on me, as I was impelled to respond. First I said, very gently, slowly and tenderly as if to a sobbing child, 'It's all right – it's all right – it's all right – it's all right'; then, very slowly, over and over, 'I love you – I love you – I love you – I love you'. Then to my astonishment this became 'I forgive you – I forgive you – it's all right – I forgive you' – astonishment, because I am not (alas) a quick forgiver, and would normally have held on to my grievance for some time. But this forgiveness was instantaneous and heartfelt in a way

I had never experienced: it was as if it came through me – as though it wasn't *I* who forgave, but I couldn't help it because she was so beautiful, in such distress, and she needed it so much. It felt to me like a reflection of God's love and forgiveness of us all when we truly ask for it.

The vision ended more faintly with a couple of intimate cameos that seemed to answer a question I'd had in my mind, and which gave added authenticity and had me laughing: a typical Sally touch. The effect of the whole was overpowering. While the earlier vision gave information and reassurance, this one brought a two-way interaction that still amazes me when I think of it. . . . it extended my understanding of what may be possible beyond the divide of death.

. . .

. . . they have left me with an enhanced sense of wonder and privilege, and of closeness to Sally.

. . .

She had a very powerful energy about her; she was psychic; she was full of fun; and as an Alister Hardy member she was intensely interested in this field. [from 005374][141]

Instances of people communicating through mediums and even materializing during special séances are fairly well-known but a notable recent case is that of Montague Keen. A well-known researcher into the paranormal, he died suddenly while asking a question at the Royal Society of Arts. Since then, his widow, Veronica, has had communications from all over the world from mediums who did not know her husband, but who have relayed messages from him to her. She has even heard his voice through a medium. This was recorded on tape and played on TV. They had promised each other that whoever passed on first would do their utmost to communicate with the other, and indeed Veronica is continuing Montague's work on survival with his continued help. There are regular communications which are posted on a website, www.montaguekeen.com.

Death, dying and the afterlife seem to be in need of re-evaluation in the light of such experiences, perhaps reflecting more closely what is contained in the scriptures of the world's religions, that death is not the end.

10. Mystics

In all times and places there have been people with a special awareness of ultimate reality. Through these mystics, we are able to glimpse the beyond, as the finite touches the infinite. A mystical experience is usually thought of as being one of unity with Ultimate Reality, an intense form of spiritual experience.

Mystical experiences tend to happen in two main ways: an introvert experience, achieved through inner realization or an extrovert experience, outside the self, of merging with the universe. The immanent experience is within, a personal relation with God or Allah, who is closer than the jugular vein according to the Qur'an. Within other religious traditions this might be interpreted as Christ within or the realization of the Buddha nature. The extrovert experience is a sense of the individual merging into unity with the transcendent, whether this is viewed as the Godhead, understood as the absorption into the impersonal Brahman, or as attaining the Buddhist state of Nirvana. These states can lead from one to the other and indeed it is often held that the immanent is a stage on the path to the transcendent experience.

The inner way can be through meditation, as the mind is calmed and probed, thoughts watched and allowed to disappear. In *How to Practise, the Way to a Meaningful Life*, the Dalai Lama quotes the Buddha.

> In the mind, the mind is not to be found; the nature of the mind is clear light.[142]

Radhakrishnan (1888–1975) explains the outward way:

> The way of growth lies through a gradual increase in impersonality by an ever deeper and more intense unifying of the self with a greater than itself. In this process prayer, worship, meditation, philosophy, art, and literature all play their part, since all help in purifying the inner being and disposing it more and more for contact with the divine.[143]

Although often alleged to be ineffable, that is, impossible to describe, mystical experiences have given the human race some of its most profound and exquisite writings. Mystics attempt to express their sublime states, yet are constantly aware of the shortcomings of language, whether conceptual or poetic. Mystical experiences may also include supranatural manifestations, such as visions, voices or presences and in some cases physical marks such as the stigmata.

There are mystics in most religious traditions, who very often bring a new vision. However, it has to be admitted that they are often completely different from the norm. There is at times a thin line between mental imbalance and life lived within a consciousness of another level of existence. Their behaviour sometimes does not conform to what is generally accepted. The ecstasies of Ramakrishna and Teresa of Avila are challenging. However, many profound insights have come through mystics, who have deepened our understanding: Plotinus (205–270), Muhammad Ibn 'Arabi (1165–1240), St John of the Cross (1542–1592) and Meister Eckhart (1260–1327) to name but very few. Ramakrishna (1836–1886) explored the mystical experiences at the heart of Hinduism, Islam and Christianity and found them to be the same. In his view God had made many religions to suit the needs of different times and places, just as a mother cooks different dishes for the members of her family.

There are schools of thought supporting this, such as Aldous Huxley in *The Perennial Philosophy,* who sees a similarity between the mystical experiences within different religious traditions. This leads them to claim a common core. Many interpreters, however, look closely at the differences between the experiences of various religious traditions, and maintain that all experience, including that of the mystics, is determined by prior expectation as well as subsequent interpretation and thus deny any common core.

Mystical experiences may come after specific practice, and most religious traditions have mystical branches and techniques associated with them. Hindus use various types of yoga; the Greeks had their Mysteries, reserved for the initiated; Buddhists use various forms of meditation and in Zen impossible questions known as *koans* are used to pierce logical thought; the Sufis of Islam have the poetry of love, music and the dance of the whirling dervishes; the Jewish Kabbalists use the Tree of Life. These are just a few ways in which individuals can prepare themselves for an experience of the divine, but it cannot be induced. Many experiences take the mystics beyond the boundaries of their tradition, sometimes revealing greater depths of understanding of doctrine, but often moving beyond the teachings. It has often been the case that the mystics, although they were trained within their specific religious traditions, they have found themselves on the margins when their extraordinary experiences became known. Their revelations did not always conform to received doctrine. In fact, Meister Eckhart was condemned by the church. Yet mystics are often innovators and can offer a deeper understanding of faith.

Such experiences can also happen with no preparation at all. Blaise Pascal (1632–1662) was a French mathematical genius, who excelled in the fields of physics and geometry and invented an adding machine called 'la pascaline'. He was also known for his wager: that as we cannot know whether there is a God or not, it is more sensible to believe, as if you believe and are right, you gain paradise, if you believe and are wrong, that is the end anyway, as it would be if you disbelieve and are right. However, if you disbelieve and are wrong, you risk eternal damnation.

This rational approach was shattered by Pascal's pivotal religious experience, which took place on 23 November 1654. He wrote down what happened to him on this 'Night of Fire' and afterwards kept his 'memorial' or 'amulet', sewn into his clothes. The parchment was discovered after his death and it recounted his realization of the

> God of Abraham, God of Isaac, God of Jacob, not of the philosophers and savants.[144]

This was certainty, this was a revelation of God as a powerful reality and of Jesus Christ. It caused Pascal tears of joy and led to complete submission. He subsequently led a semi-monastic life and composed the *Lettres Provinciales* (Provincial Letters) on Jesuit theology and began a treatise on miracles which developed into a work of 'Thoughts' or Pensées, which were published posthumously.

Dionysius the Areopagite

A Syrian monk writing in the sixth century took the pseudonym of St Paul's convert, Dionysius the Areopagite, who was mentioned in the New Testament (Acts 17:34). Such seeming subterfuge was not an unusual practice in those days and gave his work added authority. When his true identity was discovered, he became known as Pseudo-Dionysius. His work, Neoplatonic in content, had a seminal influence on the Western mystical tradition.

Dionysius also wrote *The Divine Names* as well as *The Mystical Theology* and The *Celestial Hierarchies*. The anonymous author of the *Cloud of Unknowing* translated Dionysius' *Mystical Theology* as *Deonise Hid Divinite*, and based the Cloud of Unknowing on it. The main thesis of Dionysius' work is that all one can say of God is what he is not, this is known as the Apophatic Tradition or Via Negativa. Dionysius describes the absolute truth by the use of negatives, because it so infinitely excels all qualifications:

> ... He is neither soul nor intellect; nor has He imagination, opinion, reason, or understanding, nor is He any act of reason or understanding. Nor can He be expressed or conceived, since He is neither number nor order; nor greatness nor smallness; nor equality nor inequality; nor similarity nor dissimilarity. Neither is He standing, nor moving, nor at rest. Neither has He power nor is power, nor is light. Neither does He live nor is He life. Neither is He essence, nor eternity nor time. ... nor is He spirit, in the sense that we understand it ... Neither does anything that is know Him as He is ... the all-perfect and unique Cause of all things transcends all affirmation, and the simple pre-eminence of His Absolute Nature is outside of every negation – free from every limitation and beyond them all.[145]

This way of describing God begins with creation and multiplicity and moves upward through a process of negation to the Godhead. Its opposite is the *Via Positiva* which begins from an intellectual understanding of the universal First Cause and proceeds downwards to affirm the divinity in all things. For Dionysius, God could neither be experienced as an object of direct perception nor known by the intellect, but only experienced through contemplation. Dionysius suggested stages of mysticism:

> The Active Life through the Way of Purification, whereby we may become true servants of God;
> The Inner Life, the Way of Illumination, and of real sonship with God;
> The Contemplative Life, which is the Unitive Way, whereby we may attain to true friendship with God.[146]

Dame Julian of Norwich (1342–Circa 1416)

A devout woman, Julian of Norwich was deeply steeped in the Christian tradition but gave a new understanding of God as Mother as well as Father. She lived in a time of turbulence, when fourteenth-century England faced a devastating mass reduction in the population through the Black Death and of social upheaval, culminating in the Peasants' Revolt of 1381. It was, however a time when mystics flourished, from

Mystics

Richard Rolle and Walter Hinton in England, Meister Eckhart in Germany and Jan van Ruuysbroek (John of Ruysbroeck) in Holland.

Julian of Norwich is known for the 16 'shewings' or visions, which she received during a 12-hour period on 8 May 1373. There are two accounts of her experience, a shorter, believed to have been written soon afterwards, and a longer, more developed account, *Revelations of Divine Love* written 20 years later, which includes her subsequent reflections upon her experiences.

> She had asked for three gifts from God:
> (i) to understand his passion, (ii) to suffer physically while still a young woman of thirty; and (iii) to have as God's gift three wounds[147]

She wanted to be actually there with Mary Magdalene and the others to suffer with Christ as he was crucified. The illness she desired was to

> undergo all those spiritual and physical sufferings she would have if she were really dying so that she would be cleansed and live more worthily afterwards.[148]

It was as she had wished. At the age of 30, she became so desperately ill that the priest had given her the last rites. She was supported to sit up, and was just able to fix her eyes on the crucifix which the priest had set before her. She recounts:

> Then my sight began to fail, and the room became dark about me as if it were night, except for the image of the cross which somehow was lighted up; but how was beyond my comprehension. Apart from the cross everything else seemed horrible as if it were occupied by fiends.
> Then the rest of my body began to die, and I could hardly feel a thing. As my breathing became shorter and shorter I knew for certain that I was passing away.
> Suddenly all my pain was taken away, and I was as fit and well as I had ever been; . . . I was amazed at this sudden change, for I thought it must have been a special miracle of God, and not something natural.[149]

Her visions took place over about five hours. She vividly saw Christ's suffering on the cross, and shared his pain as he slowly approached death. The outward, physical side of her nature suffered, yet the inward, ultimately superior side, was filled with love and peace. She came to understand how the two aspects of human nature, the higher and lower are united. The higher part of our nature was united to God when we were created, and God united himself to our nature in its lower part when he became incarnate. Thus through Christ the two parts are made one. She says:

> God makes no distinction in the love he has for the blessed soul of Christ and that which he has for the lowliest soul to be saved. . . . How greatly we should rejoice that God indwells our soul! Even more that our soul dwells in God! . . . I could see no difference between God and our substance: it was all God, so to speak.[150]

She saw

> the whole Godhead concentrated as it were in a single point, and thereby I learnt that he is in all things.[151]

She still assumed that she was dying, and indeed was not comforted by feeling better, as she thought that she would much rather have been taken from this world but,

> . . . he showed me more, a little thing, the size of a hazelnut, on the palm of my hand, round like a ball. I looked at it thoughtfully and wondered, 'What is this?' And the answer came, 'It is all that is made.' I marvelled that it continued to exist and did not suddenly disintegrate; it was so small. And again my mind supplied the answer, 'It exists, both now and for ever, because God loves it.' . . . In this 'little thing' I saw three truths. The first is that God made it; the second is that God loves it; and the third is that God sustains it. In short, everything owes its existence to the love of God.[152]

Here she realizes the 'littleness of creation'. Her understanding is that we need to become detached from 'trivial things which cannot satisfy' in order to seek God. Detachment is necessary for spiritual rest. She explains that prayer, rather than petitionary, should be a source for revitalization of grace and virtue, and for the loving contemplation of our Maker. To understand the love of God, Julian uses the image of motherhood, seeing God as Mother as well as Father and Jesus too as Mother.

> The human mother may put her child tenderly to her breast, but our tender Mother Jesus simply leads us into his blessed breast through his open side, and there gives us a glimpse of the Godhead and heavenly

joy – the inner certainty of eternal bliss . . .. In essence *motherhood* means love, kindness, wisdom, knowledge, goodness.[153]

This strange vision was given in the tenth of her showings. Julian draws the analogy of bringing up a child, allowing the infant to fall in order to learn the hard way. Thus humans learn through suffering. However, it was not until years later that she finally understood the meaning of the revelations.

> You would know our Lord's meaning in this thing? Know it well. Love was his meaning. Who showed it you? Love. What did he show you? Love. Why did he show it? For love. Hold onto this and you will know and understand love more and more. But you will not know or learn anything else – ever![154]
>
> 'You will not be overcome' was said very distinctly and firmly to give us confidence and comfort for whatever troubles may come. He did not say, 'You will never have a rough passage, you will never be overstrained, you will never feel uncomfortable' but he *did* say, 'You will never be overcome' . . . So all will be well.[155]

The process begun with her illness and visions, was one which continued all her life, leading her to learn to read and write and to live the life of an anchoress. This meant renouncing the world and living in a cell adjacent to a church, devoting herself to her own spiritual progress and that of others. Her shrine and cell can still be visited today in Norwich and there is a Friends of Julian group, continuing her spirituality. Julian of Norwich is perhaps best known for her saying 'All shall be well, and all shall be well, and all manner of thing shall be well,' cited by T. S. Eliot in 'Little Gidding' in his *Four Quartets*. She enriched much Christian teaching, and her writings remain a potent source of devotion. Her stress on the motherhood of Christ is one which appeals greatly to contemporary thinkers, in particular feminist theologians, as the male hegemony of the church is questioned.

Rumi (1207–1273)

Born in Balkh, Afghanistan, Mawlana Jalal-ad-Din Muhammad Rumi (Jalaluddin Rumi) grew up in Turkey. His family had fled there from the Mongol invasion. His education included the spiritual practice of fasting and meditation as well as the study of Sufi texts. Sufism is a mystical branch of Islam, the name alluding to *suf* or wool, as traditionally worn by those mystics. Often cited as America's most popular poet, Rumi's work was originally written in Persian.

By the age of 37, Rumi had taken over his father's position as sheikh and teacher in Konya and had acquired a large following. His life was transformed in 1244, when he met Shams-e Tabrizi (Shams of Tabriz). The name Shams means 'sun'. He was a wandering dervish, who had spent years travelling around India, and had longed to meet someone with whom to share his advanced spiritual knowledge. Legend has it that Shams had learned the secrets of divine love and had passed beyond what could be communicated in words and concepts. He had asked for someone with whom he could share what he had found, and had offered his life for that. He had been made aware of Rumi, and various stories are told of their meeting.

> Rumi . . . was leaving his college situated in the coffee trader market, on his way to the bazaar riding a mule. His students were following him on foot. Suddenly Shams ran after him, grasped the mule's bridle, and asked Rumi who was the greatest, Bayazid (a great Sufi mystic in the tradition of Al-Hallaj), or Mohammed? Maulana (Rumi) answered that it was a strange question, Mohammed being the seed of the prophets. 'What is the meaning then of this,' answered Shams. 'The Prophet said to God, "I have not known Thee as I should have," and Bayazid said, "Glory be to me. How high is my dignity." ' At this moment Rumi fainted. When he recovered, he took Shams by the hand and led him to the college on foot, where they kept to themselves in a cell for forty days.[156]

Their intense relationship aroused jealousy in Rumi's family and students. Shams fled. Rumi was beside himself with grief and begged all travellers arriving in Konya for any news of Shams. When he heard that Shams was in Damascus, he sent his son to fetch him. It took three months for them to walk back. When Shams and Rumi were reunited, once again they became inseparable, united in mystical love. Rumi's son Sultan Walad tells us that that when Shams and Rumi met after that long agony of separation, they ran into each other's arms and 'you could not tell the lover from the beloved.'

Again Shams and Rumi went into the deepest mystical union. They went into ecstatic communion, they danced, they sang and they exchanged divine secrets, and the transmission continued with furious power. Again, the jealousy of the disciples grew, wilder and wilder, until the moment, that terrible moment in December 1247, when there was a knock at the

Mystics

door of Rumi's house. Shams got up calmly and said, 'It is time. I am going. I am called to my death.' And he went out into the night and was never seen again.[157]

Rumi was broken with grief. He suffered terribly and this led to his writing the moving *Divan-I Shamsi Tabriz* and the *Mathnawi*. Rumi's love for Shams and his loss led to a profound understanding of the love of God.

> Love is the remedy of our pride and self-conceit, the physician of all our infirmities. Only he whose garment is rent by love becomes entirely unselfish.[158]

Still on the theme of loss of ego, in *Mathnawi,* Rumi writes of worship,

> Go and contemplate God's wonders, become lost to yourselves from the majesty and awe of God. When the one who beholds the wonders of God abandons pride and egoism from contemplating God's work, that one will know his proper station and will be silent concerning the Maker. Such a person will only say from their soul, 'I cannot praise You properly,' because that declaration is beyond reckoning.[159]

He also explains how the love for God is in fact reciprocal, as humans are responding to the love of God and through this are led to a mystical marriage of unity.

> One night a certain devotee was praying aloud, when Satan appeared to him and said, 'How long wilt thou cry, "O Allah"? Be quiet, for thou wilt get no answer.' The devotee hung his head in silence. After a little while he had a vision of the prophet Khadir, who said to him, 'Ah, why hast thou ceased to call on God?' 'Because the answer "Here am I" came not,' he replied. Khadir said, 'God hath ordered me to go to thee and say this:
> "Was it not I that summoned thee to service? Did not I make thee busy with My name? Thy calling 'Allah!' *was* My 'Here am I,' Thy yearning pain My messenger to thee. Of all those tears and cries and supplications I was the magnet, and I gave them wings." '[160]

After Shams' disappearance, Rumi began the dancing which led to the establishment of the Mevlevi Order of whirling dervishes. Dressed in white, with full skirts, the dancers circle, like the planets round the sun, the right arm extended towards heaven, receiving divine grace, the left directing this grace down to the earth. These Sufis use poetry, music and movement to reach spiritual ecstasy.

Rumi died at sunset, and was mourned by people of all faiths, who had found illumination of their own traditions through Rumi's poetry.

Swami Paramahansa Yogananda (1893–1952)

Born Mukunda Lal Ghosh, Paramahansa Yogananda recounts his extraordinary life in *Autobiography of a Yogi*. In the book he tells of his profound spiritual experiences, as well as his meetings with Mahatma Gandhi and Rabindranath Tagore. He gives a deep insight into the life of a mystic, right from his very earliest memories of being aware of a previous incarnation as a yogi in the Himalayas and impatience with the limitations of his infant body. His mother died when he was young, and he was warned in a vision that she was on her deathbed far from home, arranging the wedding of his elder brother. She left him a mystic amulet, with a message foretelling his future as a yogi.

Paramahansa Yogananda saw his guru (referred to in the quote below as 'gurudeva', meaning divine teacher) Sri Yukteswar, while walking in Benares and was then guided to him by being unable to walk in any other direction.

> Retracing my steps as though wing-shod, I reached the narrow lane. My quick glance revealed the quiet figure, steadily gazing in my direction. A few eager steps and I was at his feet.
>
> 'Gurudeva!' The divine face was the one I had seen in a thousand visions. . . .
>
> 'O my own, you have come to meet me!' My guru uttered the words again and again in Bengali, his voice tremulous with joy. 'How many years have I waited for you!'
>
> We entered a oneness of silence; words seemed the rankest superfluities. Eloquence flowed in soundless chant from the heart of master to disciple. With an antenna of irrefragable insight I sensed that my guru knew God and would lead me to Him. The obscuration of this life disappeared in a fragile dawn of prenatal memories. Dramatic time! Past, present, and future are its cycling scenes. This was not the first sun to find me at these holy feet![161]

Mystics

Paramahansa Yogananda gave an account of his experience of cosmic consciousness, induced by his Guru, Sri Yukteswar, who gently struck him on the chest above the heart:

> My body became immovably rooted; breath was drawn out of my lungs as if by a huge magnet. Soul and mind instantly lost their physical bondage and streamed out like a fluid piercing light from my every pore. The flesh was as though dead; yet in my intense awareness I knew that never before had I been so fully alive. My sense of identity was no longer narrowly confined to a body but embraced the circumambient atoms. People on distant streets seemed to be moving gently over my own remote periphery. The roots of plants and trees appeared through a dim transparency of the soil; I discerned the inward flow of their sap.
> . . . The unifying light alternated with materializations of form, the metamorphoses revealing the law of cause and effect in creation.
> An oceanic joy broke upon calm endless shores of my soul. The Spirit of God, I realized, is exhaustless Bliss; His body is countless tissues of light. . . .
> I cognized the centre of the empyrean as a point of intuitive perception in my heart. Irradiating splendour issued from my nucleus to every part of the universal structure. . . . The creative voice of God I heard resounding as *Aum* . . .
> Suddenly the breath returned to my lungs. With a disappointment almost unbearable, I realized that my infinite immensity was lost. Once more I was limited to the humiliating cage of a body, not easily accommodative to the Spirit.[162]

Yogananda learned to live a two-fold existence, in the world yet in a state of constant awareness of the eternal, in unity with God. In 1915 he obtained his degree and became a monk in the Swami Order, taking the name of Yogananda, meaning *ananda* – bliss, through *yoga*, divine union. In 1920 he visited the USA and set up the Self-Realization Fellowship to disseminate the teachings of Kriya Yoga. His technique of *Yogoda* was based on the idea of recharging the life force from cosmic energy, and meditation as a path to God, through direct experience.

In 1935 Sri Yukteswar gave Yogananda the highest spiritual title of Paramahansa, literally *parama* – highest, *hansa* – swan', traditionally the mount of Brahma the Creator, signifying someone who lived in a state of constant unity with God. Not long afterwards Sri Yukeswar died, but subsequently reappeared to Yogananda and divulged a huge amount of information about the afterlife. Paramahansa Yogananda died of a heart attack in California, at the end of a banquet in honour of the Ambassador of India. Yogananda had just finished speaking about closer ties between the two countries. His passing was viewed as *mahasamadhi*, a conscious exit from his body, which showed no signs of decay for 20 days afterwards.

Contemporary Accounts

Many people have sudden, unexpected experiences of being outside time and space, or an experience of the unity of all things including themselves, which they would term mystical. They try to describe what has happened to them, perhaps some time later, but find this difficult. Even if they do not talk about the experience it remains of great importance to them as an indication of having touched another dimension. The first two accounts although from the RERC archive, are taken from *The Common Experience* by J. M. Cohen, J. M. and J-F. Phipps.

> On the first occasion (aged 8–10) I was in the garden, muddling about alone. A cuckoo flew over, calling. Suddenly, I experienced a sensation I can only describe as an effect that might follow the rotating of a kaleidoscope. It was a feeling of timelessness, not only that time stood still, that duration had ceased, but that I was myself outside time altogether. Somehow I knew that I was part of eternity. And there was a feeling of spacelessness. I lost all awareness of my surroundings. With this detachment I felt the intensest joy I had ever known, and yet with so great a longing – for what I did not know – that it was scarcely distinguishable from suffering . . .
>
> The second occurred a good while after the first. It was an absolutely still day, flooded with sunshine. In the garden everything was shining, breathless, as if waiting expectant. Quite suddenly I felt convinced of the existence of God; as if I had only to put out my hand to touch Him. And at the same time there came the intensest joy and indescribable longing, as if in exile, perhaps, for home. It seemed as if my heart were struggling to leap out of my body.
>
> How long I stood, or would have gone on standing, I do not know; the tea-bell rang, shattering the extra dimension into which I had seemed to be caught up. I returned to earth and went obediently in, speaking to no one of these things. [1263]

Mystics

The following occurred at a time when I had no feeling for religion. It was not the result of religious ecstasy or a joyous heightening of the spirit. A certain event had hurt and humiliated me. I rushed to my room in a state of despair, feeling worthless as an empty shell. From this point of utter emptiness it was as though I were caught up in another dimension. My separate self ceased to exist and for a fraction of time I seemed part of a timeless immensity of power and joy and light. Something beyond this domain of life and death. My subjective and painful feelings vanished.

The intensity of the vision faded, but it has remained as a vivid memory ever since.... [1146][163]

There are many experiences of a mystical nature in the archive.

I have experienced a heightened awareness and this has enabled me to become extra-sensitive to surroundings, people etc. This has given me an increased perception of being in a state of 'Oneness' with circumstances and people but at the same time I have at the same time a definite awareness of my 'a-lone-ness'. At times I have an experience of expansion and a feeling of suffusion from within me – an expanding consciousness of myself and an intensification of my inner awareness which brings a feeling of union and relationship with creation. [0750]

It seemed to me that, in some way, I was extending into my surroundings and was becoming one with them. At the same time I felt a sense of lightness, exhilaration and power as if I was beginning to understand the true meaning of the whole Universe. [0712]

Rapt in Beethoven's music, I closed my eyes and watched a silver glow which shaped itself into a circle with a central focus brighter than the rest. The circle became a tunnel of light proceeding from some distant sun in the heart of the Self. Swiftly and smoothly I was borne through the tunnel and as I went the light turned from silver to gold. There was an impression of drawing strength from a limitless sea of power and a sense of deepening peace. The light grew brighter but was never dazzling or alarming. I came to a point where time and motion ceased. In my recollection it took the shape of a flat-topped rock, surrounded by a summer sea, with a sandy pool at its foot. The dream scene vanished and I am absorbed in the Light of the Universe, in Reality glowing like fire with the knowledge of itself, without ceasing to be one and myself, merged like a drop of quicksilver in the Whole, yet still separate as a grain of sand in the desert. The peace that passes all understanding and the pulsating energy of creation are one in the centre in the midst of conditions where all opposites are reconciled.[164]

We spent the latter half of August 2000 on a walking holiday in Galicia and Minho (the northern most part of Portugal). On our return I was interested in finding out a little more about the origin of Portugal as a nation. On Sunday 3 September I started to thumb through a history of Spain and Portugal. Eventually I found that Minho was the dowry given by a certain king Alfonso of Spain (or what is now part of Spain) to one of his daughters, when she married a French knight, in the twelfth century. Although the land was supposed to be subject to Castille, both the daughter and her husband had other ideas. As I understood it, on a rather hurried reading, they and their heirs subsequently carved out a country which is today Portugal.

While reading this account I suddenly saw the hot, dusty, countryside where we had been staying a few days before, the sparse vegetation, the hills and small villages. I became aware of a man and a woman surveying the land and gradually conquering the surrounding area. History and life became part of a grand, sweeping, movement through time, with the general development, but probably not the details, preordained. This applied to everything, individuals, countries, the universe itself. It was as though events and particularly humans were waves of various size and duration on a limitless ocean. The waves were born, developed and died out, to be reunited with the ultimate – the universal ocean. Somehow this put everything that we experience, good, bad, indifferent, into its place. In a non-intellectual way everything was 'all right'.

I must stress that this experience was not deliberately sought and was not a vision, although I did see in my mind an area of countryside and was aware of two people in it. The experience can best be described as an overwhelming feeling, which though it gradually faded, stayed with me for several days and was (and is) immensely comforting. [005446]

Here is an account from someone who has had many mystical and religious experiences throughout life:

Since my youth I have had quite a number of what may be religious or mystical experiences. Some would say they are just imagination but to me they have felt like intense absolute reality.

It is difficult or perhaps impossible to express these experiences in words.

Mystics

My best experiences may to some degree be 'indicated' by the following quotes.

Happold in 'Mysticism' (p.122) writes 'Suddenly the timeless moment is there, the morning stars sing together, a sense of utter joy, utter certainty mingle, and in awe and wonder it murmurs I KNOW.' Anne Miller writing (Aug.1998) on Zen Buddhism in the *Scientific and Medical Network Journal* states 'Kensho (Sartori) may occur quite unexpectedly. In this state the mind is unfocussed but instantly acquires a sense of absolute reality, intrinsic rightness, ultimate perfection and an enhanced sense of reality. Impressions enter that this is an eternal state of affairs. There is nothing more to do and nothing to fear.'

I did not start making notes until 1991. Feelings that have been present during these experiences have included certainty of survival of death (the most frequent), the existence of a higher world, certainty of meeting deceased relatives and friends again (especially my mother), eternity is perpendicular to time, that I have a guardian angel or guide, a sense that I am experiencing absolute reality, a call to return to my real residence in a higher dimensional world etc.

I have tried to classify these experiences as intense, moderate or slight. Since 1991 I have recorded just over a hundred such experiences. Of these I would describe about 20% as intense, 30% as moderate and the rest as slight. Perhaps I have been very lucky or very imaginative as the sceptical scientist within me says.

They have been triggered in various ways. Some types of music have often helped, particularly mass being sung in cathedrals and churches, chanting of monks and songs with a possible spiritual interpretation have also helped. Beautiful sights such as mountains have played their part I was once transported by observing a beautiful ginger cat sitting on a wall. Another stimulus has been reading certain spiritual or religious texts. On one occasion I was put into a receptive state by listening to the accounts of some victims of violence in Belfast. My one visit to Lourdes also had an intense effect. Often there has been no obvious trigger.

Sadly the frequency of these experiences has decreased in the last few years.

I have never found meditation very useful except as an aid to relaxation. I have never had an NDE or an OBE. I have been given some vaguely correct information from mediums. I have observed the strange behaviour of my mother's cat at the exact time she died in hospital 20 miles away. I have been in contact with Rupert Sheldrake about this. A few days after my father's death, suddenly to my astonishment (he was a convinced atheist) I felt with certainty his presence indicating survival. He seemed to be saying 'I'M .OK'. A few years later a very similar occurrence happened with my mother.

I have only once tried hypnotic regression to former incarnations. During this session I made a statement about a fact that I did not consciously know. I was very surprised that later investigation showed that I had made a true statement.

Since 1991 I have also kept a record of what I call 'Lucky Misses'. By these I mean events which at the time have seemed like bad luck but have turned out to be the reverse, saving me from something possibly worse. To give one example, in July 2006 I had an accident which made me cancel a flight to Central Asia. It transpired that taking this flight would have caused very considerable problems.

I have recorded about 50 of these 'blessings in disguise', but most were less significant than the one mentioned above. It is tempting to imagine a 'guardian angel'.

My background is Scientific with qualifications in Mathematics, Physics and the History of Science. I spent most of my working life lecturing on Mathematics in Colleges and Universities. I have been a member of the Scientific and Medical Network since 1987.

I do not subscribe to any religious faith. Indeed I even consider it wrong to do so. I try to remain an unbiased Scientific Observer. [100050]

Mysticism Across Religions

There have always been those who have regarded mysticism as the unifying path, which brings all religions together. The mystical experiences of the different traditions seem to show a similarity which is greater than the variations between them. Some mystics have been particularly involved with more than one religion. They have found that in transcending their own tradition to a deeper level of consciousness, they have discerned deep affinities with other traditions. Some have fused two traditions, others many, bringing them together in innovative and enriching ways.

Hinduism and Christianity

Bede Griffiths (1906–1993)
In his last term at school, Alan Griffiths had an experience of nature mysticism, which awoke him to another dimension in life. He was alone, listening to the birdsong at sunset.

Mystics

> I remember the shock of surprise with which the sound broke on my ears. It seemed to me that I had never heard the birds singing before and I wondered whether they sang like that all the year round and I had never noticed it. As I walked on I came upon some hawthorn trees in full bloom and again I thought I had never seen such a sight or experienced such sweetness before. If I had been brought suddenly among the trees of the Garden of Paradise and heard a choir of angels singing I could not have been more surprised. I came then to where the sun was setting over the playing fields. A lark rose suddenly from the ground beside the tree where I was standing and poured out its song above my head, and then sank still singing to rest. Everything then grew still as the sunset faded and the veil of dusk began to cover the earth. I remember now the feeling of awe which came over me. I felt inclined to kneel on the ground, as though I had been standing in the presence of an angel; and I hardly dared to look on the face of the sky, because it seemed as though it was but a veil before the face of God.
>
> These are the words with which I tried many years later to express what I had experienced that evening, but no words can do more than suggest what it meant to me. It came to me quite suddenly, as it were out of the blue, and now that I look back on it, it seems to me that it was one of the most decisive events of my life.[165]

He suggests that such an experience is not uncommon, particularly in adolescence, and may be triggered by a number of things, including nature, art, music, adventure, war, illness or falling in love.

> [I]t is as though a veil has been lifted and we see for the first time behind the façade which the world has built round us. Suddenly we know we belong to another world, that there is another dimension to existence. It is impossible to put what we have seen into words; it is something beyond all words which has been revealed. . . . we see our life for a moment in its true perspective in relation to eternity.[166]

This experience awakened Alan to the challenge of finding out more about what had been opened to him. It set him on an unexpected adventure, a search for God, which continued for the rest of his life, as he found that the more he learned, the more there was still to learn. After studying at Oxford, he and two friends tried to 'return to nature' in an experiment of simple living in the Cotswold village of Eastington without any 'mod cons'. During that time he found the Christian faith, which led him to the Benedictine community at Prinknash in Gloucestershire, where as a novice, he took the name of Bede.

> The presence of God had been revealed to me on that day at school beneath the forms of nature, the birds' song, the flowers' scent, the sunset over the fields; but now it was another presence which I perceived, the presence of God in the mystery not of nature but of Grace. Externally it was shown in the white habits of he monks, in the chant and ceremonies of the choir, in the order and dignity of the life which they led, and it was not long before I discovered the inner secret of the life. It was something which had been hidden from me all these years, something which I had been seeking without knowing exactly what it was, the secret of prayer. [167]

At the beginning of *Return to the Centre*, Bede reflects on that mystical experience at school, as he watches the sun set behind the trees, but now they are palm trees and it is the Indian robin singing. Bede emigrated to India in 1955 to 'discover the other half of his soul', as he put it in *The Marriage of East and West*. Although in some ways fulfilled by the monastic way of life, Bede had long wanted to go to India, convinced that he would find the intuitive awareness of the presence of God in man and nature missing in the West. He wanted to combine the Western, conscious, rational approach to life with the Eastern, unconscious, intuitive awareness.

Eventually he set up an ashram in Tamil Nadu called Shantivanam, meaning forest of peace, where he brought the Hindu teachings of eternal truth, *sanatana dharma*, and Christianity together in a way of life centred on silent prayer or meditation.

> When the mind in meditation goes beyond images and concepts, beyond reason and will to the ultimate Ground of its consciousness, it experiences itself in this timeless and spaceless unity of Being, and this is expressed in the 'great sayings' of the Upanishads: I am Brahman, 'Thou art That' ... the Ultimate is experienced in the depth of the soul, in the substance or Centre of its consciousness, as its own Ground or Source, as its very being or Self (*Atman*). This experience of God is summed up in the word *saccidananda*. God, or Ultimate Reality, is experienced as absolute being (*sat*), known as pure consciousness (*cit*), communicating absolute bliss (*ananda*).[168]

He evolved a pattern of worship, which included readings from the Bible, the Vedas, the Qur'an and the Granth Sahib. Bede recognized the Truth behind all religious traditions and a spark of divinity in everyone, glimpsed in religious experience.

Mystics

> All religion derives from a mystical experience, transcending thought, and seeks to express this experience, to give it form, in language, ritual, and social organization.[169]

At the end of his life, Bede lived as a sannyasi.

> [C]alled to go beyond all religion, beyond every human institution, beyond every scripture and creed, till he comes to that which every religion and scripture and ritual signifies but can never name. In every religion it has been recognized that the ultimate Reality cannot be named and the Sannyasi is one who is called to go beyond all religion and seek the ultimate goal.[170]

The story of Bede Griffiths' life is told by Shirley du Boulay in *Beyond the Darkness*. The ashram still thrives and Bede's teachings are kept alive by the Bede Griffiths Sangha, which as its newsletter states, 'is committed to the search for the truth at the heart of all religions'. www.bedegriffithssangha.org.uk

Buddhism and Christianity

Thich Nhat Hanh (1926–)

A Vietnamese Zen Buddhist monk, Thich Nhat Hanh is affectionately known as 'Thay' (teacher). He has given his life to making peace and in 1967, Martin Luther King nominated him for the Nobel Peace Prize shortly before his assassination. The result of Thay's efforts at reconciliation during the Vietnamese War (between North and South Vietnam, backed by the communists and the USA respectively) was for him to be condemned by both sides and forced into exile in 1966. He now lives in Plum village in the South East of France. There he has established a community which welcomes all, Buddhist or not. Before his exile Thich Nhat Hanh had established a movement of 'engaged Buddhism' in Saigon and the An Quang Pagoda there.

His message is one of integration and wholeness and mindfulness, being aware of each moment. He himself is a prolific author and travels widely leading mindfulness retreats and giving teachings. I took part in a retreat in Scotland and joined hundreds of others in a walking meditation with Thay across the famous Old Course in Gleneagles. The astonished golfers halted their game as we slowly, mindfully made our way across the links to the beach, where we sat in meditation as the sun rose before us.

In *The Miracle of Mindfulness* Thich Nhat Hanh describes such walking, remembering his own village in Vietnam:

> I like to walk alone on country paths, rice plants and wild grasses on both sides, putting each foot down on the earth in mindfulness, knowing that I walk on the wondrous earth. In such moments, existence is a miraculous and mysterious reality. People usually consider walking on water or in thin air a miracle. But I think the real miracle is not to walk either on water or in thin air, but to walk on earth. Every day we are engaged in a miracle which we don't even recognize: a blue sky, white clouds, green leaves, the black, curious eyes of a child – our own two eyes. All is a miracle.[171]

His own practice of mindfulness and constant meditation enabled Thich Nhat Hanh to deal with the opprobrium heaped upon him during the war years. He was criticized by all sides for his role as peacemaker. James Forest tells of when he was travelling with Thay in 1968 in America. During a visit to a Christian church in St Louis a man in the congregation stood up and vented his anger at the Vietnamese monk, suggesting that he should go and spend his time with his own people. Thay reacted calmly, speaking about dealing with the roots of the problem in Vietnam, which lay in America and advocating overcoming hatred with love. But the altercation was costly for him, and afterwards he left the room. In order to calm himself, he had taken breaths that were too deep and slow and needed to recover. Experience is at the heart of his teaching.

> Religious experience is inevitable human experience. It has to do with the human consciousness, both individual and collective. In Buddhism, religious practice begins with mindfulness. As the practice deepens and mindfulness becomes more sustained, the practitioner is able to touch, feel, see and understand more deeply. Understanding makes love and compassion possible, and when love and compassion are present, understanding deepens. The practitioner learns how to practice to maintain mindfulness and help it grow. She knows that while mindfulness is alive, transformation can take place.[172]

Thich Nhat Hanh has written with deep insight of Christianity and Buddhism, bringing the two traditions together, despite Vietnam's history of Christian-based denigration of Buddhism under French colonial rule.

> On the altar in my hermitage in France are images of Buddha and Jesus, and every time I light incense, I touch both of them as my spiritual ancestors.[173]

He has drawn parallels between the wisdom of the two teachers and the traditions in *Living Buddha, Living Christ* and *Going Home, Jesus and Buddha as Brothers*, where he imagines the Buddha and Jesus meeting for tea and helping each other for the sake of humanity. Thay's focus is on genuine underlying experience within religion.

> Authentic experience makes a religion a true tradition. . . . The absence of true experience brings forth intolerance and a lack of understanding. Organized religions, therefore, must create conditions that are favourable for true practice and true experience to flower.[174]

He does not ignore the aspects which make harmony difficult, such as statements affirming that Jesus is the only Son of God and salvation is only possible through him, which excludes other religious traditions. He brings the same instinct to the reconciliation of the religions as to peacemaking, here quoting the second precept of the Order of Interbeing, founded within the Zen Buddhist tradition during the Vietnam War.

> Do not think the knowledge you presently possess is changeless, absolute truth. Avoid being narrow-minded and bound to present views. Learn and practice non-attachment from views in order to be open to receive others' viewpoints.[175]

Thich Nhat Hanh has a huge following of people attracted to his homely, practical form of mysticism. He has turned his exile into a new beginning and in the midst of conflict has brought peace. The Community of Interbeing co-ordinates his visits, retreats and book sales in the United Kingdom.

Mystical Experience within All Religions

This is the view that all traditions are a response to the same ultimate reality.

Sri Ramakrishna (1836–1886) was an almost illiterate Hindu who lived near Calcutta. As a child he had trance-like experiences, completely carried away by the beauty of nature.

> One day as a child, Ramakrishna was crossing a paddy field holding a large bowl of rice; when some cranes flew across a black storm cloud, the sense of beauty was so overwhelming that he fainted, and the rice

flew all over the place. Later in life, Ramakrishna became subject to moods of 'God-intoxication' – 'samadhi' – in which he was overwhelmed by ecstasy, and would lose consciousness.[176]

He was initially a priest at the temple of Kali in Dakshineswar, where he had an ecstatic revelation of Kali in and as everything. This took place during a period of intense absorption known as *nirvikalpa Samadhi* which lasted for six months. He was kept alive during that time by a monk.

When he 'came down' from his prolonged ecstasy, he was transfigured and visibly divinely empowered. The Mother herself, it is said, asked him to remain in *bhavamukha* – at the threshold of relative and absolute consciousness – so as to be able to teach, embody and witness her reality.

It was in this extraordinary state of unity that Ramakrishna then proceeded on what remains the most revolutionary aspect of his journey: his diving first into the depths of Islam . . . with the help of a Sufi adept he realized union with Allah; and then eight years later . . . his plunging into Christianity. After three days absorption in Christ, he met and merged with him in the garden of Dakshineswar.[177]

He concluded that the mystical experience at the heart of all religions was the same and thus the different religions are paths to the same ultimate truth, that of God-consciousness. He drew followers of many religious traditions, as all were able to relate to the guru's experiences, those of a pluralist:

The substance is one under different names, and everyone is seeing the same substance: only climate, temperament and name create differences. Let each man follow his own path. If he sincerely and ardently wishes to know God, peace be unto him, he will surely realize him.[178]

Swami Vivekananda (1863–1902) was the most famous among Ramakrishna's followers, and made a great impression on the Western world at the 1893 World Parliament of Religions in Chicago. It was said at the time that the way to fill the main hall was to announce Vivekananda as the final speaker. He underpinned Ramakrishna's experiential side with a philosophical approach, which understood God as ultimately without qualities, yet known at a lower level in many different forms.

He set up the Ramakrishna Mission which continued the master's teachings, the main thrust of which was that all have the divine within as God is in everything and we live in Him. Social service was an important aspect of the mission's work.

Mysticism with No Religious Tradition

Jiddu Krishnamurti (1895–1989) had a remarkable life. Born into a poor family in South India, he lost his mother, whom he adored, very early in life. Krishnamurti and his younger brother, Nityananda were spotted by C. W. Leadbeater (1854–1934), who was involved with the Theosophical Society. Throughout his life, Krishnamurti had episodes of a psychic or spiritual nature, in particular seeing his deceased mother and sister when he was young.

This endeared him to the Theosophists and both boys were eventually taken to England by Annie Besant, President of the Society. She proclaimed Krishnamurti the new World Teacher and Head of the Order of the Star in the East. However, Krishnamurti became increasingly uneasy about the role imposed upon him, the expectation of psychic powers and the adoration and riches heaped upon him. In 1929 he dissolved the Order and turned his back on all that had accumulated around him.

Despite renouncing his position, such was his charisma, that he still attracted devotees and was in constant demand as a speaker. He denounced all formal religious traditions, advocating that each individual should find his or her own path to inner realization. In his speech announcing the dissolution of the Order, he said,

> I maintain that Truth is a pathless land, and you cannot approach it by any path whatsoever, by any religion, by any sect. . . . Truth, being limitless, unconditioned, unapproachable by any path whatsoever, cannot be organized; nor should any organization be formed to lead or coerce people along a particular path. . . . Truth cannot be brought down, rather the individual must make the effort to ascend to it. You cannot bring the mountain-top to the valley. [179]

He discouraged followers and forbade any movement to be created in his name. His teachings, while simple, are not easy, aiming to bring the individual to an honest and self-reliant path of spiritual progress through freeing the mind. The mind needs to be clear, to transcend time and reveal the silence of truth. Although he recommended meditation, he was against mantras, saying one might as well chant 'Coca Cola' as the holy sound of

'Om' (pronounced 'aum', it is Sanskrit for God and is considered the primal word). In fact his approach to meditation was to eschew all methods as the mind should be free of any authority or control.

> Probably you have played with meditation – transcendental meditation, Tibetan meditation, Hindu meditation, Buddhist meditation, Zen meditation – seriously or flippantly. As far as one can understand, the whole concept of these meditations is that thought must be controlled, that you must subjugate your own feelings to something other than 'what is', through control, through constant alertness. . . . There must be no authority, because then you depend, you struggle, you imitate and conform.[180]
>
> Meditation is one of the greatest arts in life – perhaps *the* greatest, and one cannot possibly learn it from anybody. That is the beauty of it. It has no technique and therefore no authority. When you learn about yourself, watch yourself, watch the way you walk, how you eat, what you say, the gossip, the hate, the jealousy – if you are aware of all that in yourself, without any choice, that is part of meditation.
>
> So meditation can take place even when you are sitting in a bus or walking in the woods full of light and shadows, or listening to the singing of the birds or looking at the face of your wife or child.[181]

Much of what he taught is recorded in dialogue form. There is a retreat and study centre in Brockwood Park in Hampshire dedicated to preserving his memory and teachings. Mary Lutyens gives a detailed account of Krishnamurti's life and extraordinary spiritual experiences in *Krishnamurti, The Years of Awakening* and *Krishnamurti, The Years of Fulfilment*.[182]

Direct Path

Andrew Harvey (1952–) feels that *The Direct Path, Creating a Journey to the Divine Using the World's Mystical Traditions* is what his whole life had been leading up to. Born in India, educated in England, he became the youngest ever Fellow of All Soul's College, Oxford. He then turned his back on academia and returned to India to follow a journey of spiritual discovery. This led him to Aurobindo's ashram, to Mother Meera, to Ladakh to learn from Tibetan Buddhist Thuksey Rinpoche, to a vision of Christ. Meanwhile he read widely, especially Rumi.

Growing up in India, Harvey had been surrounded by devotion to God expressed through different religious traditions, through his Protestant family, Muslim driver, Catholic ayah (nursemaid) and Hindu servants. So he was naturally drawn to the teachings of Ramakrishna. Harvey saw an inner unity within all mystical traditions and compiled an anthology of mystical quotations from the world's religious traditions, *The Essential Mystics, The Soul's Journey into Truth*. In *The Direct Path* he goes further. Drawing on those traditions for universal wisdom, he proposes eschewing religious teachers and organizations in favour of a kind of spiritual DIY. He offers 18 spiritual exercises from different mystical traditions so that by following Harvey's guidelines, readers can create their own path.

Harvey has had various mystical experiences during his life, notably these:

> I was walking along the sea ... It was night ... All at once my mind seemed to split apart like a coconut flung against a wall, and I saw with open eyes all the fishermen's boats and the beach itself glitter with brilliant white light. I heard the waves singing *om* as they crashed on and on. The experience lasted for about fifteen minutes. Reality, I realized, was revealing to me its divine face without a mask, its face of light.[183]

The second was while he was spending time at the bedside of his dying father, a Christian:

> After the priest had finished, I happened to look up at the crucifix at the back of the church. There is only one way I can describe what happened then; the Christ on the cross became alive. For fifteen astounding minutes, with open eyes, my entire being racked by the glory of what I was witnessing, I saw Christ on the cross extending his arms in a gesture of all-embracing, absolute, and final love to the whole of reality.
>
> Wave after wave of divine love invaded me; nothing in any of the many experiences of the Divine I had had up to that moment prepared me for the volcanic ecstasy and passion and sheer frightening force of what streamed into me from the living Christ.[184]

His work brings the wisdom and practice of many traditions together, offering them as a way of finding truth.

These mystics offer an insight into the profoundest of mysteries, and their experiences are perhaps the nearest humans ever come to understanding the divine.

11. Spiritual and Mystical Experiences of Well-Known People

Apart from the founders of the traditions, there have always been people with a deep sense of the spiritual, whose influence has been enduring. Many have gained followers of their own. A wide range of people has been chosen to reflect the different ways in which spirituality is expressed. Plato, St Paul and C. G. Jung still have an impact on the way we think today. The life of Mother Teresa is an extraordinary testament to her religious faith. There have been inspiring leaders such as Mahatma Gandhi and the Dalai Lama. William Wilberforce and Francis Younghusband changed the world around them. Some people lead inspirational lives of courage, as they face down political opposition, as did Dietrich Bonhoeffer and Nelson Mandela, and Aung San Suu Kyi continues to do today. Two remarkable women kept company with the dying, Elisabeth Kübler-Ross and Cicely Saunders, while Chad Varah's experience of a funeral triggered his life's work. Less likely candidates are a couple of rock stars, but Yusuf Islam and Eric Clapton have extraordinary stories to tell.

Plato (427–347 BCE)

There is a saying that the whole of Western philosophy is but footnotes to Plato. His influence is such that although not primarily a religious thinker, he must be included in any study of religious thought. He left the first written records of the classical philosophy of Ancient Greece. Plato was a pupil of Socrates (470–399 BCE) whose life, death and ideas, he recounted. There is no record that Socrates himself ever wrote anything, as his method of enquiry was one of dialogue. He challenged the Athenians to question their beliefs and knowledge of basic concepts, which resulted in his being considered subversive. Eventually he was tried, convicted and sentenced to death. Plato described the death of Socrates in the *Phaedo*, in an account which shows the calm with which Socrates drank poison, in graphic confirmation of his belief in the immortality of the soul.

Spiritual and Mystical Experiences

Plato began his own work by recounting the thought of Socrates, but soon developed his own ideas. In *The Republic* Plato tells the story of the cave to illustrate just how little we really understand through the use of our senses. The reference to a guardian in the passage, is to someone who, in an ideal state, would be in a position of authority.

> [T]hose who are destitute of philosophy may be compared to prisoners in a cave, who are only able to look in one direction because they are bound, and who have a fire behind them and a wall in front. Between them and the wall is nothing; all they see are shadows of themselves, and of objects behind them, cast on the wall by the light of the fire. Inevitably they regard these shadows as real, and have no notion of the objects to which they are due. At last some man succeeds in escaping from the cave to the light of the sun; for the first time he sees real things, and becomes aware that he has hitherto been deceived by shadows. If he is the sort of philosopher who is fit to become a guardian, he will feel it his duty to those who were formerly his fellow-prisoners to go down again into the cave, instruct them as to the truth, and show them the way up. But he will have difficulty in persuading them, because, coming out of the sunlight, he will see shadows less clearly than they do, and will seem to them stupider than before his escape.[185]

Plato drew a distinction between the world around us, perceived with the senses, and the realm of eternal Forms or Ideas. We might see something beautiful on earth, but it would be transient and imperfect, merely a reflection of an eternal Idea of beauty beyond time and space. He considered that the world which the senses revealed was not the real world, which he contrasted with the eternal world of the immortal soul.

This is an extract of a dialogue between Socrates, shortly before he was to drink the poison, and Cebes in the *Phaedo*:

> 'And did we not say earlier that when the soul uses the aid of the body for any investigation, through the instrument of sight or hearing or any other sense – for investigation through the body means through the senses – she is torn away by the body into the region of constant fluctuation, and she herself wanders about like a drunken man, because of her contact with things in similar confusion?'
> 'Certainly'
> 'But when she pursues her inquiries by herself, she goes to the region of the pure, the eternal and immortal and ever-unchanging, and being akin thereto she ever dwells in it, when she is by herself and it is possible for her to do so: and she has ceased from her wanderings and

remains ever constant and changeless with the unchanging, because of her contact with things similarly immutable: and this condition of hers is called wisdom, is it not?'

'After death',

'... the soul, the unseen, which departs to a place resembling itself, pure and noble and invisible, to Hades in the true sense of the word [meaning "unseen"] to dwell with a God good and wise – whither, if God so will, my soul must shortly depart – can it ever be that with such a nature and origin she is straightway dissipated and destroyed when once she leaves the body, as most men tell us?'[186]

Plato recounted a NDE in the tenth book of *The Republic*. It is the story of Er, who was thought to have been killed in battle and was put onto the funeral pyre. He awoke and told of his journey into the afterlife, recalling a judgement, after which the righteous went to the right and upwards to heaven, but the unjust went to the left and downwards. He explained that reincarnating souls drank of the River of Forgetfulness. However, he was not allowed to drink, but was to remember and return to earth as a messenger, in order to tell people of this other world. Er also recounted a vision of the cosmic axis of the universe seen as a column of light.

These ideas, of an eternal realm of the soul and the impermanence of earthly things drew Plato towards a spiritual attitude to life, a focus on what is beyond the everyday. As the New Testament was written in Greek, many of Plato's ideas were absorbed into Christianity through the early thinkers. Later, Plotinus (204–269) drew on those ideas for a mystical Neo-Platonism which in turn influenced St Augustine (354–430) and St Thomas Aquinas (1225–1274).

St Paul (Circa 10–67)

One of the best known of all religious experiences is that of Paul on the Road to Damascus. Some time in the first century, as Saul of Tarsus was bent on persecuting followers of 'the Way' of Jesus of Nazareth, he was stopped in his tracks by a dramatic vision of the resurrected Jesus Christ.

Now as he journeyed he approached Damascus, and suddenly a light from heaven flashed about him. And he fell to the ground and heard a voice saying to him, 'Saul, Saul, why do you persecute me?' And he said, 'Who are you, Lord?' And he said, 'I am Jesus, whom you are persecuting; but rise and enter the city, and you will be told what you

Spiritual and Mystical Experiences

are to do. The men who were travelling with him stood speechless, hearing the voice but seeing no-one.'[Acts 9:3–7]

Saul had been struck blind and was led into the city of Damascus, where the blindness lasted for three days, during which time he neither ate nor drank. Ananias was instructed in a vision to go to Saul and heal him. Ananias was reluctant, well aware of Saul's reputation as a persecutor of followers of Jesus, but he went to Saul, laid hands on his eyes and Saul's sight was restored.

The effect on the early Christian movement by the man who changed his name to Paul, and was later canonized, was seminal. His was an overwhelming experience of revelation which completely reversed the course of his life, and changed history. From persecuting the followers of Christ, he had changed dramatically to become the foremost missionary of the new faith to non-Jews and the most important teacher in Christianity after Jesus himself.

Later in life, Paul had another experience which he described in the third person,

I know a man in Christ who fourteen years ago was caught up to the third heaven – whether in the body or out of the body I do not know, God knows. And I know that this man was caught up into Paradise – whether in the body or out of the body I do not know, God knows – and he heard things that cannot be told, which man may not utter. [2 Corinthians 12:2–4]

Yet Paul referred to a thorn in the flesh, something he never described, but which he felt was to prevent him from too much elation after his visions.

An educated Jew as well as a Roman citizen, Paul travelled widely, spreading the Gospel of Christ, often in the face of strong opposition. He preached salvation for Jews and Gentiles through the death and Resurrection of Jesus Christ. In all he made three missionary journeys with Barnabas, Titus and Timothy, which took in Cyprus, Asia Minor (present day Turkey), Corinth and Athens. In Athens he gave a speech at the Areopagus, a hill on which the judicial council (the Areopagites) met. There he told the Athenians that the 'Unknown God' whom they worshipped was the God who had raised Jesus. It was here that Paul converted Dioysius the Areopagite.

Eventually opposition to his message led to his being imprisoned in Caesarea and later in Rome and it is thought that he was martyred there. Paul is considered to have been the author of 13 epistles (letters)

to various congregations in the region, many of which he himself had established, such as to the Thessalonians; Galatians; Corinthians, Philippians, Philemon and Romans. They reflect Paul's understanding of faith in the risen Christ and constitute part of the New Testament widely read in church services today.

C. G. Jung (1875–1961)

The renowned Swiss psychiatrist, Carl Gustav Jung recounted his life in *Memories, Dreams and Reflections* which is something approaching an autobiography. As Jung believed that one's earliest memories are not the beginning, and the end unknown, he was left with the psychic processes in between. His view of a lifetime was that of a plant, sustained by invisible, long-lasting roots but which itself fades and dies in a season.

> Yet I have never lost a sense of something that lives and endures underneath the eternal flux. What we see is the blossom, which passes. The rhizome remains.
>
> In the end the only events in my life worth telling are those when the imperishable world interrupted into this transitory one. That is why I speak chiefly of inner experiences amongst which I include my dreams and visions.[187]

During his intense and solitary childhood, Jung became aware of a secret side of himself. He carved a manikin which he kept hidden in the attic in a pencil box to which he added letters written in code. He had dreams which had a profound effect on him, but which he did not share with anyone. He created a fantasy world for himself and became aware of himself as two personalities: No. 1 the normal child, No. 2 who had lived in the eighteenth century, close to dreams and to a sense of God.

After studying medicine, Jung specialized in psychiatry and sent a book he had written to Freud. When they met they talked for 13 solid hours. They then worked together for some years until there was an acrimonious split between them. One of the reasons for this was that Jung found Freud's thinking too reductionist. Jung maintained that there was a 'collective unconscious', a level of ideas common to all humanity, underlying the thinking mind, composed of 'archetypes'. He regarded these as psychic structures, yet also neurological, unifying mind and matter into the unitary world of the mystics. The archetypes impinge on the personality in various ways in life, through apparent coincidences, which he called synchronicity, but principally through dreams.

Spiritual and Mystical Experiences

Jung's psychotherapy used an approach which involved both therapist and patient being active, rather than the passive therapist model of Freud. Patients were encouraged to face up to their own responsibility for their situation and to grow through it.

Throughout Jung's life, he had dreams which made such an impression on him that he followed them up, searching out their meaning. Often they foretold events, sometimes the death of someone he knew. Jung felt that recognition of this mythic level of consciousness was necessary for the wholeness of a person, but was not to be found in organized religion.

In 1944, Jung broke his foot and subsequently had a heart attack, after which he had something like an NDE. The nurse told him that he had been surrounded by a bright glow as he was being given oxygen and camphor injections. This experience opened something in him, giving him a deeper insight into life.

> It seemed to me that I was high up in space. Far below I saw the globe of the earth, bathed in a gloriously blue light. . . .. Later I discovered how high in space one would have to be to have so extensive a view – approximately a thousand miles!
>
> . . . Something new entered my field of vision. A short distance away I saw in space a tremendous dark block of stone, like a meteorite. . . . An entrance led into a small antechamber. To the right of the entrance, a black Hindu sat silently in lotus posture upon a stone bench. He wore a white gown, and I knew he expected me. . ... As I approached the steps leading up to the entrance into the rock, a strange thing happened: I had the feeling that everything was being sloughed away; everything I aimed at or wished for or thought, the whole phantasmagoria of earthly existence, fell away or was stripped from me – an extremely painful process. Nevertheless something remained; it was as if I now carried along with me everything I had ever experienced or done, everything that had happened around me. I might also say: it was with me, and I was it. I consisted of all that, so to speak. I consisted of my own history, and I felt with great certainty: this is what I am. 'I am this bundle of what has been, and what has been accomplished.'
>
> This experience gave me a feeling of extreme poverty, but at the same time of great fullness. There was no longer anything I wanted or desired . . ... On the contrary: I had everything that I was, and that was everything. [188]

Then Jung's doctor appeared, according to Jung, in his primal form, and Jung realized that he was to return to earth rather than enter the rock temple. He was so disappointed, that he was subsequently hostile to the doctor who had brought him back to life. It was three weeks before he decided that he actually wanted to live and by then he was worried about the doctor, who he felt sure was to die before long. In fact Jung was his last patient, as he died of septicaemia very soon afterwards. Jung then began a rhythm of sleep followed by lying awake in ecstasy in the night as he seemed to revisit those realms in his visions. He found ordinary life on earth extremely drab and irritating in comparison.

> I can describe the experience only as the ecstasy of a non-temporal state in which present, past, and future are one.[189]

The illness and experience brought Jung a sense of acceptance of fate and of his thoughts, without judging them and liberated him to write his principal works.

William Wilberforce (1759–1833)

Here was a man whose whole life became a struggle to liberate the oppressed. It took William Wilberforce 20 years to get the bill to abolish the Atlantic slave trade through parliament, and it was not until he was on his deathbed in 1833 that the Abolition of Slavery was enacted. Wilberforce was not born to religion, rather the opposite, in fact. While staying with an Aunt and Uncle as a young boy, he became influenced by their Methodism, and this so horrified his mother that she instantly removed him from his relatives and ensured that he was then exposed to all the pleasures and distractions of life which came with his prosperous family standing in Hull. He enjoyed life to the full, became a Member of Parliament and was a good friend of the Prime Minister William Pitt.

However, as a young man, Wilberforce was converted and a fundamental change took place.

> In the autumn of 1875 Wilberforce experienced a classic conversion to Christian evangelicalism, a mental and spiritual experience of enormous power.

> . . .

> It is not possible to pinpoint Wilberforce's own conversion to a single day, nor did he report the intervention of an other-worldly vision or

Spiritual and Mystical Experiences

voice. Yet the time which elapsed between his going about his normal business in the late spring of 1785 and the adoption of an entirely new and rigorous approach to life that December was unusually short.

. . .

Wilberforce was clear in later life that true religious conviction could only emerge after a period of self-examination, doubt and often agony.

. . .

. . . Wilberforce clearly felt an ineluctable pull towards an enthusiasm for Christianity which would guide and dictate all his future actions in every aspect of life.[190]

After this, Wilberforce relinquished a life of pleasure and dissipation to follow a regime of prayer and reading of scripture and theology. His life and career were henceforth guided by Christian principles. He gave much of his salary and fortune away, particularly supporting causes close to his heart, like that of educating those who had wasted their opportunities in early life, as had he himself. Although he had changed his priorities, such was his charm that he managed not to lose his former friends while making new ones who shared his new view on life.

He turned his attentions to the Reformation of Manners, a campaign against prostitution, gambling and excessive drinking. In 1787 Wilberforce, having heard reports of the conditions of the West Indian slaves and the high death rate during their crossing of the Atlantic, took up the cause of the Abolition of the Slave Trade.

God Almighty has set before me two great objects, the suppression of the slave trade and the reformation of manners.' . . . As soon as I had arrived thus far in my investigation of the slave trade, I confess to you, so enormous, so dreadful, so irremediable did its wickedness appear that my own mind was completely made up for the abolition . . . let the consequences be what they would, I from this time determined that I would never rest until I had effected its Abolition.[191]

Although in all it took him years of persistent campaigning, he never wavered, despite stiff opposition within and outside parliament especially from those whose wealth depended on the trade. Eventually the bill to abolish the slave trade was passed in 1807, paving the way for complete abolition of slavery. This actually took place long after he had retired from active politics. As Wilberforce lay dying in 1833 the news was brought to him that the bill for the Abolition of Slavery was finally secure in its passage through parliament.

His story is told in William Hague's *William Wilberforce, The Life of the Great Anti-Slave Trade Campaigner*.

Sir Francis Younghusband (1863–1942)

The founder of the World Congress of Faiths was a military figure, a colonel whose life was changed by an experience in Tibet. Francis Younghusband's biography was written by Patrick French, who vividly describes Younghusband's life of adventure, how he had explored Central Asia, finding a new route across the Gobi desert and had led an unauthorized military invasion of Tibet. Younghusband's life was changed by a vision, which took place after he had ridden off alone towards the mountains, and dismounted to sit on a rock.

> Suddenly he found himself suffused with the most intense, inexplicable, 'untellable joy. The whole world was ablaze with the same ineffable bliss that was burning within me.'

The experience remained pivotal for him and years later he wrote,

> There came upon me what was far more than elation or exhilaration . . . I was beside my self with an intensity of joy, such as even the joy of first love can give only a faint foreshadowing of. And with this indescribable joy came a revelation of the essential goodness of the world. I was convinced past all refutation that men were good at heart, that the evil in them was superficial . . . in short, that men at heart were divine.[192]

A later experience of 'The Power of the Spirit' confirmed Younghusband in his spiritual quest.

> In the middle of the night – about three – I awoke and I immediately knew the Power was coming. I made one desperate effort to resist and then it was on me. I felt it in my legs first. They were convulsed and shook violently.
> Then it came all over me till I was filled with it. And I gave great puffs – as it were to blow the spirit out of me before it could overwhelm me. But I was filled and filled with it and could no more fight

against it. It took absolute possession of me and I just settled down and lay there. And then a wonderful peace came on me – most beautiful and sweet.[193]

This left him feeling like a 'clear sky after a storm'. He subsequently spent much of his time speaking and writing on spiritual matters and ultimately set up the World Congress of Faiths, an interfaith organization which is still going strong.

Mahatma Gandhi (1869–1948)

Born Mohandas, later entitled Mahatma (great soul), Gandhi grew up in India, surrounded by various religions and was able to value the best in them all, taking from them an eclectic view which remained with him all his life. He studied law in England but it was in South Africa, where he experienced racial prejudice at first hand, that his political consciousness was awakened. From then on, he fought for the rights of his people, first in South Africa and later in India against British colonial rule.

Gandhi's adherence to non-violence – *ahimsa* – in his struggles became legendary. His was a life lived religiously, one in which political engagement was undertaken with strict adherence to spiritual principles. A familiar figure in his dhoti (long loin cloth), Gandhi had hardy any possessions and used fasting as a weapon against injustice and violence. He protested against the imposition of a tax on salt by the colonial masters by leading the salt march to the sea in order to make illegal salt. This gained him an international reputation and got him arrested, but moved independence a step further forward. India became independent in 1947, but Gandhi was heartbroken over Partition, the split of Muslim Pakistan from predominantly Hindu India and the ensuing killing of each other by Hindus and Muslims.

He was martyred six months later on 30 January 1948 by a Hindu fanatic, Nathuram Godse, who was unable to accept Gandhi's rapprochement with Muslims. It is said that Gandhi died with the words 'Hey Ram' (Oh God) on his lips. Thus a religious life was terminated in the name of religion: tolerance snuffed out by bigotry. Jawaharlal Nehru, the first Prime Minister of India had to announce Gandhi's death on All India Radio, but could hardly bring himself to say the words,

> The light has gone out of our lives, and there is darkness everywhere, and I do not quite know what to tell you or how to say it.

Mother Teresa (1910–1997)

Gonxa Agnes Bojaxhiu was born in Skopje, Macedonia, and lost her father at the age of eight. At 18, Gonxa left her home to go to Ireland to join the Institute of the Blessed Virgin Mary, known as the Sisters of Loreto. After a few months there, when she received the name Sister Mary Teresa after St Thérèse of Lisieux, she was sent to India and undertook her training and First Profession of Vows in Darjeeling. She was then sent to Calcutta where she taught at St Mary's Bengali Medium School for girls, eventually becoming principal. On 24 May 1937 she made her Final Profession of Vows, becoming known as Mother Teresa. In 1942 she made another vow, which remained secret for many years, that she would not refuse God anything, whatever might be demanded of her.

Her life changed with an experience on 10 September 1946 on a train from Calcutta to Darjeeling, where Mother Teresa was going for a retreat. It was a mystical encounter with Jesus Christ and was followed by months of conversation with him. Mother Teresa heard what she would later refer to as 'The Voice'. It was Christ's voice and he begged her to 'Come, be My light'. It was a 'call within a call' for her to leave her post and set up a mission to the poor. Mother Teresa would call this her Inspiration Day. She never revealed the exact nature of her experience, fearing that it would thereby lose its sanctity. From then on, she never wavered in her conviction that despite her sorrow at leaving the Loreto sisters and her fear at not being able to fulfil Christ's demand, this was what she was to do. Her spiritual directors tested her vocation, to ensure that it was indeed authentic before she was given permission to proceed.

It took Mother Teresa two years to set up her own religious order, the Missionaries of Charity (M. C.), who were to wear the now familiar blue and white robes. Her work among the poorest of the poor in Calcutta became widely known and in 1979 she was awarded the Nobel Peace Prize. In the same year, the Missionaries of Charity – Contemplative, of brothers and sisters was established and in 1984, the Charity Fathers. Her organization continued to grow and by the time of her death 610 foundations had been set up in 123 different countries. She was beatified in 2003.

It was not until after her death that it became known just how she struggled with her own faith, feeling a terrible separation from God. This is described in her letters, published in *Mother Teresa, Come Be My Light: The Private Writings of the 'Saint of Calcutta'* edited by Father Brian Kolodiejchuck, who knew her well. This alienation began in 1949 or 1950 and caused her great suffering. It lasted for the rest of her life and although over time she was able to come to terms with it, nevertheless, it was a constant source of distress to her. Yet throughout those years of darkness, she continued with her work, her own pain enabling her more fully to identify with the poor and dying.

Dietrich Bonhoeffer (1906–1945)

One of the greatest examples of fortitude in the face of oppression is that of Dietrich Bonhoeffer's resistance to the Nazis. He is probably far better known for his personal courage than for his theology. His life has been recounted by his close friend in *Dietrich Bonhoeffer, A Biography by Eberhard Bethge*. Despite not coming from a particularly religious family, Dietrich decided at the age of 14 to study theology and become a minister, and he never changed his mind. He was aware of death from an early age, being deeply affected by the loss of a brother and other close relatives in the Great War. This turned his thoughts to the afterlife and religion and set his course. Even in such a seemingly smooth progression from childhood vocation to martyrdom, there was a noticeable change in Bonnhoeffer in 1931, which he alluded to in correspondence but upon which he did not elaborate. It was a change of heart, from being a theologian to becoming a Christian. From the rather ambitious author of *Act and Being*, based on his doctoral thesis, which he then came to dislike, he changed to one for whom the Bible and prayer became central. This inner conviction was to see him through his trials and made a deep impression on all who came into contact with him.

After studies in Tübingen and Berlin, Bonhoeffer spent a year in Spain, another in America and between 1933 and 1935 he led the German congregations in St Paul and Sydenham in London. On his return to Germany he preached in opposition to the Nazis even before Hitler came to power and was much involved in setting up the 'Confessing Church' which stood out against the regime. When the Second World War broke out, Bonhoeffer was in America, but bravely took the decision to return and work for the resistance, which he did at a very high level. Despite being banned from Berlin and from preaching by the Gestapo, his influence was such that he was recruited to the *Abwehr* or military intelligence. Thus he was able to travel extensively. However, he led a double life, ostensibly working for the regime, but in fact supporting the Confessing Church and keeping in contact with those opposing Hitler abroad. This was all done under cover, at great risk as Bonhoeffer was part of a small circle of dedicated opposition, which included men like his brother-in-law, Hans von Dohnanyi. In those extremely challenging times, Bonhoeffer's interest in theological ethics had a practical dimension. His writing and work became inextricable entwined, as in 'What is Meant by "Telling the Truth"', an issue which at the time could spell life or death.

He was arrested in April 1943 and imprisoned in Tegel, Berlin. There he wrote the poem *Who am I?* in which he draws a comparison between how he is seen, as in control, almost heroic and how he feels within, resentful and weak, yet his faith remains,

Whoever I am, Thou knowest, O God, I am thine![194]

His *Letters and Papers from Prison* are a poignant legacy of his incarceration. Through his contacts with the resistance, he was well aware of the 20 July 1944 Stauffenburg plot to assassinate Hitler, in the aftermath of which his conditions of imprisonment became more stringent and his ultimate fate was sealed. He was moved to Buchenwald, Schönberg and then to Flossenbürg, where he was executed in a barbaric fashion on 8 April 1945, only weeks before Hitler committed suicide. It was said by fellow prisoners that Bonhoeffer radiated serenity and even joy in captivity and he managed to earn the respect of his guards too. In Flossenbürg he was with allied prisoners from many nations, who asked him to conduct a service for them. It was a moving act of worship after which he was called away by the guards. His last words as he left were to an Englishman, Payne Best,

This is the end – but for me the beginning of life.[195]

Chad Varah (1911–2007)

Rev. Chad Varah was the founder of the Samaritans, an organization to listen and support the suicidal, the lonely and the depressed. He tells his story in *Before I Die Again,* a reference to his belief in reincarnation. The son of a vicar, Chad Varah had no intention of following in his father's footsteps. However, at a loose end after Oxford University, he worked with the Anthroposophists. His father disapproved, brought him home and Chad Varah found himself at theological college, on the understanding that he need not be ordained at the end of it.

He finished the course and the dreaded ordination loomed. Varah tells how he made a last desperate attempt to escape by going to see the very old and extremely ill Bishop Hine. Three times he tried to explain to the bishop his reasons for not wishing to be ordained. Chad Varah feared ordination because he couldn't face being lumped with vicars and maiden aunts. The bishop merely said 'Scruples', by which he meant avoiding doing one's duty by pretending that something is against one's convictions. Varah felt unable to argue, found himself accepting ordination and left the room. Within minutes the bishop died. As Varah put it:

> So what chance did I have, being press-ganged by a saint on his deathbed? I felt that I had just received a life sentence, and that, of course, is what it was.[196]

The next significant event for Chad Varah followed soon after. His first duty as a curate was to take a funeral service. To his distress he found that not only was he was burying a 13-year-old girl, but that it was to be in unconsecrated ground, because she had committed suicide. Apparently she had taken her life because she was bleeding and thought she was dying of a venereal disease. In fact it was her first period, and she had had no idea what had happened to her. She had no-one she could talk to about it. Such ignorance was, unfortunately not uncommon in 1935 and Varah was so moved that he made a vow:

> Little girl, I never knew you, but you have changed my life. I promise you that I, who was taught about sex by a saintly old man when I was younger than you, will teach children your age what they need to know, and be someone they can ask, even if I get called a dirty old man at the age of twenty-four.[197]

This is what Varah then did. At his own youth club he established a pattern of answering any question put to him. At first, of course, all the questions were about sex, but gradually bigger issues were discussed. Varah established a good relationship with the youngsters and later wrote for the popular comics *Eagle* and *Girl*. Through his counselling work, he became more and more aware of the high rate of suicides, particularly in Greater London, and he also realized that many of them could be prevented by simply talking to someone. He was, however, extremely busy in the parish and had a young family, including triplets. So while he felt that there was a need for a telephone service for suicidal people, which would have to be available day and night, he

> said to God, 'Don't look at me. Surely you can see I'm busy? This mission to save people from suicide, if it's done at all, will have to be done by one of those parsons who has a church in the City with no parishioners to speak of, and the possibility of spending the whole time in some specialization.' And so, having kindly instructed God how

to proceed further if He wished to do so, I set off for my holiday in Knokke.

During the holiday, which was in fact a period in charge of a church on the Belgian coast, a cable arrived, offering him the benefice of St Stephen Walbrook, right in the heart of the City of London. The job exactly met the requirements he had spelled out as necessary for a telephone service for the suicidal. He took it and his course was set. The telephone exchange there was MAN and Varah wanted a number which was easy to remember for the suicide line. He had decided on MAN 9000, so he dialled the operator to ask if his number could be changed to that, fearing, however, that it would be too expensive. The operator asked him what number he was calling from and so he wiped the grimy telephone dial clean – to reveal MAN 9000.

Chad Varah had accepted that he was to set up the Samaritans and from then on, he worked tirelessly to provide the service staffed by volunteers, which is now established all over the world.

Elisabeth Kübler-Ross (1926–2004)

Known for her best-selling work *On Death and Dying*, which has been of enormous help to those treating or caring for terminally ill patients, Elisabeth Kübler-Ross was an early pioneer in NDE research. She wrote the Foreword to Raymond Moody's groundbreaking *Life After Life*.

Elisabeth Kübler-Ross was a Swiss physician, who had to struggle from birth. The first of triplets, she was a scrawny two-pound baby and later felt that this gave her the feeling that she always had to prove herself worthy of life. She needed to be tough, as she eventually qualified as a doctor in the face of her father's opposition. After the war, she travelled to Poland and went to the erstwhile concentration camp at Maidenek, where 300,000 people had died.

> I personally saw trainloads of baby shoes, trainloads of human hair from the victims of the concentration camps being taken to Germany to make pillows. When you smell the concentration camps with your own nose, when you see the crematoriums when you are very young like I was, when you really are an adolescent in a way, you will never ever be the same again.[198]

She was also changed by Golda, whom she met there. Golda had survived the gas chamber by a miracle and after a period of rage, had realized that in fact we are all capable of being like Hitler, if we allow hatred to dominate in life. Golda had chosen to forgive and love. Elisabeth Kübler-Ross also saw hundreds of drawings on the walls of the barracks where the prisoners had spent their final days, drawings of butterflies. It was many years before she understood that they represented the spirit being liberated from the cocoon of the body and the image remained with her.

> Death is simply a shedding of the physical body like the butterfly shedding its cocoon. It is a transition to a higher state of consciousness where you continue to perceive, to understand, to laugh, and to be able to grow.[199]

Years later, when she was practicing medicine in the USA, Elisabeth Kübler-Ross began spending time with her terminally ill patients, and found herself listening to them. In those days, there was a denial of the inevitability of death in the medical profession. The patients, however, were unhappy at being fobbed off with excuses and wanted to talk about death and make preparations to leave this life, rather than endure denial. Elisabeth Kübler-Ross began to study the stages these patients went through from their diagnosis onward: anger, denial, bargaining, depression to acceptance. This was the basis of her book, and she found the pattern applicable in all situations of loss or hardship, in life as well as in death.

She set up a seminar at the University of Chicago to study death and dying, for students of medicine, sociology, psychology and theology, which was also attended by hospital staff and relatives of patients. Patients too, would contribute from time to time, and a Mrs Schwarz recounted an OBE, which was a completely new experience for the class. Sometime after that, Mrs Schwarz died and she appeared to Elisabeth, encouraging her to continue her work. This led to Elisabeth Kübler-Ross's increasing involvement into research on what happens after death. She began to interview people who had been revived after their vital signs had indicated that they were dead. She discovered more about NDEs and began to understand death as a transition from one state of consciousness to another.

Convinced that her second task in life was to tell people that death does not exist, she lectured and wrote widely, using her patients' stories as examples. Her life-story, *A Memoir of Living and Dying, The Wheel of Life* includes accounts of her many mystical experiences, and ends with the words,

> Dying is nothing to fear. It can be the most wonderful experience of your life. It all depends on how you have lived.

Death is but a transition from this life to another existence where there is no more pain and anguish.
Everything is bearable when there is love.
My wish is that you try to give more people more love.
The only thing that lives for ever is love.[200]

Dame Cicely Saunders (1918–2005)

Dame Cicely Saunders, who almost single-handedly founded the Modern Hospice Movement, bringing scientific excellence and spiritual care together to help the dying, had a profound experience of conversion. Afterwards, throughout her life she had a sure faith that she would receive the necessary support – spiritual and material – for her venture to succeed. She did. Her movement has now spread all over the world and care of the terminally ill has been transformed.

Religion had not been not part of Cicely Saunders' home life but when she began her spiritual exploration, she did so with all the intensity of such a remarkably persistent character. As her biographer Shirley du Boulay put it,

> Cicely did not do things by halves and soon the search was on. She thought, she talked, she argued, she went to church again, and she read, most of all she read. . . . All this, however, was in her head, her heart was not yet touched. It was as if she knew how electricity worked but lived in the dark. She longed for the light to be turned on, for the real conversion she had read about and heard of from her friends, but it eluded her.[201]

It was the idea of letting go to God which eventually led to her conversion experience as she prayed,

> Oh God, I must have been emotional or not really meaning it when I said I wanted to try and believe and serve you before, but *please* can it be alright this time? And the Lord as it were said to me, 'It's not you who has to do anything, I have done it all.' At that moment I felt that God had turned me round and that it was alright. It was for all the world like suddenly finding the wind at your back instead of battling against it all the time.[202]

During the war years Cicely trained as a nurse, but was unable to practise due to a spinal problem. She retrained as an almoner, today's social worker, and fell in love with a patient, David Tasma. He was a young Polish refugee, who was dying. They shared a vision for the care of the dying, discussing how terminally ill patients could be helped. He felt that his life had been wasted but in thinking through with Cicely the idea of a special home, he realized that he could leave a legacy. He left her all his money, £500, saying that he would be a window in her home. She would later say that it took her 19 years to build the home around his window. But she did it, even though it meant retraining in medicine in her late thirties, finding land and funds and also battling the medical establishment. St Christopher's Hospice was opened in Sydenham in 1967. However, in running the hospice, funds were an ever-present problem, but much to the distress of her accountants, Cicely continued as she had begun, to rely on faith and an overdraft. They managed and St Christopher's became a model for the rest of the world to emulate.

His Holiness the Dalai Lama (1935–)

One of the world's most popular spiritual leaders has only achieved that prominence through exile. On 31 March 1959 the Fourteenth Dalai Lama left Tibet secretly by night. He was forced to flee because his country had been taken over by the People's Republic of China, a situation which endures to this day. Before leaving he had consulted his oracle and prayed, visualizing a safe journey and a return. After a perilous three week journey, the Dalai Lama and his companions reached India. Some time later, he set up the Tibetan Government in Exile in Dharamsala. The reverence in which he is held is a measure of the Dalai Lama's living example of Buddhist teaching, that it is through suffering that liberation is attained.

It is believed that the Dalai Lama, whose title is sometimes translated as meaning 'ocean of wisdom', is an incarnation of Avalokiteshvara or Chenresig, Bodhisattva of Compassion. Bodhisattvas are regarded as those who have become enlightened, who have achieved Buddhahood, but who remain involved in human affairs to bring all to enlightenment.

The choice of Dalai Lama is dependent upon a spiritual process, reflecting the belief in reincarnation. When a major Buddhist figure dies, his successor is chosen through identifying his reincarnation. Born in Takster in north-east Tibet, Lhamo Thondup was picked out by a search party looking for the reincarnation of the Thirteenth Dalai Lama, Thupten Gyatso. By visions and signs, they were led to Kumbum monastery and then to Lhamo Thondup's parents' house nearby. They gave no indication of their mission and the leader, Kewtsang Rinpoché pretended to be a servant, while carefully observing the three-year-old child. But Llamo Thondup recognized him, calling him 'Sera Lama', Sera being the name of Kewtsang Rinpoché's monastery. The party returned the following day, bringing various articles, some of which had belonged to the Thirteenth Dalai Lama. The boy correctly picked out those items, saying that they were his. He was subsequently pronounced the Fourteenth Dalai Lama and officially installed in 1940.

This led to separation from his parents and life in the Potala Palace in Lhasa. It was there that tutors for different subjects came to give him lessons, on temporal and spiritual subjects as well as allowing a little time for play. As an adult, the Dalai Lama has a great interest in science and has co-operated with research on meditation and advanced practices. In the late 1970s he permitted Dr Herbert Benson from Harvard to undertake experiments on monks in the most advanced states of meditation. This showed that the mind was able to control the body to such an extent that the monks were able to remain outside, sitting naked on the snow in freezing temperatures and to dry sheets which had been soaked in cold water simply through their body heat. In recent years the Dalai Lama has taken part in dialogues with the scientific community, particularly on the subject of consciousness under the auspices of the Mind Life Institute.

He travels the world teaching love and compassion, which he reflects in his own life. There has never been any question in his mind that the Chinese, who have taken over Tibet, should be resisted with anything but peaceful means. He remains steadfast in his refusal to countenance violence and in 1989 he was awarded the Nobel Peace prize. He has said that he finds it hard to love his enemy, the Chinese, but accepts that they are probably his greatest teachers. This is a figure whose life has been centred on the spiritual since childhood, yet who remains fully engaged in the world; an exile who has turned into one of the most inspirational citizens of the world.

Nelson Mandela (1918–)

Viewed by many as a kind of secular saint for the way he forgave those who had kept him in jail for 27 years, Nelson Mandela became the first President of South Africa after the fall of the Apartheid system of racial segregation. Anthony Sampson's biography tells of the background to Rolihlahla Mandela, who was a Xhosa and the scion of the Transkei Tembu royal dynasty. From childhood he was imbued with the concept of *ubuntu*, African brotherhood, which involves compassion for and solidarity with others. He was also influenced by the Methodism of his mother and missionary teachers. His education was befitting to his station, undertaken by his uncle at Mqhekezweni or the Great Place, among the Tembu elders. Later he studied law and his opposition to the system of Apartheid hardened. He joined the African National Congress and developed into a fiery rebel. He stressed to his biographer that he was 'no angel'.

He was arrested several times and each time made a stand against the system, which made an impression world-wide. At the age of 46 he was imprisoned for life on the notorious Robben Island. Prison brought about a change in him, which was to have far-reaching consequences for his country and the whole world. There he reflected on the situation in South Africa and realized that in order to avoid the bloodbath widely seen as inevitable, he needed to negotiate with the enemy. He also learned to control his temper and despite very much seeing political opposition as a team effort, he began to emerge as the leader. He established links with the major churches in South Africa as they mobilized against the regime, particularly with Desmond Tutu. Once President, Mandela established freedom for all religions, recognizing the part that the different faiths had played in the transformation of the country, from providing education and health care for blacks when the regime did not, to supporting the struggle for change.

Universal protest against Apartheid turned him into the world's most famous prisoner. It is a measure of the man that he was able to cope with his iconic status on his release, retaining an engaging, natural, humorous manner. He and President F. W. De Klerk managed to put aside their considerable differences and over a long period, work out a transition of power. They were rewarded by the Nobel Peace Prize in 1993. Nelson Mandela had not only forgiven his oppressors, but had managed to bring his colleagues in the ANC with him – no mean feat. They often baulked at his compassion, his leniency towards prison guards and Afrikaners, but Mandela was not to be moved. As president, Mandela set up The Truth and Reconciliation Commission, an imaginative way of coming to terms with the past based on forgiveness, an example of *ubuntu* in action. Mandela gave a third of his presidential salary to a charity, handed over to his successor gracefully and now lives a simple life. His life is an example of true humanity in the face of adversity.

Aung San Suu Kyi (1945–)

In Rangoon, the capital of Myanmar (Burma), there is a leafy lane near Inya Lake, called University Avenue. It is there that 'The Lady', Aung San Suu Kyi has been under almost constant house arrest since 1990. That was the year in which her National League for Democracy (NLD) won a general election with 81% of the vote. The SLORC (State Law and Order Restoration Council) set up by the ruling military junta has refused to recognize the results and Aung San Suu Kyi has been denied her freedom ever since. She is the world's most famous prisoner of conscience.

Her credentials as a political figure stem from her parents. Her father Bogyoke (General) Aung San, having led the fight for freedom from British colonial rule, became head of the first government of the newly independent state in 1947. Only a few months after taking that position, he was assassinated. Suu Kyi was then only two years old and she grew up revering his memory. Her mother Daw Khin Kyi then took a more prominent role in public life and in 1960 was appointed ambassador to India and Nepal.

Aung San Suu Kyi studied Philosophy, Politics and Economics (PPE) at Oxford University, where she met Michael Aris, whom she married in 1972. They had two sons, Alexander and Kim and for some years Suu Kyi enjoyed life as a wife and mother, while researching her father's life and the political history of Burma. It was in 1988 that her life changed. A phone call informed her that her mother had had a stroke and the following day Suu Kyi flew back to Burma to nurse her. During that year Suu Kyi became politically active. The National League for Democracy (NLD) was formed to oppose the government and to pave the way for free and fair elections. Suu Kyi was appointed General Secretary and she gave her first public speech outside the Shwedagon Pagoda in Rangoon, calling for democratic government. When her mother died in 1989, Suu Kyi vowed to serve her country as her parents had done, little realizing what sacrifices would be demanded of her.

The NLD continued to oppose the regime and later that same year Suu Kyi and her supporters found themselves facing armed soldiers.

> On 5 April 1989, Aung San Suu Kyi and her colleagues confronted an army unit whose rifles were pointed at them. She motioned for her colleagues to step aside while she walked alone towards the soldiers, offering herself as an easy target. An army major finally intervened and the rifles were lowered. This poignant scene, of an unarmed solitary figure advancing towards the aimed weapons of a paranoid military dictatorship, can be seen as an allegory of her struggle for freedom in her land. In those few minutes, Aung San Suu Kyi showed extraordinary physical courage in the face of an acute mortal threat, adding still farther to her stature as the leader of democracy in the face of tyranny.[203]

SLORC remains in power to this day and despite brief periods of respite from house arrest in 1995 and in 2002, Aung San Suu Kyi has never been able to resume normal life since those elections in 1990. At first her family was allowed to visit her, but when it became clear that Michael Aris would not persuade his wife to leave the country, he and the children were used against her. The regime refused to grant visas to her family to visit her and cut off all communication between them, encouraging her to leave the country. Suu Kyi would not do so, as she knew that she would be denied re-entry. Even when her husband was diagnosed with incurable prostate cancer in 1998, he was denied entry into Burma, and so they were unable to say goodbye to each other.

In 1991 Aung San Suu Kyi was awarded the Nobel Peace Prize. She heard about it on the BBC World Service. Her sons accepted the award on her behalf and Alexander Aris in his acceptance speech said,

> I know that if she were free today my mother would, in thanking you, also ask you to pray that the oppressors and the oppressed should throw down their weapons and join together to build a nation founded on humanity in the spirit of peace.
>
> Although my mother is often described as a political dissident who strives by peaceful means for democratic change, we should remember that her quest is basically spiritual. As she has said, 'The quintessential revolution is that of the spirit', and she has written of the 'essential spiritual aims' of the struggle. The realization of this depends solely on human responsibility. At the root of that responsibility lies, and I quote, 'the concept of perfection, the urge to achieve it, the intelligence to find a path towards it, and the will to follow that path if not to the end, at least the distance needed to rise above individual limitation. . . .' 'To live the full life', she says, 'one must have the courage to bear the responsibility of the needs of others . . . one must want to bear this responsibility.' And she links this firmly to her faith when she writes, '. . . Buddhism, the foundation of traditional Burmese culture, places the greatest value on man, who alone of all beings can achieve the supreme state of Buddhahood. Each man has in him the potential to realize the truth through his own will and endeavour and to help others to realize it.' Finally she says, 'The quest for democracy in Burma is the struggle of a people to live whole, meaningful lives as free and equal members of the world community. It is part of the unceasing human endeavour to prove that the spirit of man can transcend the flaws of his nature.'[204]

Aung San Suu Kyi has a profound Buddhist faith which has informed her peaceful protest based on the concept of *metta* or loving-kindness and also sustained her throughout her long, lonely years of imprisonment.

Yusuf Islam (1948–)

Heart-throb pop star Cat Stevens gave up fame and its attractive trappings to become Yusuf Islam. He was very successful while still a young man, with a string of hits and plenty of money, and he fully enjoyed the high life. In 1968, aged 19, he suffered a bout of TB, which brought him to a halt. It was a time of reflection and he became more spiritually aware. Many of his songs written after this period reflected his search for meaning in life. Despite a Christian upbringing, he felt that was not his path and when his brother gave him a Qur'an, he was very taken with the teachings.

However, it was in 1975 that his life changed. He almost drowned in Malibu and vowed 'Oh God, if you save me I'll work for you.' It was a promise he took seriously and he converted to Islam in 1977, taking the name Yusuf Islam the following year, when he gave up music as incompatible with his faith. He spent the following years engaged in altruistic work.

It was the tragedy of 9.11 which brought him back into the limelight. He spoke out against the attacks on the World Trade Centre in New York, making it clear that the Qur'an did not condone murder and sang 'Peace Train' in public for the first time in 20 years. This heralded a return to music-making, but he chooses carefully, playing in concerts for Nelson Mandela, for the Tsunami victims and the Adopt-A-Minefield Gala. His is a life which reflects his beliefs.

Eric Clapton (1945–)

Once hailed as 'God' in graffiti for his legendary guitar playing, Eric Clapton fought a lifelong battle with drink and drugs. When he decided to write his autobiography he admitted to having to look himself up on the web, to find out when he had been where, so many of his memories having been wiped out through substance abuse. Unsuccessful attempts at 'detox' and 'rehab' had failed and his life was spiralling out of control. In 1987 he went back into treatment, admitting that he was 'a mess'. After a month, with the period drawing to a close, Clapton realized that he needed to change within, but had not. In his autobiography Clapton describes how in his despair, he fell on his knees and surrendered.

> I was absolutely terrified, in complete despair. At that moment, almost of their own accord, my legs gave way and I fell to my knees. In the privacy of my room I begged for help. I had no notion who I thought

Spiritual and Mystical Experiences

I was talking to, I just knew that I had come to the end of my tether. I had nothing left to fight with. Then I remembered what I had heard about surrender, something I thought I could never do – my pride just wouldn't allow it – but I knew that on my own, I wasn't going to make it, so I asked for help and, getting down on my knees, I surrendered.

Within a few days I realised that something had happened for me. An atheist would probably say it was just a change of attitude, and to a certain extent, that's true, but there was much more to it than that. I had found a place to turn to, a place that I'd always known was there, but never really wanted, or needed, to believe in. From that day until this, I have never failed to pray in the morning, on my knees, asking for help, and at night to express gratitude for my life and most of all for my sobriety. I choose to kneel because I feel I need to humble myself when I pray, and with my ego, this is the most I can do. If you were to ask why I do all this, I will tell you . . . because it works, as simple as that.[205]

Years later, Eric decided that smoking also had to go. He had smoked since his twenty-first birthday party and by then he was smoking at least 40, sometimes 60 cigarettes a day. He went to a hypnotherapist and stopped, and has not missed it since. He says,

I really believe it is about spiritual application, no matter how poverty-stricken I feel my application may be.[206]

Here the transformative effect of spiritual experience has been seen in an enormously varied group of people, whose names have become well-known and whose influence continues to this day. It has also been seen that worldly fame and fortune have not been enough to satisfy the spirit.

12. Fruits of Spiritual Experience

The evaluation of religious experience has frequently been through the effects on the lives of the experients. In the Bible Jesus says,

> For no good tree bears bad fruit, nor again does a bad tree bear good fruit; each tree is known by its own fruit. . . . The good man out of the good treasure of his heart produces good, and the evil man out of his evil treasure produces evil; . . . (Luke 6:43, 46)

William James too stresses the importance of fruits,

> If the *fruits for life* of the state of conversion are good, we ought to idealize and venerate it, even though it be a piece of natural psychology; if not, we ought to make short work with it, no matter what supernatural being may have infused it.

> . . .

> The real witness of the spirit to the second birth is to be found only in the disposition of the genuine child of God, the permanently patient heart, the love of self eradicated. And this, it has to be admitted, is also found in those who pass no crisis, and may even be found outside Christianity altogether. [207]

For those who are prepared to accept them, spiritual experiences are revelatory and of deep significance, and the result is an empowerment of the individual and enhancement of life. According to French social anthropologist Emile Durkheim (1858–1917),

> The believer who has communicated with his god . . . is *stronger*. He feels within him more force, either to endure the trials of existence or to conquer them.[208]

Sir Alister Hardy found that religious experience was,

> . . . being in touch with some Power which appears to be outside and beyond the individual self and from which he can receive grace: help in

the conduct of his life and a sense of renewed vitality . . .. On so many occasions men and women have achieved, by what they call divine help or grace, that which they, and others who knew them, would have regarded as being beyond their normal capabilities.[209]

One interesting result of a mystical experience was in the case of St Thomas Aquinas, learned theologian, author of many works, including the *Summa Theologica*, which he worked on from 1265 to 1273. He did not complete it, however, for a vision during mass on 6 December 1273, the Feast of St Nicholas, resulted in him not writing any more. He proclaimed his theology mere straw in comparison to what had been revealed to him.

Many experiences lead to a complete change of attitudes to life and often in moral behaviour, as this account shows.

I find it difficult to describe my experience, only to say that it seems to be outside of me and enormous and yet at the same time I am part of it, everything is. It is purely personal and helps me to live and to love others. It is difficult to describe, but in some way because of this feeling I feel united to all people, to all living things. Of recent years the feeling has become so strong that I am now training to become a social worker because I find that I must help people: in some way I feel their unhappiness as my own.[210]

However, not everyone follows the promptings of such experiences. Here is one which was ignored, and the fruits, which may well have been to affect lives for the better, were not brought about.

In December 1983 I literally bumped into a woman who had often been seated near me on the evening commuter train; we apologized to each other with a smile. The next day the trains were in chaos and I found myself advising her which platform to head for. We soon discovered that we were both Christians, and before long she confided in me that her husband, a deacon of their church, had deserted her and their children for another woman. My wife and I helped support her through the years of trauma that followed.

One day, when I had just bought Jack Dominian's book *Marriage, Faith and Love*, two words flashed into my mind, as if relating to their marriage, 'Nox praecessit'. My Latin was already rusty, but I managed to confirm that they were real words; but what did they signify? Where did they come from? Eventually I decided that they would be found in the Latin Vulgate Bible in Romans 13, and knowing that there was a copy in the library, I went there and opened it. There it was, *nox praecessit*: 'The night is far spent' – and then it goes on, 'daylight is at hand: let us therefore cast away the works of darkness, and let us put on the armour of light.' I felt that these words were intended for my friend's husband, and the conviction grew that I must write to him about them. I was astonished to find that he too had been given the same words (though he knew no Latin whatsoever) and taken them to Christian counsellors who had told him he must cast away the works of darkness and return to his wife! Unfortunately he chose to ignore what God was saying to him: 'God will forgive me', he said, and went on to divorce and remarriage. I have reason for believing that he deeply regrets doing so. 'O God, why did I do it?' he was heard to exclaim some years later as he revisited his old church. When his ex-wife visited him in hospital years later, they put their arms round each other; but, he said, 'I could not stand another divorce.' (005433)

Many works of art have been created in different media to express the spiritual. Writers, artists and musicians all move beyond the everyday world as they create, and those enjoying the results of their work respond on a profound level.

Paintings of Ken Butler-Evans

A most unusual incidence of an artist being in touch with another level of existence is that of Kenneth Butler-Evans (1924–1987). A self –taught artist, he became well-known as a cartoonist and illustrator. He began to paint in egg emulsion and during his lifetime he produced paintings which he 'saw' and then did his best to recreate. He did not discuss their meaning, wanting them to speak for themselves. After his sudden death, his widow was frequently woken in the early hours and seemed to be given the meaning behind the paintings. She was convinced that Ken was explaining the paintings to her, and she kept notes. The paintings and what Ann received, have been compiled in *An Artist's Life After Death*.[211]

The World's Largest Book: Kuthodaw Pagoda

An unusual manifestation of the inspiration of religion in art is the world's largest book. In Mandalay in Myanmar (Burma) is the Kuthodaw Pagoda, which houses 729 white Sagyin marble slabs, on which the *Tipitaka* or the Three Baskets of the Buddhist Pali canon is carved. Each slab, 5ft by 3.5ft, is housed in its own beautifully carved, marble shrine. The carving took eight years to complete. This was completed under the auspices of King Mindon (1852–1878), who was inspired by a tradition, according to which the Buddha once went to Mandalay Hill and prophesied that in the 2400th year of his religion, a royal city would be established there and a king would rule who would promote his religion. Indeed, King Mindon established the Royal City in 1859 and also the most permanent of all presentations of the Buddha's teachings, the Dharma.

Charities

Many charitable organizations owe their foundation to spiritual experiences and often continue through the support of volunteers similarly inspired.

The Müller Orphan Houses

These orphanages were established in Bristol through a remarkable venture of faith. Nancy Garton tells the story in *George Müller and his Orphans*. George Müller (1805–1898) was a German, who married Mary Groves in England and moved to Bristol in 1832. He was a man who prayed for everything he needed and received it. That is how he set up his Müller Orphan Houses for boys and girls.

George had been happy living a dissolute life, had no Bible and hardly ever went to church. One evening he decided to accompany a friend to a meeting where a chapter from the Bible was read and a sermon, followed by a hymn and a prayer.

> He scarcely remembered afterwards what he did in getting back to his lodging, except that he lay peaceful and happy in bed. 'This shows that the Lord may begin His work in different ways. For I have not the least doubt that on that evening He began a work of grace in me, though I obtained joy without any deep sorrow of heart, and with scarcely any knowledge. That evening was the turning point in my life. The next day, and Monday, and once or twice besides, I went again to the house of this brother; for it was too long to wait until Saturday came again.'[212]

He changed completely, foreswearing the tavern for religious observance and from then on lived not merely a devout life, but one entirely dependent on God. He would pray and then wait for guidance, after which he left it all up to God and he was not disappointed, for even when he and his wife were down to their last penny, ultimately they were always provided for.

In the wake of an outbreak of cholera in Bristol, Müller decided to establish homes for orphans, which he saw as part of his missionary work. He began with one for girls between seven and twelve years old, soon after he began a home for younger children and then one for boys, all in Wilson Street. Before long, he was able to move to premises he had specially built on Ashley Down. From the very beginning, all this was funded by donations, which Müller received in answer to prayer. This was a precarious method of financing such a project, but despite times of difficulty, donations would come and eventually various large gifts and legacies ensured the survival of the Houses. George Müller himself never doubted that his venture would succeed, as he was certain that he was doing God's will and therefore the means would be provided.

The Prison Phoenix Trust

This is an orgnaization which brings yoga and meditation to prisoners, often transforming their lives. It came about as a result of someone being inspired by the religious experiences of others. Ann Wetherall began working with Sir Alister Hardy on the categorization of the experiences sent in by the public in 1983. Considering that 'imprisonment' might be a trigger, Ann contacted people who had suffered periods of incarceration – hostages, and prisoners, including IRA prisoner Jimmy Boyle, infamous for his 'dirty protests'. As a result of her request published in prison newspapers, she received letters from prisoners, describing spiritual experiences which most were admitting for the first time, as they feared being sent to the psychiatrist.

Here is an extract from the kind of letter Ann read, describing the experience of a prisoner on the 58th day of a hunger strike:

> I suddenly felt the most holy benediction flood my heart with a physical warmth so comforting so absolutely unworldly that I felt my sins (which were many and grievous) were wiped away ... as the feeling gradually matured in me all my lifelong grief and sadness all the loneliness and self recrimination all the hate was washed away and healed. In their place was the Holy Ghost. It did not go away. It remained there where the physical heart is like an infinitely tender and live warmth-cum light. It expressed itself as Life and intelligence

and Love – all in one. Words are inadequate to describe the experience. It can only be expressed by living one's life consistently in a way that can express ones gratitude and admiration, love and loyalty to it.[213]

This caused the prisoner to decide to stop the hunger strike, co-operate with the Home Office, deal with the borstal sentence, give up smoking and drinking and live a completely different life.

Ann felt that the prisoners who wrote to the RERU (as it was known at that time) deserved support, reassurance as to their sanity and help to build on their experiences, so she left the research in order to set up 'The Prison Ashram Project' with Rupert Sheldrake and Bede Griffiths among the original patrons. Later renamed 'The Prison Phoenix Trust', it is now an organization in contact with over 2,000 prisoners all over the country. Its aim is stated in its newsletter:

The opportunity for spiritual growth exists in a prison cell. The Prison Phoenix Trust encourages young prisoners in their spiritual lives through the practices of meditation and yoga, working with silence and the breath. We offer personal support to prisoners through teaching, workshops, correspondence, books and newsletters – and to prison staff too.

www.prisonphoenixtrust.org.uk

The Allan Sweeney International Reiki And Healing and Training Centre

This was set up by Allan Sweeney Hon. PhD (Medicina Alternativa) following a dream.

In May 1999 I had a vision in dream at night that I should phone Clive Emson property auctioneers at 0900 on 19 June 1999. I should then buy a large property on the beach in Margate to use as a healing centre to help those suffering around the world. This simply felt Truth, as if those above were saying I had no choice, that this was part of my spiritual Destiny. Even though I had no money for a large healing centre, it felt like all I needed to do was follow what had been pre-ordained.

On 19 June at 0900 I phoned Clive Emson. They said, 'Hurry, there's a viewing now!' The property was on the beach in Margate. It had been a nursing home (the previous owners had paid £210,000 for it) with planning permission for ten overnight stays + staff – perfect for a residential healing centre. But I could never afford it. However, it was a bank repossession, and the bank and other bidders thought it was subsiding, so the other bidders dropped out, and the bank sold it to me pre-auction for £40,000 (+ fixtures and fittings). Even though everyone thought it was subsiding, I trusted the vision to buy it. Before I moved in, two surveyors both said there was no subsidence!

The day I moved in, a 'shooting star' fell into the sea opposite.

The day we had our first guests, a small white cloud hovered over us, exactly shaped like an angel.

Following the vision changed my life dramatically. The centre became world-renowned, with people travelling here from most countries on earth. Two full time house-keepers and three secretaries could hardly cope. Most patients did not leave with the problems they arrived with. Some days the queue for healing started at 0800 and finished at 0100 the next morning. With so many patients, and so many students wanting to study here, I had to buy two houses next door to accommodate them all.

Over ten years, thousands of people have been helped, and the properties on the beach are now worth about £2m.

Very soon after I moved in, guests saw Jesus, Mary, Krishna, Aesclepius, and other Gods in the therapy and teaching rooms – never anywhere else. Hundreds of people have now witnessed these religious and spiritual beings appear. Some were shocked, because they had not believed in appearances before.

It seems as if this was my spiritual path, the Destiny for my soul. The regular appearances of Jesus and so on, seemed like signs I was on the right path. For example, after I moved in, I decorated all rooms in themes, for example, Grecian, Egyptian, Indian, Japanese, Angel and so on rooms. When my ex-wife visited, she said, 'Do you remember, about 30 years ago, you had a vision that one day you would have a large property overlooking the sea and each room would have themes of Greece, Egypt, India, Japan and so on?' I had forgotten. But it just seemed one more sign on the path to a spiritual Destiny. [100055]
http://www.reiki-healing.com/healcent.html

Religious Orders

The decision to enter a religious order is often the result of a religious experience. In many religious traditions, individuals have felt called to leave their families and renounce marriage, possessions and the world. The founders of such orders were often remarkable figures, who had a specific vision for their community. Although most Christian monks and nuns take vows for life, many Buddhist boys and sometimes girls spend a period of time as monks and then re-emerge into the world, usually much the wiser for the period of renunciation and reflection. The Dalai Lama, although leader of his nation, describes himself as a simple Buddhist monk, for that is how he lives. Monks and nuns of different traditions share a vision and a way of life of simplicity and withdrawal from everyday life, even when they are not sequestered, which instantly makes them brother and sister despite different religious traditions.

St Benedict (480–543)

What is known of Benedict comes mainly from St Gregory's account in his *Dialogues*. Benedict, who was the founder of Western monasticism was born in Nursia, in what is now Italy, one of twins. His sister Scholastica played a prominent part in his life although he left home at an early age to renounce the life of a nobleman in Rome. He took with him his nurse, as a servant and it was said that his first miracle was to mend an earthenware wheat-sifter for her. The ensuing attention led him to flee to Subiaco, where he lived as a hermit for some years. His first attempt at leading a community was unsuccessful – the monks attempted to murder him. Yet later, due to the following he had acquired, he established a dozen monasteries, each with 12 monks and a superior. He formulated his Rule, based on prayer and work within a community, a moderate but spiritually-based way of life which survives to this day in the Benedictine communities. Although he did not begin the monastic tradition, Benedict's 'Twelve Steps to Humility' offered a practical synthesis of preceding practice which proved a success.

Scholastica lived nearby in a religious community linked to her brother's establishment, so women were part of the movement from its inception. It is said that a few days before she died, Benedict visited her and was prevented from leaving by a storm, which erupted suddenly as she prayed. After her death, Benedict saw what he described as her spirit rising up to heaven and he too then had profound visions of God.

St Francis of Assisi (1182–1226)

The Italian founder of the Franciscans was a man who found holiness after enjoying life to the full as a young man. After being on the losing side in a fight between Assisi and Perugia, Francis was taken prisoner and then became ill. He was changed by a conversion experience and renounced wealth for a life closely modelled on that of Jesus. He abandoned ordinary clothes and donned a dark robe bound with a rope and took to a life of poverty, charity and preaching the Gospel. As he attracted followers, Francis formulated rules for them to live by which eventually led him set up the Order of the Franciscans and with St Clare (1194–1253), the Poor Clares for women. Francis lived a life of utter simplicity and poverty, in tune with nature, apparently even preaching to the birds. There are many extraordinary events associated with St Francis, the most significant being the stigmata. After a period of retreat and fasting, contemplating Christ's passion, Francis had a vision of a crucified seraph. It was well attested that his hands thereafter showed nail imprints and his side the marks of a wound.

The order, in three versions, survives as the Friars Minor, usually just referred to as the Franciscans; the Poor Clares and the Tertiaries, the Third Order or Society of St Francis, who live in the world but follow the rule.

Outside the Walls: The Beguines

In the Middle Ages, originating in the Netherlands and spreading throughout the continent were communities of lay women, who devoted themselves to the care of others. They were of mystical inclination and not bound by vows. These independent women were not looked upon with favour by the established churches as their frugal way of life was indeed a reproach to some clergy.

Of varied background, some women had means, some not but they were not obliged to renounce any property. They would initially live in the Beguinage and after training would leave and live alone in the town. There they would teach or care for the sick and poor. Such centres sprang up all over Europe as the movement spread and men formed parallel communities of Beghards. The mother of the Belgian mystic Jan van Ruuysbroek (John of Ruysbroeck) ended her days in the Beguinage in Brussels. Today there is an American Beguine community following this pattern of life.

Repentance and Forgiveness

Repentance and forgiveness are at the heart of Christian practice, offering a chance of renewal. In services, the congregation confess their sins and are then absolved by the priest. Sometimes in order to move towards peace in the world, people need to say sorry on behalf of nations, even if they personally were not involved in the deed. Such acts pave the way for forgiveness and are not exclusive to Christianity.

An organization for peace and reconciliation in the Middle East, Jerusalem Peacemakers recently hosted an event about work being done to help build bridges between Syria and the West, Building Bridges for Peace with Syria, with Marc Gopin, 9 January 2008. This is the report:

> At the same moment that the Prime Minister of Israel was hosting a dinner for President George Bush and Israel's top politicians just a few blocks away, we hosted over 40 Israelis and Palestinians for a peace gathering and discussion with Rabbi Prof. Marc Gopin. Marc Gopin is the James Laue Professor of World's Religions, Diplomacy and Conflict Resolution at George Mason University. Marc Gopin shared about his mission of reconciliation and recent journeys to Syria.
>
> Invited by the Syrian government, Marc Gopin has been the only American rabbi to address the Syrian nation. Marc Gopin reported: 'we have in the last three years set up over five conferences and press conferences in Damascus, as well as at some universities on the issues of interfaith tolerance and interfaith cooperation in building civil society. All were broadcast on Syrian television and sometimes Al Jazeerah.'
>
> On a journey to Aleppo in 2006, Marc Gopin was invited to be a guest of honor in the central mosque in Aleppo by his friend the mufti of Syria. After the mufti gave the Friday speech at the mosque he pointed out one man in the audience, an Iraqi refugee who had been tortured by American soldiers in the Abu Ghraib prison in Iraq. In front of 2,000 people, Marc Gopin made a gesture of apology as a religious leader from America, to this man. The mufti asked his followers to record this moment. It was recorded on people's cell phones and broadcast all over Syria. The leader of Syria responded that was more important as a gesture of reconciliation than any speech by the US president.[214]

The Truth and Reconciliation Commission

We all require forgiveness from time to time, and also need to show it, which is not always easy. In South Africa, after apartheid, Nelson Mandela was determined that a way to forgive but not forget had to be found, in order that the nation should move forward as a whole. Instead of any kind of war crimes tribunal of the former regime, the Truth and

Reconciliation Commission was set up. As Archbishop Desmond Tutu took over the Chairmanship with interfaith support, it acquired a more religious character. People would be pardoned, but they were required to confess, to tell the truth. What emerged was uncomfortable for both sides, and neither the ANC nor the former leaders were happy with the five volumes of findings published in October 1998. But Mandela and Tutu stood firm with both black and white South Africans, knowing that without reconciliation, the country would have gone up in smoke. Although not perfect, this approach was innovative and successful and an important feature of building the Rainbow Nation.

This chapter has shown that spiritual experiences have led to some very worthwhile projects, movements and initiatives. Although not exclusively the result of particular experiences, the underlying attitudes of altruism and forgiveness have their roots in a spiritual approach to life.

13. Spiritual Experience Research

If we look at spiritual experience as a whole, and think in contemporary terms, the question of who has such experiences leads to a rather surprising answer. Over half of the population of the United Kingdom today would consider that they had had what they would describe as a spiritual experience of one kind or another. Most people do not talk about these things for fear of being thought odd, yet despite that, the experience almost always remains clear and meaningful for them, indeed it is often the most important event in their lives.

The Religious Experience Research Centre

Although surveys and accounts of religious experiences had been undertaken in the USA by Edwin Starbuck and William James, in the United Kingdom it was Alister Hardy, a professor of marine biology, who first attempted to elicit a response on the subject of spiritual experience from the general public. After failing to get a satisfactory response from the religious press, where he originally imagined he would make contact with people aware of such experiences, Alister Hardy repeated the exercise in the secular press. In 1969 he gave an interview in *The Guardian* describing the work he was doing on spiritual experience based on accounts of spiritual experiences collected by a press agency. He broadened his appeal across the spectrum from *The Times* to the *Daily Mail*. In *The Observer* he used an account by Beatrice Webb describing her 'apprehension of a power or purpose outside herself' which led her to 'a religious interpretation of the universe'. This was followed by this statement:

> Professor Hardy proposes, if readers will kindly cooperate, to study and compare as many personal records of such experiences as possible. He invites all who have been conscious of, and perhaps influenced by, some such power, whether they call it the power of God or not, to write a simple and brief account of these feelings and their effects.[215]

To his astonishment, he then received over a thousand accounts of spiritual experiences from a wide range of age groups. He was then able to begin his research by building up data in accordance with the scientific principles of the time, in order to formulate a natural history of the human experience of the spiritual. In order to facilitate this work, he set up the Religious Experience Research Unit at Manchester College, Oxford in 1969. He began by recording and classifying the data into 92 different categories. Since those days many studies have been undertaken using the data.

Hardy thought of humans as spiritual animals, and spiritual experience as a natural phenomenon. He found that many quite ordinary, unreligious people had had extraordinary experiences of this greater power. He also found that many were not church-goers before or after their experiences, but had nonetheless been transformed. In *The Spiritual Nature of Man* he traces his own career and thinking leading up to the setting up of the unit. He then offers a wide range of different spiritual experiences and draws some conclusions. Apart from building up academic knowledge, Hardy felt that he was pointing the way towards an experimental faith, encouraging people to try, sincerely, something like,

> God, if there is a God, help me to find you, and having found you, help me to have the strength and courage to do what I feel to be Thy will. [216]

Hardy admits that this is child-like, but maintains that the spiritual nature of man is not intellectual. It is more fundamental. The material he gathered showed that spiritual experience is widespread in the United Kingdom and Hardy wanted to show that it was universal, as Huxley described in the *Perennial Philosophy*. He further expounded his vision in the Gifford Lectures, the first series published as *The Living Stream* and the second as *The Divine Flame*.

Today, the renamed Religious Experience Research Centre is located in The University of Wales, Lampeter. The archive now holds over 6,000 accounts of spiritual experiences which have been computerised for easy access to researchers. The Alister Hardy Society, which supports the research and provides a forum for those interested in the subject to explore religious experience and contemporary spirituality, has well over 400 members and holds an annual Open Day and an annual conference. Groups in different parts of the United Kingdom hold meetings throughout the year to listen to speakers and to discuss spiritual experiences and their implications in various fields.

Spiritual Experience Research

From Sir Alister Hardy onwards, the centre's directors have furthered the research. These are some of their publications. Hardy published the first summary of the research in *The Spiritual Nature of Man*. Edward Robinson, who succeeded Sir Alister as Director of the RERU (as it was known then) published the first study of the children's experiences drawn from the accounts in the archive collected by Hardy, in *The Original Vision*. He later wrote *This Time Bound Ladder* and *Living the Questions*.

David Hay undertook various surveys of people's religious experiences, published in *Exploring Inner Space* followed by *Religious Experience Today* and later with Rebecca Nye, focused on childhood in *The Spirit of the Child*. His most recent works are *Something There, the Biology of the Human Spirit* and *Why Spirituality is Difficult for Westerners*.

Peggy Morgan, Director during 1996–2002, wrote and launched a distance learning MA Unit on Religious Experience. With Clive A. Lawton, she edited *Ethical Issues in Six Religious Traditions* and with Owen Cole has written a sympathetic and comprehensive study of *Six Religions in the Twenty-First Century*: Hinduism, Judaism, Christianity, Buddhism, Islam and Sikhism.

Current director Paul Badham discussed NDEs in his book (with Linda Badham) *Immortality or Extinction?* and in his occasional paper *Religious and Near-Death Experiences in Relation to Belief in a Future Life*. His book *The Contemporary Challenge of Modernist Theology* has a chapter devoted to Modern Religious Experiencing. With another director Xinzhong Yao, he has recently published *Religious Experience in Contemporary China*.

Wendy Dossett is also a director of the RERC, as well as Secretary of the Shap Working Party for World Religions in Education and Director of the MA in Religious Experience. She has written widely for A level students in Buddhism, Psychology of Religion and Religious Experience. Her helpful guide for A Level students entitled *Religious Experience* was published in 2006. She has also published research in Japanese Pure Land Buddhism, and in Religious Education.

Meg Maxwell and Verena Tschudin's *Seeing the Invisible*[217] brings together a wide-ranging selection of spiritual experiences from the archives of the Religious Experience Research Centre.

Contemporary Research

An excellent overview of the subject is to be found in *Religious Experience Today* by David Hay. He gives a comprehensive account of research into spiritual experience from the early years and his own work in Nottingham as well as that undertaken in America. He also tells the story of Sir Alister Hardy and the setting up of the Religious Experience Research Unit.

Dr Hay gives details of his research and examples of different types of spiritual experience and looks into the implications for education, organized religion and society in general. What comes out of the research is evidence that the phenomenon is widespread, found among people of all types, and in no way confined to those of limited education who might be suspected of succumbing to a simple credulity. Far from reflecting a Marxist view of religion as merely the opium of the masses, Hay found that not only do these experiences occur across social classes, they are even more prevalent among the better educated. In David Hay's survey in 1978 he found that over a third of all adults in Britain would answer the Hardy question in the affirmative.[218]

In a later survey, in 1986, the Alister Hardy Research Centre survey using Gallup Poll found that almost half of the population claimed to have had an experience of a religious kind and if premonitions were included, this rose to two-thirds. So, depending on the question, between half and two-thirds of the population felt that they had had a meaningful, spiritual experience.

In 1998 Olga Pupynin and Simon Brodbeck took a random sample of people in London, simply by accosting them on the street and found that about 65% answered in the affirmative to the question 'Have you ever had an experience that you would describe as sacred, religious, spiritual, ecstatic, paranormal or mystical?'[219]

Research Worldwide

In China, Turkey and India, research has begun. The Hardy Question,

> Have you ever been aware of or influenced by a presence or power, whether you call it God or not, which is different from your everyday self?

continues to be used, but is often rephrased to accommodate different cultural understandings. The terminology used in the questionnaires reflects the religious understanding of the country to be studied. So far results have been obtained from China and Turkey and there are plans to widen the research to include Japan, Brazil and the USA.

China

The RERC and the Centre for Chinese Studies at the University of Wales, Lampeter with the Ian Ramsey Centre at the University of Oxford received a grant from the John Templeton Foundation to undertake research in China. This vast land has been officially atheist since 1949 but since 1980, religion has once again been tolerated. The project involved four years work, beginning in 2004 and was undertaken by Professor Xinzhong Yao and Professor Paul Badham. The survey was of the Han Chinese and with the help of 110 Chinese researchers they collected 3,196 questionnaires, each 24 pages long, on many aspects of Chinese religious experience and belief, as well as conducting in-depth interviews. The equivalent of the Hardy Question was posed, followed by a list of suggestions, such as the power of the Lord of Heaven, Dao, Qi or Buddha.

> Some people have experienced that they were once and/or are frequently influenced by a kind of power that ordinary people cannot control and explain clearly. Have you ever had such an experience?[220]

Although China has a history which includes three major traditions, Confucianism, Daoism and Buddhism, the Chinese do not follow one spiritual path to the exclusion of others, but are quite happy to pray to different gods or take part in various rituals according to the situation. The traditions have become so intertwined that altars to representatives of all three at once are not at all uncommon.

When initially asked if they were religious, only about 8% thought so. However, the researchers found an astonishing response to the question about experiencing the influence or control of spiritual powers. 46.2% respondents claim to have experienced the God of fortune, 25.7% the Will of heaven, 21.2% their ancestors, 18.2% the Buddha; 6.1% have experiences of the Christian God, 5% had encountered spirits or ghosts, and 4.2% the Dao or Qi and 0.4% others. If one were simply to add these up one would get the impossible figure of 127% but this was because most Chinese have had had experience of more than one 'spiritual power'. In another question, they were asked to say which of these powers they had experienced most deeply or most often. 55.9% claimed to have experienced one or other spiritual power, and this figure accords closely with the response in China to the Hardy question about experiencing 'a power or presence different from everyday life'. This led to a result of 56.7%. The answers to these three questions taken together are sufficiently consistent to be taken as a reliable report of experiences people had had.

Overall the results from China indicate levels of spiritual experience very much in line with that in the West. Despite suppression, religion had not died out and the basic human response to another dimension had survived.

Turkey

A predominantly Muslim country, Turkey has been governed by a secular regime for about a century. In 2006–2007 Professor Dr Cafer Sadik Yaran of Istanbul University undertook a national survey of Muslim religious experience in Turkey, travelling through all of the seven regions from East to the West and interviewing people from various backgrounds based on random sampling. He collected 1,236 valid questionnaires which include 36 questions and a space for writing the most exceptional experience the participants had. He reported his findings in a paper entitled *The Varieties of Religious Experience Of Muslims in Turkey: Some Results of a National Survey In 2006–07,* given at the British Association for the Study of Religions Conference 2006.

He explained that although the *fact* of religious experience is found among the Muslims in Turkey, the *concept* of religious experience (*dini tecrübe*) is a new concept translated from English and is not readily understood by many people in the street. He defined it with simple words in the first main question, and described its various types in the second one in similarly plain terms. He took the classical 'Alister Hardy Question' and other similar questions into consideration and transformed them into the most easily understandable and culturally appropriate form of question. Thus, his first question was:

> Have you ever had an extra-ordinary, exceptional or supranormal experience which you would qualify as 'religious or spiritual' experience (state or event)?

The percentage of the answers given to this question was:

a. Yes   45.9%
b. Perhaps but not sure   19.6%
c. No   34.5%

Once the substance of the question had been clarified, with the use of examples, those in group b. above were able to decide, and the following result obtained.

In this case, the precise percentage of the answers of Muslims living in Turkey concerning whether they have ever had a religious experience or not is as follows:

a. Yes   63.7%
b. No   36.3%

In conclusion, Professor Yaran sums up:

Our first question was concerned with the proportion of having religious experience among Muslims in Turkey; and it came out that 64% of people report to have a kind of religious experience.

The second question was about the varieties of religious experiences lived in Turkey. And it came out that receiving God's help in answer to the prayer is the most widely reported religious experience. After that, awareness of the presence of God, awareness of God's guidance, awareness of God's punishment, experiencing that prayers for healing are effective, having a guiding dream coming true, having intuition and insights coming true, are the other varieties of religious experience that are frequently experienced. There are some other types of experience which is reported much less than these.

India

A Religious Experience Study Project was set up in Tamil Nadu, South India. This was a pilot study project set up by Jonathan Robinson in 2006 through the Alister Hardy Society and with the help of Rev. Peter Ravikumar at Tamilnadu Theological Seminary in the city of Madurai. An orientation day was held at the college for the people who were to carry out the interviews, who came from different parts of the state of Tamil Nadu.

Interviews were conducted at random, for people of all religious backgrounds and none. The interview paper itself sought to strike a balance between appropriate inculturation and a form that could be related to other global projects, with an individual page for different categories of religious experience, namely experience of power, new understanding of life, dreams, mysterious feelings, mysterious events, experience of 'one body' and any other experiences. It also sought some information about the background of the person being interviewed and questions about their ideas and beliefs.

206 case studies were carried out, and from this it was estimated that 68.4% of the people interviewed had what could be regarded as a valid religious experience. Also that 78.5% of the people would see themselves as 'religious' – a very high figure, but for those who know this part of Southern India it will not perhaps come as a surprise. For those who claim a belonging to a particular religious tradition, 68.8% of Hindus claimed a particular religious experience, 75.9% Christian and 70.5% Muslim. So it would seem that belonging to a religious tradition increased the chances of people having a religious experience (as a few people said they did not belong to any tradition). The most common type of religious experience was for Hindus, a sense of power, and for Christians and Muslims, miraculous answers to prayer.

Consciousness Studies

A great deal of work is being done at the moment on the study of consciousness. Neuroscientists in particular are studying the brain, not just in isolation, but incorporating a study of the mind. This is a fairly recent phenomenon in the West, where study of the brain has long been established, but that of the mind has been a separate field, the province of psychology. Buddhists have been in the field of consciousness studies for two and a half millennia, but have been less interested in the workings of the brain. The two fields are now being looked at together by a wide range of scientists, and the Dalai Lama too is keen to be involved in scientific discussion. Spiritual experience has a place in such studies as it looks at unusual human experiences and the relation between mind and brain. Brain-imaging techniques enable researchers to observe the brains of people in deep meditation and various physical triggers can result in experiences which could be interpreted as spiritual. It is a field of study in which the function of the brain is considered in relation to how humans experience the transcendent.

Interesting work on the link between the mind and the brain has been done by Rupert Sheldrake, with books such as *Seven Experiments that Could Change the World*, *Dogs That Know When Their Owners Are Coming Home* and *The Sense of Being Stared At and Other Aspects of the Extended Mind*. His thesis is that the mind is not confined to the brain, but extends beyond it. Thus he is able to explain telepathy and mind over matter effects as quite natural. He sees science as constantly moving forward with new discoveries building on what is known, which is what he is doing in his innovative work.

As much evidence for religious experience is dismissed as 'anecdotal', it is interesting to read Sheldrake's appraisal.

> The boundaries of scientific 'normality' are shifting again with a dawning recognition of the reality of consciousness. The powers of the mind, hitherto ignored by physics, are the new scientific frontier.
>
> . . .
>
> . . . to brush aside what people have actually experienced is not to be scientific, but unscientific. Science is founded on the empirical method, that is to say on experience and observation. Experiences and observations are the starting point for science, and it is unscientific to disregard or exclude them.[221]

In the late 1970s, Rupert Sheldrake spent many months at Bede Griffiths' ashram, writing *A New Science of Life* there, discussing it with Father Bede as he wrote it.

The Scientific and Medical Network brings science and spirituality together, looking at the latest research into consciousness. Its aims as stated on the website www.scimednet.org are:

> To provide a safe forum for the critical and open minded discussion of ideas that go beyond conventional paradigms in science, medicine and philosophy
> To integrate intuitive insights with rational analysis in our investigations
> To encourage a respect for Earth and community which emphasizes a spiritual and holistic approach
> To challenge the adequacy of 'scientific materialism' as an exclusive basis for knowledge and values.

Spiritual experience, particularly of meditation, is of interest in this field, as it can be monitored for research. As we become more aware of how the mind works and are able to track changes in brain activity, we are beginning to be able to understand the process of thought and the relation between the mind and the brain. Experiences of being outside the body in an OBE or NDE need to be considered in such research.

14. The Interpretation of Spiritual, Religious and Mystical Experience

Spiritual, religious and mystical experiences come in many different guises and are capable of a great variety of interpretations. Examples of all kinds have been given. Although in many cases experiences are in line with the religious tradition of the experient, it is by no means the case that only the expected is experienced. Many Christians who have had NDEs have been unable to confirm any specifically Christian interpretation of the Being of Light. Some people who have had spiritual experiences actually leave their former religion and abandon any specific practice, whereas others are subsequently drawn to a specific form of worship or belief. Interpretation plays a major role – but before, during and after? Theorists disagree.

The fact that there seems to be a remarkable similarity in these immediate and profound experiences of ultimate reality, has led to the view that all such experiences are similar, or at least of the same ultimate truth although differently interpreted. This was the opinion expressed by Aldous Huxley in *The Perennial Philosophy* and is held by scholars such as W. T. Stace and R. C. Zaehner. Holding opposing views are other scholars such as Steven Katz who maintain that as all experiences are mediated, one only has experiences within one's own frame of reference. Some interpret the experiences as purely psychological, while others investigate brain physiology.

This section will give an introduction to the thinking of some of the most important interpreters of spiritual, religious and mystical experience. This is not a comprehensive summary, and an indication of further reading is given.

Interpretation of Experience

Friedrich Schleiermacher (1768–1834)

In 1799 Friedrich Schleiermacher published his early, Romantic work, *Über die Religion: Reden an die Gebildeten unter ihren Verächtern* (On Religion: Speeches to its Cultured Despisers). The speeches were directed at the cynical critics of religion (his own circle of friends in particular) in a direct challenge. He told them that religion was not about doctrine or philosophy, but based on feeling and intuition. He aimed to dispel his readers' opinions of religion as something contemptible and suggested that by searching for metaphysics or morals, they were looking for the wrong thing. He encouraged them to see that true religion is not about dead texts. Although most people need some kind of mediator or exemplary figure, each individual should move on and listen to their innermost nature, their deepest feelings. For Schleiermacher, religion is to be found in experience, in particular the feeling of dependence and a sense of the infinite.

> To be one with the infinite in the midst of the finite and to be eternal in a moment, that is the immortality of religion.[222]

He put it clearly in his later work *The Christian Faith*:

> [T]he consciousness of being absolutely dependent, or, which is the same thing, of being in relation with God.[223]

In Schleiermacher's view, the different religions have developed from the original vision but in such a way that the 'cultured despisers' are right to disavow. Schleiermacher suggests a return to the vision of the originator.

> I invite you to consider every faith humanity has confessed, every religion you designate with a definite name and character and that has perhaps long since degenerated into a code of empty customs and a system of abstract concepts and theories. If you investigate them at their source and their original components, you will find that all the dead slag was once the glowing outpouring of the inner fire that is contained in all religions ... Each religion was one of the particular forms eternal and infinite religion necessarily had to assume among finite and limited beings.[224]

Rudolf Otto (1869–1937)

In *The Idea of the Holy* Rudolf Otto coined the adjective 'numinous' from the latin 'numen' meaning holy power, to describe a mental state which he saw as sui generis, a category of its own. For Otto this was the *mysterium tremendum et fascinans,* a sense of awe before the majesty of God as well as an attraction to it. He writes that in order to explain the concept,

> the reader is invited to direct his mind to a moment of deeply-felt religious experience, as little as possible qualified by other forms of consciousness.

and continues immediately with a startling piece of advice,

> Whoever cannot do this, whoever knows no such moments in his experience, is requested to read no farther.[225]

So, according to Otto, it is only through experience that the concept can really be understood, through direct perception of a transcendent power which is totally 'other' and which fills the human with a sense of his own insignificance, his 'creature consciousness'.

In *Mysticism East and West. A Comparative Analysis of the Nature of Mysticism* Otto turns his attention to the similarities and differences within mysticism as expressed, 'from the East by the great Indian Acharya Sankara, and from the West the great German Meister Eckhart.'[226] He contends that there are similarities of the inner spiritual life which are unaffected by differences of race or location or historical period, yet

> that it is false to maintain that mysticism is always just mysticism, is always and everywhere one and the same quantity.[227]

He shows the cross-cultural similarities to be found between the inward way of retreat into one's own soul, 'The Way of Introspection' and the outward way of reaching unity through multiplicity, 'The Way of Unifying Vision'. It is Otto's contention that both ways converge within Eastern and Western mysticism. Otto also shows how both mystics transcend the concept of the ultimate as expressed in their respective traditions. Sankara refers to the personal deity Isvara and to Brahman as Being itself, and Eckhart has the personal God, Deus with the Godhead, Deitas.

William James (1842–1910)

Still the acknowledged starting point for the study of religious and mystical experience, William James gave the Gifford Lectures of

Interpretation of Experience

1901–1902, published in 1902 as *The Varieties of Religious Experience*. He proposed

> four marks which, when an experience has them, may justify us in calling it mystical.[228]

These defining characteristics were ineffability, meaning difficult to put into words; noetic quality, meaning that something had been learned; transiency, they did not last long; and passivity, they seemed to happen to the experient. James believed that the mystical experience defies expression, being more like a state of feeling than a state of intellect, an experience which only those who have had it can fully comprehend, but find it hard to describe. Yet mystical states are also states of knowledge,

> states of insight into depths of truth unplumbed by the discursive intellect. [229]

Thus ineffablility and noetic quality constitute the main characteristics of the mystical experience according to James. However, transiency, the limited duration of the experience, and passivity, the sense of being grasped by a superior power are also usually found. Examples from various religions are given, showing the paradoxical yet universal nature of mystical utterance.

In *The Varieties of Religious Experience* James concentrates on the more dramatic instances of conversion and mystical experience. The book is filled with examples of the experiences of both well-known and ordinary people, many collected by his colleague Edwin Starbuck (1931–1996), and gives a clear approach to the subject as a whole.

James draws a contrast between the healthy-minded individual, not much given to spirituality, and the 'sick soul'. It is the latter person, aware of the deeper side of life, often dissatisfied, full of angst, who is in need of change and so often one who experiences a transformation through religious experience. He discusses Tolstoy's *My Confession,* in which the Russian author tells of his existential despair, which lasted for two years and was only overcome by the realization that he had to acknowledge God in order to make sense of life.

As 'the fountain-head of Christian mysticism', James cited Dionysius the Areopagite, whose apophatic approach to the absolute, assumes that nothing one can posit of it can be accurate, we can only say what it is not. Despite this, James concluded that mystical experience does point in the philosophical directions of optimism and monism, that all is well and one, leading to a state of reconciliation and unification.

Lynn Bridgers (1956–)

Lynn Bridgers herself had a profound conversion experience which changed her life and brought her to the work of William James. In her *Contemporary Varieties of Religious Experience*, published in 2005, she has taken another look at William James's work in the light of modern research and theory. In a wide-ranging reappraisal of James' methodology Lynn Bridgers examines the personality types of the prophet, monk and the mystic, on which James's work was based. She finds them still valid in the light of modern research. In particular, she finds a link between trauma and Post-traumatic Stress Disorder and sudden conversion experiences. She shows the traumas in the lives of the great mystics, which may well have triggered their experiences.

She suggests that the churches would do well to pay more attention mystical experience. People reporting such experiences are often innovators and are necessary for the healthy development of religious institutions.

Evelyn Underhill (1875–1941)

Mysticism was published ten years after William James's work. Evelyn Underhill moved beyond his four criteria, and proposed 'four other rules or notes which may be applied as tests to any given case which claims to rank among the mystics'.[230]

First, mysticism is seen as active and practical, involving the whole self and not just the intellect. Second, it is not concerned with this universe but has wholly transcendental and spiritual aims, so that although not neglecting his duties, the mystic's 'heart is always set on the changeless One'. Third, this One, for the mystic, is more than mere Reality, it is 'a living and personal Object of Love.' Finally, it is a living union with this One which is the aim of the spiritual process of the Mystic Way. Intellectual realization and emotional longing are part of this, but not enough. An 'arduous psychological and spiritual process' leads to the transformation of the mystic's consciousness and to the Unitive State, summarized as a gradual process of a growing relationship with the Absolute.

Evelyn Underhill also highlights a central issue within mysticism: the apparently contradictory doctrines of 'Emanation' and 'Immanence'. Simply expressed, the former envisages the divine as completely separate from the human, the latter sees humans and the universe as infused with the divine. She notes, however, that some mystics in fact combine both.

Some of the least lettered and most inspired amongst them – for instance Catherine of Siena, Julian of Norwich – and some of the most learned, as Dionysius the Areopagite and Meister Eckhart, have actually used in their rhapsodies language appropriate to both the theories of Emanation and of Immanence.[231]

Martin Buber (1878–1965)

A Jewish philosopher of religion, Marin Buber, with a colleague, translated the Hebrew Bible into German. He wrote *Ich und Du* (I and Thou) in 1923 and it was translated into English in 1937. Buber explains two kinds of relationships humans have, with the world and other people as objects, I-It; or an engagement with the others, I-Thou. Both relationships can take place with people and things, the distinctions change as the focus and involvement alter. We need both.

> [W]ithout It man cannot live. But he who lives with It alone is not a man.[232]

We have relationships of both types with nature, with other people and with God. We use the world as I-It, but the I-Thou relationship is one of meeting. God is taken as separate from the world and humanity, and met through grace, not by seeking.

> Men do not find God if they stay in the world. They do not find Him if they leave the world. He who goes out with his whole being to meet his *Thou* and carries to it all being that is in the world, finds Him who cannot be sought. . . .
>
> Of course God is the 'wholly Other'; but He is also the wholly Same, the wholly Present. Of course He is the *Mysterium Tremendum* that appears and overthrows; but He is also the mystery of the self-evident, nearer to me than my *I*.

> If you explore the life of things and of conditioned being you come to the unfathomable, if you deny the life of and of conditioned being you stand before nothingness, if you hallow this life, you meet the living God.[233]

Aldous Huxley (1894–1963)

The Perennial Philosophy expresses just that, Aldous Huxley's conviction that underlying the world's religions is a common core of wisdom, shared by all but expressed in different forms. In the book, Huxley brings together wisdom from mystics, poets and spiritual teachers, rather than philosophers of religion, to illustrate this 'Highest Common Factor' of religions. The book begins:

> Philosophia perennis – the phrase was coined by Leibniz; but the thing – the metaphysic that recognizes a divine Reality substantial to the world of things and minds and lives; the psychology that finds in the soul something similar to, or even identical with, divine Reality; the ethic that places man's final end in the knowledge of the immanent and transcendent Ground of all being – the thing is immemorial and universal.[234]

A. J. Ayer (1910–1989)

In 1936, at the age of 24, A. J. Ayer published *Language, Truth and Logic* which established him as a Logical Positivist philosopher. He had been influenced by the Vienna Circle of philosophers as well as the British empiricists, Locke, Berkeley and Hume. His main thesis was that metaphysics was meaningless. The 'Principle of Verification' had to be applied to all statements and led to just two kinds of sentence being acceptable: analytic, sentences of definition, in which no new data was introduced and sentences which could be empirically verified by evidence from the senses. Nothing beyond sense data could be verified, so talk of God or spirituality was meaningless.

It is particularly interesting therefore that A. J. Ayer had a NDE. In 1988 Ayer's heart stopped for four minutes while he was in London University Hospital. On resuscitation, Ayer apparently admitted to his doctor that he had seen a Divine Being, and would have to revise all his previous books and opinions. He did not speak so openly again, and as this would have indeed have entailed a complete reversal of his philosophy, he subsequently altered his language in articles in *The Sunday Telegraph* and *Spectator* which were written later. There he referred to a red light which seemed to be responsible for governing the universe and the River Styx, but continued to maintain that

> My recent experiences have slightly weakened my conviction that my genuine death, which is due fairly soon, will be the end of me but I continue to hope it will be.[235]

Interpretation of Experience

W. T. Stace (1886–1967)

The ways of the mystical extrovert and introvert, rather than being in opposition, are seen by W. T. Stace as being different stages on the same path. Extrovert mysticism, seeing the unity in diversity is a stage on the way to the ultimate goal of the introvert mystical experience of full unity with the divine.

Stace maintains that experience and interpretation are separate, and that students of mysticism will inevitably be dealing with accounts of experience and thus interpreted experiences. He feels that the normal criteria of logic break down as attempts are made to describe the mystical experience which is beyond words, leading to apparent paradox and ineffability.

Steven Katz (1944–)

If in fact the mystic does not mean what he says and his words have no literal meaning, then nothing at all can be proved, pluralistic or otherwise, according to Steven Katz. In his view, interpretation affects not only post-experiential evaluation but is fundamental to the mystical experience itself. He maintains that preconditioning leads to the type of experience one has, mystical or otherwise. For him there are no pure or unmediated experiences.

In his paper *Language, Epistemology, and Mysticism*, Katz takes the view that all experiences of ultimate reality within the different traditions are inherently different because these are all defined within their own context. Any attempt to abstract low ramification descriptions, which omit specific understandings associated with them, in order to arrive at a comprehensive theory, renders them meaningless. In other words, Nirvana cannot be compared with God.

Ninian Smart (1927–2001)

The author of many wide-ranging works on the world's religious traditions, Ninian Smart made a major contribution to religious studies through his classification of religion into seven dimensions: ritual, mythological, doctrinal, ethical, social, material and experiential. *The Religious Experience of Mankind* gives a global overview of all these aspects of religion from the primal world to today. Of the experiential dimension, he suggests that not only were the inaugural experiences vital in the founding of the religious traditions, but that personal experience is what keeps religion alive for the practitioner.

He looks at the two main strands of mystical thought, the contemplative or mystical, leading to peace and serenity, and the numinous sense of fear, awe and humility. He also maintains that a religion must incorporate both the numinous and mystical strands if it is to have universal appeal. Smart illustrates the difficulty of keeping any one-strand religion pure, with the examples of Sufism in Islam (an explosion of unitive experience within a religion stressing the gulf between man and God) and Pure Land Buddhism (in which one attains salvation by worshipping Amida Buddha in a tradition which at its origin had no place for such worship).

Robert Sharf (1953–)

Religious experience as a meaningful concept is critiqued by Robert Sharf. He considers the terms religious and mystical experience, often used to describe what many people feel to be the most important and even fundamental aspect of religion is in need of reappraisal. While Asian religions have been seen as experience-based, Sharf feels that this has come about through Asians who made use of Western scholarship and concepts to formulate the experiential side of religion and to promote it. When analysed, the experience per se disappears as only the account is available, which already involves language, culture and an interaction with the external world. Along with Daniel Dennett, Sharf does not accept that *qualia*, subjective experiences, exist, considering that individual experiences of taste or colour are in fact extrinsic or outward, relational properties, not events in the individual brain.

Sharf compares accounts of mystical experience with accounts of alien abductions, which he assumes normal people would discount, despite the proven sanity of the 'experiencers'. We may not understand what is going on, but we can be sure that the beliefs of the 'experiencers' are false. Here, for Sharf, is a clear case showing there is no 'originary event' but a narrative which is culturally generated and often induced by therapists. He compares accounts of these events with reports from mystics, showing that we never deal with unmediated inner experiences, only with conditioned narratives, and in fact they are all that exist.

Richard Swinburne (1934–)

In his most celebrated work, *The Existence of God*, Richard Swinburne considers the many arguments for belief in God. While he concludes

Interpretation of Experience

that none of them are deductively valid, and so cannot conclusively decide the matter, he suggests that religious experience tips the balance in favour of belief as part of a cumulative argument. He formulated two principles which are important in the evaluation of religious experience, the 'Principle of Credulity' and the 'Principle of Testimony'.

> The assumptions that things are (probably) as others claim to have perceived them has two components. One is the Principle of Credulity – that (in the absence of special considerations) things are (probably) as others are inclined to believe that they have perceived them. The other component is the principle that (in the absence of special considerations) the experiences of others are (probably) as they report them. This later principle I will call the Principle of Testimony. I used this principle in claiming that (on the basis of what they tell us) that very many people have religious experiences.[236]

These two principles offer a foundation for the acceptance of the veracity of religious experiences, and support the case that theism is more probable than not. Swinburne does, however, suggest that a person's lifestyle gives supporting evidence of the veracity of the report of religious experience, in other words, the fruits of the experience should be evident.

Caroline Franks Davis

Another cumulative argument for the acceptance of religious experience is put forward in *The Evidential Force of Religious Experience* by Caroline Franks Davis. She considers various challenges to the acceptance of religious experiences as genuine and suggests four types of experience which although different, are not mutually incompatible.

1. Experiences of the awesome 'numen'
2. Experiences of a loving (etc.) relationship with a personal 'other'
3. Extrovertive mystical experiences of unity in multiplicity
4. Introvertive mystical experiences of unity devoid of all multiplicity.[237]

Franks Davis suggests that a sort of common core can be extracted from numinous and mystical experiences by using relatively unramified doctrines, moving toward 'broad theism'. These may be summarized as follows:

- that the physical world is not the whole or ultimate reality;
- the ego of everyday consciousness is not the deepest level of the self, that deeper self in some way depends on and participates in ultimate reality;

- ultimate reality is holy, eternal and of supreme value and everything else is dependent on it;
- this may be experienced as a loving, guiding presence with whom individuals can have a relationship;
- some mystical experiences are of union with something else, although introvertive experiences in themselves cannot show this as only the union is experienced; and
- some kind of union or harmonious relation with the ultimate reality is the human being's *summum bonum*, his final liberation or salvation, and the means by which he discovers his 'true self' or 'true home'.[238]

She explains, that although few people are such 'broad theists' but belong to religions which have far greater ramification, such broad common core claims can stand.

Pluralism

This view, reflected in contemporary studies in the work of John Hick, and taught in the East centuries ago, notably by Kabir and Rumi, is that the same ultimate spiritual reality is discovered and experienced under many guises. A similar view of our awareness of reality was also formulated by St Thomas Aquinas.

> Things known are in the knower according to the mode of the knower.[239]

It was further developed in Kant's understanding of our inability as humans to know the true nature of reality: *das Ding an sich*, the thing-in-itself, the noumenon. Humans can only know the phenomena, the world as it appears to us, not as it really is.

John Hick (1922–)

John Hick takes the Real in itself as unknowable, but suggests that all religions have a culturally based approach to it. All religious traditions are accepted as equally valid paths to the same goal. As this ultimate is considered in personal terms as God by some and as non-personal by others, it is often referred to as the Real or Ultimate Reality. Some criterion has to be drawn to rule out certain violent sects and so the fruits or consequences of the religions are the decisive factor. The pluralist perspective rules out exclusive truth claims by any faith.

There is a difference between our ordinary experience of the world around us which is universal and public, and religious experience, some of which is public but much of which is private, taking place within the psyche and so unknowable to others. The former is easily accepted and verifiable, the latter is more problematic. However, religious experiences can legitimately be considered as giving an awareness of the Real within a worldview which accepts the spiritual dimension.

Hick explains the phenomenon of religious experience:

> The hypothesis I am proposing is that the universal presence of the Real, in which 'we live, move and have our being', generates within certain exceptionally open and sensitive individuals an unconscious awareness of an aspect or aspects of its meaning for our human existence. In cybernetic terms this is 'information' about the significance of the Real for our lives. In order to be consciously received and responded to this information is transformed into inner or outer visions or voices, the psychological machinery which transforms the transcendent information into such experiences consisting of the mystic's own mind-set and creative imagination.[240]

Keith Ward (1938–)

Keith Ward suggests that ultimate reality is not wholly unknowable. His view is that the different religions, while not having complete understanding, do offer valid insights into the nature of the divine. He takes an inclusivist view that the different ways of approaching the divine are efficacious and valuable. In *Concepts of God* he compares and contrasts the doctrines relating to ultimate reality, whether conceived as Brahman, Sunyata or God. He finds a profound convergence between them, a similar understanding of the divine, approached by turning away from egoism.

However he does not consider all beliefs about ultimate reality equally true. Although none has exclusive claim to the truth, some must offer a more adequate approach to the truth than others. Yet the traditions can learn from and enrich each other, as their cultural differences lead to valuable and complementary insights.

In his paper *Is there a Common Core of Religious Experience?* Ward argues that there is a range of core experiences which reflect a convergent spirituality within religions. He considers two traditions,

Christianity and Vedanta and argues that there is a common core of religious experience.

> It is a 'core' in that it focuses on the most central and important element of religious belief, the nature of the supremely Real. The core is common, because there is an overlapping identity of description of the Real in both Vedantic and Christian traditions. Brahman and God both have the character of wisdom, infinity, intelligence and bliss. Both form the one and only self-existent, on which all other beings depend. The simplest hypothesis is that these descriptions refer to the same reality, and experience of that reality is experience of the same thing.[241]

Implicit Religion

This is a way of looking at people's ultimate values and concerns outside formal religion. As religious observance declines and contemporary society seems to be increasingly secular, is there anything which elicits a spiritual response in people? Implicit religion is the exploration of this invisible or hidden side of life.

Edward Bailey (1935–)

In *Implicit Religion: an Introduction* Edward Bailey, Founding Director of the Centre for the Study of Implicit Religion and Contemporary Spirituality, suggests three definitions of the concept which he established. These are 'commitments', referring to what is of importance in someone's life; 'integrating foci' meaning human interaction – individual and social; and 'intensive concerns with extensive effects', things which matter deeply and have a far-reaching impact. What implicit religion is really about, is what makes people tick, what means most to them. This may include religious experience, but is more likely to arise from their ordinary, daily living.

Implicit religion, then, is as real as these moments of heightened consciousness, whether they are understood in terms of transcendence, values or religion. But it is not restricted to such 'surconscious' experiences.

Don Cupitt (1934–)

This thinker does away with transcendent reality altogether, finding God within everyday life. Religious and mystical experiences are stripped of a metanarrative perspective and brought into the real world. In *The Sea of Faith* Don Cupitt begins with Matthew Arnold's poem *Dover Beach* to illustrate the dying of religion. In Cupitt's view, metaphysics has had its time. Non-realist Christianity retains moral and religious truths but they are viewed from a different perspective. God is not a separate entity but a religious ideal, the sum of our values and thus a human construct. He gave a postmodern interpretation of religious experience in *Mysticism After Modernity*.

Daniel Dennett (1942–)

An American philosopher and self-confessed 'bright' or atheist, Daniel Dennett has written widely on the problems of the mind, consciousness and mental states. In *Breaking the Spell* he discusses religion. In contrast to William James' definition of religion as solitary feelings, acts and experiences in relation to the divine, Dennett's definition is:

> Social systems whose participants avow belief in a supernatural agent or agents whose approval is to be sought.[242]

Dennett considers James' solitaries as spiritual rather than religious and sees religion as a group activity. In Dennett's view, religion is such a powerful force in the modern world that it should be investigated thoroughly by means of a multidisciplinary approach. The spell Dennett wants to break is the taboo against such an examination and his book is a comprehensive investigation into the phenomenon of religion from a scientific and philosophical point of view. The book is in three parts. In the first part the relation between religion and scientific inquiry is considered; the second part takes an evolutionary overview of the origins of religions; and in part three, 'Religion Today' the pros and cons of belief are evaluated, the benefits weighed against the dangers of extremism. Overall Dennett makes a strong case for the need for an open, informed inquiry into the nature of religion.

Richard Dawkins (1941–)

There is no God at all in Richard Dawkins' universe. *The God Delusion* took the UK by storm in 2007 and Dawkins triggered a national debate about belief, as well as ripostes such as Alister McGrath's *The Dawkins Delusion* and John Cornwell's *Darwin's Angel*. Dawkins, a biologist, is

Professor for the Public Understanding of Science and frequently writes, lectures and broadcasts his anti-religious views. He maintains that Darwin's Theory of Evolution has conclusively shown that the universe evolved over time, there never was a creator and religion is superstitious nonsense.

The God Delusion begins with a religious experience which led Dawkins' school chaplain to faith and eventually holy orders. Dawkins liked him, understood the experience, but would have interpreted it differently. He later quotes another experience which led to ordination, this time, however, there was a natural explanation – the voice experienced as that of the devil was in fact a Manx Shearwater or 'Devil Bird'. Religious experiences are illusions or constructions of the brain, convincing to those who have them, but not to others, particularly not to scientists.

D'Aquili (1940–1998) And Newberg (1966–)

In *The Mystical Mind – Probing the Biology of Religious Experience*, Eugene D'Aquili and Andrew Newberg approach the subject of spiritual experience from a neurophysiological perspective, using brain-imaging and modern research methods in neurology, psychology and psychiatry. They show that the brain is the medium through which such extraordinary spiritual experiences arise, but they also explain that 'normal' reality also comes to us through the same process. They stress however, that the brain does not necessarily generate religious experiences. They argue that, at the present time, the research cannot delineate whether religious experiences arise from an external source (i.e. God) or whether they are generated from within the brain.

Recently, Andrew Newberg with Mark Waldman published *Why We Believe What We Believe*. This is an exploration of how different kinds of beliefs are formed. The authors look at how the neural activities of the brain function under different conditions, testing people meditating, praying and even speaking in tongues. The same neurological activity can lead to quite different beliefs.

Recommended Reading

Peter Donovan

As its title *Interpreting Religious Experience* would suggest, this is a comprehensive consideration of what can and cannot be proved by religious experience. Peter Donovan looks at different types of religious experiences, their interpretation, what can be argued from them and just what we can learn through them. Despite the possibility of a naturalist explanation for some experiences, the religious interpretation is often preferred as it makes for a more coherent and integrated explanation of life as a whole.

Paul Marshall

In *Mystical Encounters with the Natural World, Experiences and Explanations* Paul Marshall looks at a range of extrovertive mystical experiences including accounts of unity, knowledge, light and love but particularly those relating to the natural world, and considers their effects. He had a spiritual experience himself, and draws on the RERC archive for examples. He gives an overview of different critical approaches, including spiritual, psychoanalytical and neurophysiological and an appraisal of the work of R. M. Bucke, Estlin Carpenter, W. R. Inge, Evelyn Underhill, Rudolf Otto, Sigmund Freud, Aldous Huxley, Steven Katz and Robert Forman. He considers explanations ranging from an acceptance of genuine experiences of a metaphysical reality to postmodern and deconstructionist perspectives.

Grahame Miles

Science and Religious Experience, Are They Similar Forms of Knowledge? is a consideration of how we acquire knowledge of different kinds: biological, personal, moral, religious and scientific. Grahame Miles looks at how knowledge is established in science and religious experience. He finds in both a pattern of perception, interpretative understanding and subsequent acceptance by the believing community (scientific or religious).

All these interpretations of religious and spiritual experiences enhance understanding, as the subject is investigated from many, often conflicting academic perspectives.

Conclusion

This book has brought together many accounts of a great variety of religious and spiritual experiences, some short, some told at length and in detail. They reflect moments and even lifetimes of awareness of something beyond the everyday world. Spiritual experiences take people outside their normal parameters and at the very least seem to indicate an extension of the limits of human consciousness. They deepen everyday experience, indicating a dimension underlying the world of the senses. More than that, they seem to be evidence of a power greater than ourselves, which some might call God. This may be experienced dramatically, perhaps as light or love, or as a deeper awareness throughout life, a sense of being guided. People become aware of a source of strength and comfort. When they sincerely respond to it, they find that it works, even if they do not quite understand it. Despite the protests of sceptics, the experients themselves have no doubt that the reality revealed to them is more real than the world around them and that the messages given are compelling.

Many who have spiritual experiences interpret them as such. They value them as grace given by God. If they are not religious, they still view them as comfort or help from somewhere other than the world around them. They take from them a renewed sense of wonder at the natural world and above all, a profound love for all creation. This has transformed many lives as such people feel a deep motivation to work for the good of others. Even in times of doubt, people have found that they can call on this power, and it works. It is hard for those who have never had any such awareness to view these experiences as anything other than merely the products – or aberrations – of the mind, interpreted according to particular religious expectations and so they are apt to dismiss them as delusions.

Whatever the interpretation, however, for those who have them, their experiences serve to deepen their apprehension of the mystery of life and intensify their appreciation of its intricate complexity. Many experiences also seem to indicate an afterlife of some kind, the possibility of a continuation of consciousness beyond death, and even contact with the deceased.

Conclusion

Spiritual experiences set life in the greater context of eternity, which is in line with the teachings of the religious traditions.

Most people would hesitate to say that such experiences offer conclusive proof of the existence of God or of divine intervention. However, as part of a cumulative argument, they strengthen the case for belief in the divine. They are in harmony with what is contained in the writings of the world's great faiths, many of which can trace their origins to similar experiences. Religious experiences and traditions are perhaps best appreciated as offering intimations of an ultimate reality beyond our comprehension, but partially revealed in many different ways.

The differences between religions might best be understood with the help of the ancient Indian story of the blind men and the elephant. One man felt the trunk and deduced that it was a kind of snake; another touched the ear and thought it like a leaf; a third put his hand around the leg and found it like a tree trunk; another felt the tail and was convinced that it was like a rope. Each man had an insight into one aspect of what he was exploring, but none had a complete understanding of the whole.

Spiritual experiences happen to men, women and children all over the world and always have done. It is as if a door opens and a new realm is revealed, in the depths of the heart as well as within and beyond the universe. The underlying message is one of love for our environment and above all, for each other. Surveys worldwide indicate that more than half of us would say that they had some kind of spiritual experience. We can choose to ignore or explore this level of awareness. However, as we are faced with an ever-growing need for mutual understanding and global co-operation, a spiritual approach to life may be our best hope for the future of the planet.

Notes

1 Alister Hardy *The Spiritual Nature of Man, A Study of Contemporary Religious Experience* (1979) OUP. p. 1.
2 Ibid. p. 18.
3 The Alister Hardy Trust website was consulted on 19 February 2008.
4 Hay, David *Religious Experience Today* (1990) Mowbray, London. p. 42.
5 Quoted in Cafer Yaran *The Varieties of Religious Experience of Muslims in Turkey: Some Results of a National Survey in 2006–07* given at the BASR Conference 2007 in Edinburgh. p. 7.
6 Keeble, John *'This Unnamed Something', A Personal Portrait of the Life of Professor Sir Alister Hardy FRS 1896–1985* (2000) RERC, Lampeter. pp. 9–10.
7 Quoted in *Religious Experience Today* by David Hay (1990) Cassel, London. p. 17.
8 *The Varieties of Religious Experience* by William James (2002 edition) Routledge, London and New York. p. 11.
9 William James *The Varieties of Religious Experience* (2002 edition) Routledge, London and New York. pp. 29–30.
10 Wilfred Cantwell Smith *The Meaning and End of Religion* (reprint 1963) Fortress Press, Minneapolis. p. 194
11 Smart, Ninian *The Religious Experience of Mankind* (Third Edition 1984) Charles Scribner's Sons, New York. p. 15.
12 Peggy Morgan in 'Continuing the work' in *De Numine* No. 35, February 2004 RERC, Lampeter. p. 20.
13 Alister Hardy *The Spiritual Nature of Man, A Study of Contemporary Religious Experience* (1979) OUP. p.1.
14 Michael Paffard *Inglorious Wordsworths* (1973) Hodder and Stoughton, London.
15 2nd Series Occasional Paper 34 *Encounters Beyond the Pond: The Limit Experiences of Senior High School Students* (2002) RERC, Lampeter.
16 Marghanita Laski *Ecstasy in Secular and Religious Experiences* (1990) Jeremy P. Tarcher, Los Angeles.
17 William James *The Varieties of Religious Experience* (2002 edition) Routledge, London and New York. p. 29.
18 *The Mediators, Nine Stars in the Human Sky*, John Macquarrie (1995) p. 7.

Notes

19 John Bowker *Worlds of Faith, Religious Belief and Practice in Britain Today* (1983) Ariel Books, BBC, London. p. 130.
20 Tariq Ramadan *The Messenger, The Meanings of the Life of Muhammad* (2007) Penguin Books, London. p. 29.
21 *A Course in Miracles* (London, Arkana 1985).
22 Griffiths, Bede *The Marriage of East and West* (1982) Templegate Publishers, Illinois. pp. 102, 103.
23 'SvetasvataraUpanishad' 1.8 in *Upanishads* translated by Patrick Olivelle (1998) OUP, Oxford. p. 254.
24 *Bhagavad-Gita As It Is* A. C. Bhaktivedanta Swami Prabhupada (1983, 1985) Bhaktivedanta Book Trust, Lichtenstein. p. 567.
25 Ibid. p. 422.
26 www.zarathushtra.com
27 Dates established by Richard Gombrich in *Dating the Buddha: A Red Herring Revealed* (1992).
28 *Tao Te Ching* by Lao Tsu, translated by Gia-Fu Feng and Jane English (1973) Wildwood House, UK.
29 Genesis Chapters 6–9.17.
30 Genesis 22. 114.
31 Exodus 34:2730.
32 Mark 1:10, 11.
33 Bahá'u'lláh, *Epistle to the Son of the Wolf* rev. ed. (Wilmette: Bahá'í Publishing Trust, 1979), p. 22.
34 George Fox – An Autobiography, CHAPTER I. Boyhood – A Seeker 1624–1648 *Christian Classics Ethereal Library*, as scanned and edited by Harry Plantinga.
35 From website of the Theosophical Society of America, The Esoteric World of Madame Blavatsky. By Vera P. de Zhelihovsky (HPB's sister) [Collated from Zhelihovsky 1894–1895, 203, 204, 203; and Sinnett 1886, 30–35, 37–39] Consulted Jan. 2008.
36 Shepherd A. P. *Scientist of the Invisible,* Rudolf Steiner (1954) Inner Traditions International, USA.
37 Rudolf Steiner *The Course of My Life* (1977) Anthroposophic , New York. p. 319.
38 Lissau, *Rudi Rudolf Steiner, Life, Work, Inner Path and Social Initiatives* (1987) Hawthorn Press, Stroud, UK.
39 Alister Hardy *The Divine Flame* (1966, 1978) RERU, Oxford.
40 Srila Prabhupada *On Chanting Hare Krishna* (1999) Bhaktivedanta Book Trust, USA. p. 12.
41 Mother Meera *Answers* (1991) Rider, London. pp. 17, 41.
42 Eckhart Tolle *Practising the Power of Now* (2001 USA) (2002) Hodder and Stoughton, London. p. 7.
43 Fritjof Capra *The Tao of Physics* (1976, 1992) Flamingo, London. p. 11.
44 Metropolitan Anthony of Sourozh *Living Prayer* (1966, 1990) DLT, London. p. 7.

Notes

45 Experience given to author in March 2008.
46 Quoted from Reynold A. Nicholson *The Mystics of Islam* in Cafer Yaran *Muslim Religious Experience* (2004) Occasional Paper No. 41 RERC, Lampeter. p. 1.
47 John Bowker *Worlds of Faith, Religious Belief and Practice in Britain Today* (1983) BBC, London. p. 147.
48 Meg Maxwell and Verena Tschudin *Seeing the Invisible* (1990, Penguin) (2005) RERC, Lampeter. pp. 69–70.
49 George H. Gorman *Introducing Quakers* (1981) QHS, London.
50 Anita Billington, first published in *The Friends' Quarterly* Vol. 25, No. 7, July 1989. p. 300.
51 Deepak Chopra *How to Know God, The Soul's Journey into the Mystery of Mysteries* (USA 2000) (2001) Rider, London. p. 17.
52 Taken from a paper entitled *The Varieties Of Religious Experience Of Muslims In Turkey: Some Results Of A National Survey in 2006–07* by Prof. Dr. Cafer Sadık Yaran of Istanbul University at the 2007 BASR Conference in Edinburgh.
53 *The Cloud of Unknowing* edited by William Johnston (1997) Fount Paperbacks, London. p. 15.
54 Ibid. p. 16.
55 His Holiness the Dalai Lama *How to Practise, the Way to a Meaningful Life* Translated and edited by Jeffrey Hopkins (2002) Rider, London. p.134.
56 Sandy & Jael Bharat *A Global Guide to Interfaith, Reflections from Around the World* (2007) O Books, Hants. p. 44.
57 Experience given to author on 21.3.08.
58 Lao Tsu *Tao Te Ching* translated by Gia-Fu Feng and Jane English (1973, 1986) Wildwood, Hants. p. 56.
59 Mother Meera *Answers* (1991) Rider, London. p. 53.
60 Experience given to author on 23.3.08.
61 Bede Griffiths *Return to the Centre* (1976) (2003) Medio Media, USA. p. 3.
62 Gélineau, Alain-René *The Poetry of Transcendence* (1984) Argel, Paris. p. 50.
63 Eric Gladwin *Peaceful Reflections for the New Millenium, Healing Poems and Prayers* (1994, 2000) Harmony Publications, England. p.12.
64 Paul Hawken *The Magic of Findhorn* (1976) Fontana GB pp. 120, 123.
65 http://news.bbc.co.uk/2/hi/middle_east/4181237.stm consulted on 24.2.2008.
66 Shirley du Boulay *The Road to Canterbury, A Modern Pilgrimage* (1994) Harper Collins, London. p. 232.
67 Blogging Ramadan Website consulted on 20.3.08.
68 Bharat, Sandy and Jael *Touched by Truth, A Contemporary Hindu Anthology* (2006) William Sessions, York. p. 116.
69 Anita Billington, first published in *The Friends' Quarterly* Vol. 25, No. 7, July 1989. pp. 298–299.
70 Sandy & Jael Bharat *A Global Guide to Interfaith, Reflections from Around the World* (2007) O Books, Hants. p. 45.

Notes

71 Meg Maxwell and Verena Tschudin *Seeing the Invisible* (1990, Penguin) (2005) RERC, Lampeter. pp.116–117.
72 Daniel O'Leary 'Mystery in a drop of wine' in *The Tablet*, 16 June 2007. http://www.thetablet.co.uk.
73 Quoted in Alister Hardy *The Spiritual Nature of Man, A Study of Contemporary Religious Experience* (1979) OUP, reprinted RERC, 1997. pp. 93–94.
74 John McCarthy and Jill Morrell *Some Other Rainbow* quoted in Madeleine Hill *Time Stood Still*. p. 102.
75 Eckhart Tolle *The Power of Now* (1999 USA) (2001) Hodder and Stoughton, London. pp.1–2.
76 Neale Donald Walsch, *Conversations with God, An Uncommon Dialogue* (1995 USA) (1997) Hodder and Stoughton, London. Book 1. p. 1.
77 Quoted in Wa'Na'Nee'Che (Dennis Renault) and Timothy Freke *Principles of Native American Spirituality* (1996) Thorsons, California. p. 35.
78 Alain-René Gélineau *The Poetry of Transcendence* (1984) Argel, Paris. p. 92.
79 Alister Hardy *The Spiritual Nature of Man*. p. 82.
80 Werner Hofmann *Caspar David Friedrich* (2000) Thames & Hudson, London. pp. 19 and 26.
81 Experience given to author on 29.2.08.
82 Experience given to author on 29.2.08.
83 Experience given to author on 29.2.08.
84 David Hay with Rebecca Nye in *The Spirit of the Child* (1998, revised edition 2006) HarperCollins, London. p. 100.
85 Ibid . p.100.
86 Paul McQuillan *Encounters Beyond the Pond: The Limit Experience of Senior High School Students* Occasional Paper 34 RERC, Lampeter. p. 44.
87 Ibid. p. 49.
88 Quoted from *Waiting on God* by Simone Weil in Stephen Plant *Simone Weil* Fount Christian Thinkers (1996) Fount, London. p. 9.
89 Hugh Montefiore *The Paranormal, A Bishop Investigates* (2002) Upfront Publishing, Leicester. pp. 234–235.
90 C. S. Lewis *Surprised by Joy* (1977) Fount Paperbacks, London. p. 182.
91 Hay, David *Religious Experience Today* 1990 Mowbray, London. p. 2.
92 Ibid. 2562. p. 101.
93 Taken from 'The contribution of the study of spiritual experience to spiritual care in the health service.' Part 1 by Hilary Knight in *De Numine* No. 34, February 2003.
94 Ibid. 4426. pp. 101–102.
95 Eileen Caddy 'My personal experience with guidance' in *Caduceus* Issue 71. p. 10.
96 www.thebrahmosamaj.org
97 *A Tagore Testament* Translated from the original Bengali of Rabindranath Tagore by Indu Dutt (1969) Jaico Publishing House, India. pp. 52–53, 68–69.

Notes

98 Quoted in Madeleine Hill *Time Stood Still*. pp. 54–55.
99 www.taize.fr/en_article338.html consulted in January 2005.
100 www.taize.fr/en_article102.html consulted in January 2005.
101 Quoted from *The Life of Saint Teresa of Avila*, tr. J. M. Cohen, (1957) Penguin Books. p. 180 in Shirley du Boulay *Teresa of Avila* (1991) Hodder and Stoughton, London. p. 52.
102 Obituary in the *Daily Telegraph*. 16.1.08.
103 Quoted from Simone Weil *Waiting on God* in *Simone Weil* by Stephen Plant (1996) Fount, London. p. 53.
104 Ninian Smart *The Spiritual Experience of Mankind* (1969) Charles Scribner's Sons, NY.
105 R. Balmer *Religion in 20th Century America* (2001) OUP quoted in Newberg and Waldman *Why We Believe What We Believe* (2006) Free Press, NY.
106 Quoted from *The Life of Saint Teresa of Avila*, tr. J. M. Cohen, (1957) Penguin Books. p. 192 in Shirley du Boulay *Teresa of Avila* (1991) Hodder and Stoughton, London. p. 54.
107 Heathcote-James, Emma *Seeing Angels* (2001) John Blake, London. p. 165.
108 Ibid. p. 125.
109 Experiences given to author on 22.3.08.
110 Aldous Huxley *The Doors of Perception* (1994) Flamingo, London. pp. 7–8.
111 Neale Donald Walsch *Communion with God, An Uncommon Dialogue* (2000) Hodder and Stoughton, London. p. 4.
112 Quoted in Peter Russell *From Science to God, A Physicist's Journey into the Mystery of Consciousness* (2002, 2003) New World Library, California. p. 115.
113 Quoted in *The Rumi Collection* edited by Kabir Helminski. p. 22.
114 John V. Taylor *The Christlike God* (1992) SCM Press, London.
115 First printed in the *Prison Phoenix Trust Newsletter* Winter 2007.
116 Jakobsen, Marete Demant *Negative Spiritual Experiences: Encounters with Evil* (1999) RERC, Lampeter. p. 8.
117 Ibid. p. 10.
118 Ibid. p. 36.
119 Stephen Parsons *Ungodly Fear, Fundamentalist Christianity and the Abuse of Power* (2000) Lion, UK. pp. 29, 31–32.
120 Elisabeth Kübler-Ross, quoted with permission from the website. www.elisabethkublerross.com
121 *Common Worship*. p. 151.
122 Account given to author in January 2008.
123 Brayne, S., & Fenwick, P. 'Is end-of-life care training ignoring the significance of End-of-Life Experiences?' *European Journal of Palliative Care* (In press) 2008.
124 Sue Brayne 'Deathbed phenomena and palliative care workers' in *The Christian Parapsychologist* Vol. 17 No. 5, March 2007. p. 149.

Notes

125 Ibid. p. 153.
126 Experience given to the author in September 2007.
127 Elisabeth Kübler-Ross *The Wheel of Life* (1997, 1999) Bantam, London. p. 219.
128 Bel Mooney *Devout Sceptics, Conversations on Faith and Doubt* (2003) Hodder & Stoughton, London. p. 44.
129 Raymond A. Moody *Life After Life* (1975) Bantam Books. pp. 94–95.
130 Peter and Elizabeth Fenwick *The Truth in the Light* (1997) Berkeley New York. p. 34.
131 Thomas-Mellen Benedict 'Through the Light and Beyond' in *The Near-Death Experience, A Reader* edited by Lee W. Bailey and Jenny Yates (1996) Routledge, NY and London. pp. 42–43.
132 Ibid. pp. 44 and 45.
133 Ibid. p. 50.
134 Quoted from John Neihardt *Black Elk Speaks* in Bailey, Lee W. and Yates, Jenny eds. *The Near-Death Experience, A Reader* (1996) Routledge, NY and London. p. 84.
135 Martin Israel *Happiness That Lasts* (1999) Cassell, London. pp. 5, 6–7.
136 Susan Blackmore *Consciousness, An Introduction* (2003) Hodder and Stoughton, London. pp. 364–365.
137 Quote from *The Tibetan Book of the Dead* p. 94 in Paul Badham *Religious and Near-Death Experiences in Relation to Belief in a Future Life* (1997) 2nd Series Occasional Paper No. 13 RERC, Oxford. p. 8.
138 'A Prospectively Studied Near-Death Experience with Corroborated Out-of-Body Perceptions and Unexplained Healing' in *The Journal of Near-Death Studies* 25 (2), Winter 2006. Penny Sartori, R.G.N., Ph.D., Paul Badham, Ph.D. Peter Fenwick, M.B.B.Chir., D.P.M.
139 Ibid. p.178.
140 Professor Paul Badham *Religious and Near-Death Experiences in Relation to a Belief in a Future Life*.
141 *De Numine* No. 35, February 2004 RERC, Lampeter. pp. 12–14.
142 Dalai Lama *How to Practise, the Way to a Meaningful Life* ((2002) Pocket Books, London. p. 171.
143 Happold, F. C. *Mysticism, A Study and an Anthology* (1963, 1990) Penguin Books, London. p. 57.
144 Cohen, J. M. and Phipps J-F *The Common Experience* (1979) Rider, London. pp. 137–138.
145 Dionysius the Areopagite *The Mystical Theology and the Celestial Hierarchies* translated by the Editors of the Shrine of Wisdom (1923, 2004) The Fintry Trust, Surrey. p. 29.
146 Ibid. p. 34.
147 Julian of Norwich, *Revelations of Divine Love* (1966) Penguin Books, London. p. 63.
148 Ibid. p. 63.
149 Ibid. p. 65.

150 Ibid. p.157.
151 Ibid. p. 114.
152 Ibid. p. 68.
153 Ibid. p. 170.
154 Ibid. pp. 211–212.
155 Ibid. p. 185.
156 Andrew Harvey *The Way of Passion* (1994, 1995) Souvenir Press, London. p. 24
157 Ibid. p. 28.
158 Quoted in Reynold A. Nicholson *The Mystics of Islam* (1989) Arkana, London. p. 107.
159 *The Rumi Collection, An Anthology of Translations of Mevlana Jalaluddin Rumi* selected and edited by Kabir Helminski (1998) Threshold Books, Vermont. p. 22.
160 Ibid. p.113.
161 Paramahansa Yogananda *Autobiography of a Yogi* (1950; 1969 in Britain) Rider, London. pp. 106–107.
162 Ibid. pp. 166–167.
163 Quoted in Cohen, J. M. and Phipps J-F *The Common Experience* (1979) Rider, London. pp. 139, 169.
164 From Warner Allen *The Timeless Moment* Quoted in F. C. Happold *Mysticism, A Study and an Anthology* (1963, 1990) Penguin Books, London. p. 133.
165 Bede Griffiths *The Golden String* (1976, 2003) Medio Media, USA. pp. 1–2.
166 Ibid. pp. 3 and 4.
167 Ibid. p. 124.
168 Bede Griffiths *The Marriage of East and West* (1982) Templegate, Illinois. p. 27.
169 Bede Griffiths *The Return to the Centre* (1976, 2003) Medio Media, USA. p. 73.
170 Bede Griffiths *The Marriage of East and West* (1982) Templegate, Illinois. p. 42.
171 Thich Nhat Hanh *The Miracle of Mindfulness* (1991) Rider, London. p. 12.
172 Thich Nhat Hanh *Living Buddha, Living Christ* (1996) Rider, London. p. 180.
173 Ibid. p. 6.
174 Ibid. pp. 194, 195.
175 Ibid. p. 2.
176 Colin Wilson *Afterlife, An Investigation of the Evidence for Life After Death* (1985) Harrap, London. p. 54.
177 Andrew Harvey *A Walk with Four Spiritual Guides* (2003) SkyLight Paths Publishing, Canada. p. 136.
178 Ibid. p. 137.

Notes

179 Mary Lutyens *Krishnamurti, The Years of Awakening* (1975) Avon, New York. p. 293.
180 Krishnamurti *Meeting Life* compiled by Mary Lutyens (1991) Arkana, London p. 204.
181 J. Krishnamurti *Meditations* (1991) Shambhala, London. p. 2.
182 Lutyens, Mary *Krishnamurti, The Years of Awakening* (1975) and *Krishnamurti, The Years of Fulfilment* (1983) Avon, New York.
183 Andrew Harvey *The Direct Path, Creating a Journey to the Divine Using the World's Mystical Traditions* (2000) Rider, London. p. 14.
184 Ibid. p. 21.
185 Bertrand Russell *History of Western Philosophy* (2004) Folio Society, London. p. 122.
186 Plato *Phaedo* in *Socratic Dialogues* translated and edited by W. D. Woodhead (1967) Nelson, London. pp. 123 and 125.
187 C. G. Jung *Memories, Dreams and Reflections* (1973) Fontana, London. p. 18.
188 Ibid. pp. 320–322.
189 Ibid. p. 237.
190 William Hague *William Wilberforce, The Life of the Great Anti-Slave Trade Campaigner* (2007) HarperCollins Publishers, London. pp. 78, 79, 81.
191 Ibid. p. 141.
192 Patrick French *Younghusband, The Last Imperial Adventurer* (2004) Harper Perennial, London. p. 252.
193 Ibid. p. 327.
194 Dietrich Bonhoeffer *Letters and Papers from Prison* (1953 SCM Press) (1968) Fontana, p.173.
195 *Dietrich Bonhoeffer, A Biography by Eberhard Bethge* (1977) Harper & Row, London. p. 830.
196 Chad Varah *Before I Die Again* (1992) Constable, London. p. 78.
197 Ibid. p. 81.
198 Elisabeth Kübler-Ross 'Death does not exist' in *On Life After Death* (1991) Celestial Arts, USA. p. 24.
199 Quoted with permission from www.elisabethkublerross.com
200 Elisabeth Kübler-Ross *The Wheel of Life, A Memoire of Living and Dying* (1997, 199) Bantam, UK. p. 288.
201 Du Boulay, Shirley and Rankin, Marianne *Cicely Saunders, The Founder of the Modern Hospice Movement* (2007) SPCK, London. p. 27.
202 Ibid. p. 28.
203 Brown, Gordon *Courage, Eight Portraits* (2007) Bloomsbury, London. p. 218.
204 Quotes from *Freedom from Fear: And Other Writings* (1991) Penguin, London. in Nobel Prize acceptance speech given on 10th December 1991 from nobelprize.org website consulted on 13.4.08.
205 Eric Clapton, *The Autobiography* (2007) Century, London. p. 257.
206 Ibid. p. 280.

Notes

207 James, William *The Varieties of Religious Experience, A Study in Human Nature* (2002) Special Centenary Edition, Routledge, London, NY and Canada. pp. 186, 187.

208 Hardy, Alister *The Spiritual Nature of Man* 1969 OUP 1979 RERC, Oxford. p. 6, quoting from Emile Durkheim *The Elementary Forms of Religious Life* 1915.

209 Hardy Alister *The Divine Flame* Collins 1966 RERU, Oxford 1978 p. 80 and p. 26.

210 Quoted in *The Spiritual Nature of Man, A Study of Contemporary Religious Experience* by Alister Hardy (1979) Oxford University Press.

211 Available from Ken Evans Prints, Eggmoor Lane Cottage, Chardstock, Devon, EX13 7BP. www.kenevansprints.co.uk

212 Nancy Garton *George Müller and his Orphans* (1987) Churchman Publishing, Sussex. p. 23.

213 RERC Archive account No. 002163.

214 Website consulted February 2008.

215 Hardy, Alister *The Spiritual Nature of Man, A Study of Contemporary Religious Experience* (1979) OUP, reprinted RERC 1997. p.140.

216 Alister Hardy, *The Spiritual Nature of Man* (1979) RERC, Oxford. p. 18.

217 Maxwell, Meg and Tschudin, Verena (eds) *Seeing the Invisible, Modern Religious and Other Transcendent Experiences* (1990) RERC, Lampeter.

218 David Hay *Religious Experience Today (1990)* Mowbray, London. pp. 79, 82 and 83.

219 2nd Series Occasional Paper 27 *Religious Experience in London* by Olga Pupynin and Simon Brodbeck (2001) RERC, Lampeter.

220 Yao, Xinzhong and Badham, Paul *Religious Experience in Contemporary China* (2007) University of Wales Press, Cardiff. pp. 200–201.

221 Rupert Sheldrake *The Sense of Being Stared At and Other Aspects of the Extended Mind* (2003) Hutchinson, UK. pp. 4, 5.

222 Friedrich Schleiermacher *(Über die Religion. Reden an die Gebildeten unter ihren Verächtern) On Religion. Speeches to Its Cultured Despisers* (1996) translated by Richard Crouter, Cambridge University Press, Cambridge.

223 Freidrich Schleiermacher *The Christian Faith* (1928, 1960) T&T Clark, Edinburgh. p. 12.

224 Friedrich Schleiermacher *On Religion. Speeches to Its Cultured Despisers* (1996). p. 99.

225 Rudolf Otto *The Idea of the Holy* (1923) (1958) OUP. p. 8.

226 Rudolf Otto, *Mysticism East and West. A Comparative Analysis of the Nature of Mysticism* (New York: The Macmillan Company, 1932).

227 Ibid. *Introduction*. p. xvi.

228 James, william *The Varieties of Religious Experience, A Study in Human Nature* (2002) Special Centenary Edition, Routledge, London, NY and Canada. p.294.

229 Ibid. p. 295.

230 Evelyn Underhill: *Mysticism* (London: Bracken Books, 1995).

Notes

231 Ibid. p.101.
232 Martin Buber *I and Thou* translated by Ronald Gregor Smith Second Edition (1958) T&T Clark, Edinburgh. p. 34.
233 Ibid. p. 79.
234 Aldous Huxley *The Perennial Philosophy* (1985, reprinted 1989) Triad Grafton, London. p. 9.
235 Quoted from Paul Edwards *Immortality* by Paul Badham in *Religious and Near-Death Experiences in Relation to Belief in a Future Life* (1997) Occasional Paper No. 13 RERC, Oxford. p. 13.
236 Richard Swinburne *The Existence of God* (2004) Oxford University Press. p. 322.
237 Caroline Franks Davis, *The Evidential Force of Religious Experience* (1989) Oxford, Clarendon Press p. 177.
238 Ibid. p. 191.
239 Quoted from *Summa Theologica II/II*, Q.1, art 2 in John Hick *An Interpretation of Religion* (1989) MacMillan, London.
240 John Hick *An Interpretation of Religion* (1989)Macmillan Press, London. p. 169.
241 Keith Ward *Is There a Common Core of Religious Experience?* (2005) 2nd Series Occasional Paper No. 44 RERC, Lampeter. p. 13.
242 Daniel Dennett *Breaking the Spell, Religion as a Natural Phenomenon* (2006) Allen Lane, London. p. 9.

Bibliography

Allende, Isabel *The Sum of Our Days* (2008) Fourth Estate, London.
Aung San Suu Kyi and Aris, Michael *Freedom from Fear: And Other Writings* (1991) Penguin, London.
Badham, Paul *Religious and Near-Death Experiences in Relation to Belief in a Future Life* (1997) 2nd Series Occasional Paper No. 13 RERC, Oxford.
Bailey, Edward *Implicit Religion: An Introduction* (1988, 2006) Middlesex University Press, London.
Bailey, Lee W. and Yates, Jenny eds. *The Near-Death Experience, A Reader* (1996) Routledge, New York and London.
Benedict, Thomas-Mellen 'Through the Light and Beyond' in *The Near-Death Experience, A Reader* edited by Lee W. Bailey and Jenny Yates (1996) Routledge, New York and London.
Bethge, Eberhard *Dietrich Bonhoeffer, A Biography by Eberhard Bethge* (1977) Fountain and Harper & Row, London.
Bharat, Sandy and Jael *Touched by Truth, A Contemporary Hindu Anthology* (2006) William Sessions, York.
Bharat, Sandy and Jael *A Global Guide to Interfaith, Reflections from Around the World* (2007) O Books, UK.
Bhativedanta, A. C., Swami Prabhupada trans. *Bhagavad-Gita As It Is* (1985) The Bhativedanta Book Trust, USA.
Blackmore, Susan *Consciousness, An Introduction* (2003) Hodder and Stoughton, London.
Bowker, John *Worlds of Faith, Religious Belief and Practice in Britain Today* (1983) Ariel Books, BBC, London.
Braybrooke, Marcus *Faith and Interfaith in a Global Age* (1998) CoNexus, USA.
Braybrooke, Marcus *A Heart for the World* (2005) O Books, Hants.
Bridgers, Lynn *Contemporary Varieties of Religious Experience, James's Classic Study in Light of Resiliency, Temperament, and Trauma* (2005) Rowman and Littlefield Publishers, USA.
Brown, Gordon *Courage, Eight Portraits* (2007) Bloomsbury, London.
Buber, Martin *I and Thou* translated by Ronald Gregor Smith. Second Edition (1958) T&T Clark, Edinburgh.
Cantwell Smith, Wilfred *The Meaning and End of Religion* (reprint 1963) Fortress Press, Minneapolis.

Bibliography

Capra, Fritjof *The Tao of Physics* (1976, 1992) Flamingo, London.
Chopra, Deepak *How to Know God, The Soul's Journey into the Mystery of Mysteries* (2000) Rider, London.
Clapton, Eric *The Autobiography* (2007) Century, London.
Cohen, J. M. and Phipps J-F *The Common Experience* (1979) Rider, London.
Cole, W. Owen and Morgan, Peggy *Six Religions in the Twenty-First Century* (2000) Stanley Thornes, Cheltenham.
Cupitt, Don *Mysticism after Modernity* (1998) Blackwell, Oxford.
Dalai Lama, His Holiness *How to Practise, the Way to a Meaningful Life* translated and edited by Jeffrey Hopkins (2002) Rider, London.
D'Aquili, Eugene and Newberg, Andrew *The Mystical Mind, Probing the Biology of Religious Experience* (1999) Fortress Press, Minneapolis.
Dennett, Daniel *Breaking the Spell, Religion as a Natural Phenomenon* (2006) Allen Lane, London.
Dionysius the Areopagite *The Mystical Theology and the Celestial Hierarchies* translated by the Editors of the Shrine of Wisdom (1923, 2004) The Fintry Trust, Surrey.
Donovan, Peter *Interpreting Religious Experience* (1988) RERC, Oxford.
Du Boulay, Shirley *Teresa of Avila* (1991) Hodder and Stoughton, London.
Du Boulay, Shirley *The Road to Canterbury, A Modern Pilgrimage* (1994) HarperCollins, London.
Du Boulay, Shirley *Beyond the Darkness, A Biography of Bede Griffiths* (1998) Rider, London.
Du Boulay, Shirley with Rankin, Marianne *Cicely Saunders, The Founder of the Modern Hospice Movement* (2007) SPCK, London.
Durkheim, Emile *Elementary Forms of Religious Life* (2001) Oxford University Press, Oxford.
Fenwick, Dr. Peter and Fenwick, Elizabeth *The Truth in the Light, An Investigation of Over 300 Near-Death Experiences* (1997) Berkeley, New York.
Fox, Mark *Religion, Spirituality and the Near-Death Experience* (2003) Routledge, London, Canada and USA.
Franklin, John *Exploration into Spirit, A History of the Alister Hardy Religio Experience Research Centre and Society* (2006) RERC, Lampeter.
Franks Davis, Caroline *The Evidential Force of Religious Experience* (1989) Oxford University Press, Oxford and New York.
French, Patrick *Younghusband, The Last Imperial Adventurer* (2004) Harper Periennial, London.
Fynn, Diana *On the Turn of the Tide* (2005) Goldpanner Books, Devon.
Garton, Nancy *George Müller and His Orphans* (1987) Churchman Publishing, West Sussex.
Gélineau, Alain-René *The Poetry of Transcendence* (1984) Argel, Paris.
Gladwin, Eric *Peaceful Reflections for the New Millenium, Healing Poems and Prayers* (1994, 2000) Harmony Publications, England.
Griffiths, Bede *The Golden String* (1976, 2003) Medio Media, USA.
Griffiths, Bede *Return to the Centre* (1976) (2003) Medio Media, USA.

Bibliography

Griffiths, Bede *The Marriage of East and West* (1982) Templegate Publishers, Illinois.

Hague, William *William Wilberforce, The Life of the Great Anti-Slave Trade Campaigner* (2007) HarperCollins Publishers, London.

Happold, F. C. *Mysticism, A Study and an Anthology* (1963, 1990) Penguin Books, London.

Hardy, Alister *The Divine Flame* (1966, 1978) RERU, Oxford.

Hardy, Alister *The Spiritual Nature of Man, A Study of Contemporary Religious Experience* (1979) OUP, reprinted RERC 1997.

Harvey, Andrew *The Way of Passion* (1994, 1995) Souvenir Press, London.

Harvey, Andrew *The Essential Mystics, The Soul's Journey into Truth* (1996) Harper, San Francisco.

Harvey, Andrew *The Direct Path, Creating a Journey to the Divine Using the World's Mystical Traditions* (2000) Rider, London.

Harvey, Andrew *A Walk with Four Spiritual Guides* (2003) SkyLight Paths Publishing, Canada.

Hawken, Paul *The Magic of Findhorn* (1976) Collins, Glasgow.

Hay, David *Religious Experience Today* (1990) Mowbray, London.

Hay, David *Something There, The Biology of the Human Spirit* (2006) DLT, London.

Hay, David & Nye, Rebecca *The Spirit of the Child* (1998) HarperCollins, UK.

Heathcote-James, Emma *Seeing Angels* (2001) John Blake, London.

Heathcote-James, Emma *After-Death Communication* (2003) Metro Publishing, UK.

Hick, John *An Interpretation of Religion* (1989) Macmillan, London.

Hick, John *The New Frontier of Religion and Science, Religious Experience, Neuroscience and the Transcendent* (2006) Palgrave Macmillan, Hampshire and New York.

Hill, Madeleine *Time Stood Still* (2003) SPCK, London.

Hofmann, Werner *Caspar David Friedrich* (2000) Thames & Hudson, London.

Huxley, Aldous *The Perennial Philosophy* (1985, reprinted 1989) Triad Grafton, London

Huxley, Aldous *The Doors of Perception* (1994) Flamingo, London.

Israel, Martin *Happiness That Lasts* (1999) Cassell, London.

Jakobsen, Marete Demant *Negative Spiritual Experiences: Encounters with Evil* (1999) RERC, Lampeter.

James, William *The Varieties of Religious Experience, A Study in Human Nature* (2002) Special Centenary Edition, Routledge, London, New York and Canada.

Johnston, William (ed.) *The Cloud of Unknowing* (1997) Fount Paperbacks, London. p.15.

Julian of Norwich, *Revelations of Divine Love* (1966) Penguin Books, London.

Keeble, John *'This Unnamed Something', A Personal Portrait of the Life of Professor Sir Alister Hardy FRS 1896–1985* (2000) RERC, Lampeter.

Kolodiejchuk, Brian ed. and commentary *Mother Teresa, Come Be My Light, The Private Writings of the 'Saint of Calcutta'* (2007) Doubleday, USA.

Bibliography

Krishnamurti, J. *Meditations* (1991) Shambhala, London. p. 2.

Krishnamurti, J. *Meeting Life* compiled by Mary Lutyens (1991) Arkana, London.

Kübler-Ross, Elisabeth 'Death Does Not Exist' in *On Life After Death* (1991) Celestial Arts, USA.

Kübler-Ross, Elisabeth *The Wheel of Life, A Memoir of Living and Dying* (1997, 1999) Bantam, London.

Lao Tsu, *Tao Te Ching* translated by Gia-Fu Feng and Jane English (1973) Wildwood House, UK.

Laski, Marghanita *Ecstasy, in Secular and Religious Experiences* (1961) Cresset Press, London; reprint (1990) Jeremy P. Tarcher, Los Angeles.

Lewis, C. S. *Surprised by Joy* (1977) Fount Paperbacks, London.

Macquarrie, John *The Mediators, Nine Stars in the Human Sky* (1995) SCM, London.

Marshall, Paul *Mystical Encounters with the Natural World, Experiences and Explanations* (2005) OUP, Oxford.

Maxwell, Meg and Tschudin, Verena (eds.) *Seeing the Invisible* (1996) RERC, Oxford.

Metropolitan Anthony of Sourozh *Living Prayer* (1966, 1990) DLT, London.

Miles, Grahame *Science and Religious Experience, Are They Similar Forms of Knowledge?* (2007) Sussex Academic Press, Eastbourne and Portland, OR in USA.

Montefiore, Hugh *The Paranormal, A Bishop Investigates* (2002) Upfront Publishing, Leicester.

Moody, Raymond *Life after Life* (1976) Bantam, New York.

Mooney, Bel *Devout Sceptics, Conversations on Faith and Doubt* (2003) Hodder & Stoughton, London.

Mother Meera *Answers* (1991) Rider, London.

Newberg, Andrew and Waldman, Mark, Robert *Why We Believe What We Believe* (2006) Free Press, New York.

Nicholson, Reynold A. *The Mystics of Islam* (1989) Arkana, London.

Olivelle, Patrick *A New Translation of Upanishads* (1998) OUP, Oxford.

Otto, Rudolf *The Idea of the Holy* (1923) (1958) OUP, London.

Otto, Rudolf *Mysticism East and West. A Comparative Analysis of the Nature of Mysticism* (1932) New York: The Macmillan Company.

Parsons, Stephen *Ungodly Fear, Fundamentalist Christianity and the Abuse of Power* (2000) Lion Publishing, Oxford.

Parsons, Tony *The Open Secret* (1995) Open Secret Publishing, Dorset.

Partridge, Christopher *Encyclopedia of New Religions, New Religious Movements, Sects and Spiritualities* (2004) Lion Publishing, Oxford.

Plant, Stephen *Simone Weil* Fount Christian Thinkers (1996) Fount, London.

Plato *Phaedo* in *Socratic Dialogues* translated and edited by W. D. Woodhead (1967) Nelson, London.

Ramadan, Tariq *The Messenger, The Meanings of the Life of Muhamad* (2007) Penguin Books, London.

Bibliography

Rankin, Marianne *An Introduction to Religious Experience* (2005) Third Series of Occasional Papers No. 2 RERC, Lampeter.

Robinson, Edward *Living the Questions* (1978) RERU, Oxford.

Robinson, Edward *The Original Vision* (1996) RERC, Lampeter.

Rogers, Ben *Pascal* (1999) Routledge, New York. The Great Philosophers Series.

Rumi, Mevlana Jalaluddin *The Rumi Collection* edited by Kabir Helminski (1998) Threshold Books, USA.

Russell, Bertrand *History of Western Philosophy and Its Connection with Political and Social Circumstances from the Earliest Times to the Present Day* (2004) Folio Society, London.

Russell, Peter *From Science to God, A Physicist's Journey into the Mystery of Consciousness* (2002, 2003) New World Library, California.

Schleiermacher, Friedrich *The Christian Faith* (1928, 1960) T&T Clark, Edinburgh.

Schleiermacher, Friedrich (*Über die Religion. Reden an die Gebildeten unter ihren Verächtern*) *On Religion. Speeches to its Cultured Despisers* (1996) translated by Richard Crouter, Cambridge University Press, Cambridge.

Sharf, Robert 'Experience' in *Critical Terms for Religious Studies* edited by Mark C. Taylor (1998) University of Chicago Press, USA.

Sheldrake, Rupert *The Sense of Being Stared At and Other Aspects of the Extended Mind* (2003) Hutchinson, UK.

Smart, Ninian *The Religious Experience of Mankind* (Third Edition 1984) Charles Scribner's Sons, New York.

Smart, Ninian *Dimensions of the Sacred, An Anatomy of the World's Beliefs* (1997) Fontana Press, London.

Smart, Ninian *The World's Religions* (Second Edition 1998) Cambridge University Press, Cambridge.

Steiner, Rudolf *The Course of My Life* (1977) Anthroposophic Press, New York.

Swinburne, Richard *The Existence of God* (Second Edition, 2004) OUP, Oxford.

Tolle, Eckhart *The Power of Now* (1999 USA) (2001) Hodder and Stoughton, London.

Tolle, Eckhart *Practising the Power of Now* (2001 USA) (2002) Hodder and Stoughton, London.

Tolle, Eckhart *A New Earth, Awakening to Your Life's Purpose* (2005 USA) (2006) Penguin Books, London.

Varah, Chad *Before I Die Again* (1992) Constable, London.

Walsch, Neale Donald *Conversations with God, An Uncommon Dialogue* (1995 USA) (1997) Hodder and Stoughton, London.

Walsch, Neale Donald *Communion with God, An Uncommon Dialogue* (2000) Hodder and Stoughton, London.

Wa'Na'Nee'Che (Dennis Renault) and Timothy Freke *Principles of Native American Spirituality* (1996) Thorsons, California.

Bibliography

Ward Keith *Concepts of God, Images of the Divine in Five Religious Traditions* (1987, 1998) Oneworld, Oxford.

Ward, Keith *Religion and Revelation* (1994) Oxford University Press, Oxford and New York.

Ward, Keith *Is There a Common Core of Religious Experience?* (2005) 2nd Series Occasional Paper No. 44 RERC, Lampeter.

White, Rhea and Dale, Laura *Parapsychology: Sources of Information* (1973) Scarecrow Pr, USA.

Yao, Xinzhong and Badham, Paul *Religious Experience in Contemporary China* (2007) University of Wales Press, Cardiff.

Yaran, Cafer *Muslim Religious Experience* (2004) 2nd Series Occasional Paper No. 41 RERC, Lampeter.

Yoganada, Paramahansa *Autobiography of a Yogi* (1950) (in UK 1969) Rider, London.

Index

Abolition of Slavery 202
Abraham 18, 34
  and Muhammad 38
Absolute Unitary Being (AUB) 16–17
Abu Bakr 37
accident 80–1
Adams, Douglas, *Hitchhiker's Guide to the Galaxy* 144
Adi Granth, holy scripture of Sikhs 39
  object of devotion 19
adolescence, conversion 100, 101
Advaita, doctrine of non-duality 48
African National Congress 215, 230
afterlife 17
Agam Sutras, Zoroastrian teachings 31
ahimsa, complete non-violence 31
  Gandhi taught 205
Ahura Mazda 30
Aitken, Jonathan, *Pride and Perjury* 109–10
Alister Hardy Research Centre 234
Alister Hardy Society 96, 168–9, 232
Alister Hardy Trust website 6, 7, 114
Allah, merciful creator 37
Allan Sweeney International Reiki and Healing and Training Centre 225
Allende, Isabel, *The Sum of Our Days* 132
altered states of consciousness (ASC) 127–8
alternative medicine 225
Amesha Spentas 30
Analects, Confucianism 33
Ananda, Buddha's cousin 20
ancient burial sites 146
Angel Jibril (Gabriel), vision of 37
angels, visions of 123–5

anger 86
Angra Mainyu 30
Anthroposophists 45–6, 208
apartheid, protest against 215
apology to Iraqi refugee 229
Aranyakas (hidden teachings) 28
Arnold, Matthew, poem, 'Dover Beach' 253
ashram (retreat centre) 47
  in Tamil Nadu 188
Atharva 28
atheism in China 235
atman, individual soul 28
Aung San Suu Kyi, Myanmar 196, 215–17
avatars (incarnations) 2, 47
awareness of other dimension 8
ayahusca 'trip' 132
Ayer, A. J., atheist philosopher 163, 164
  Language, Truth and Logic 246
  Near Death Experience 246
Ayurvedic medicine 51

Bab ('the gate') 41, 42
Bach, 'Partita in D Minor' 88
Baha'i 41
Baha'u'llah ('The Glory of God') 41
Bailey, Edward, *Implicit Religion: an Introduction* 252
'Beatitudes' 35
Beguines, lay women of charity 228
beliefs, deepening of 102
Benedictine Rule 187–8, 227
Bernadette Soubirous, France (St Bernadette) 111–12
Bernini, Gian Lorenzo, *The Ecstasy of Saint Theresa*, sculpture 124

Index

Besant, Annie, Theosophist 45, 193
Bethlehem 71
Bhagavad Gita (The *Gita*) 29, 54, 145
Bhakti, devotion to one god 38, 53
Bible 145
  accuracy of record 20
biographical portraits 1
birds and nature, St Francis 228
Black Elk (Oglala Sioux Tribe) North America 86, 159
Blackmore, Susan, on dying brain 162–3
Blavatsky, Helena 44–5
  Isis Unveiled 45
  The Secret Doctrine 45
blessing 66–7
Bodh Gaya 71
Bodhi Tree (Tree of Enlightenment) 32
Bodhisattva of Compassion 5, 213
Bojaxhiu, Gonxa Agnes (Mother Teresa) 206
Bonhoeffer, Dietrich 196, 207–8
Book of Revelation, Bible 142
Boyle, Jimmy, IRA prisoner 224
Bragg, Melvyn, out of body experience 154–5
Brahma Baba 40
Brahma Kumaris, female movement 40, 66
Brahma Kumaris World Spiritual University (BKWSU) 40
Brahman, consciousness 28
Brahmanas (hidden teachings) 28
Brahmo Dharma 41
Brahmo Samaj 40–1
Brahms symphony, religious experience 7
brain
  source of religious experience 254
  study of 238
brain-imaging techniques 238, 254
Branch Davidians 142–3
Braybrooke, Marcus
  Faith and Interfaith in a Global World 24
  A Heart for the World 24
breaking of bread 54

Bridgers, Lynn, religious experience 244
Buber, Martin, Jewish philosopher of religion 245
Buddha 18, 148, 171
  born in India 31–2
  Four Noble Truths 32
  no writing 20
Buddhism
  Aung San Suu Kyi's belief 217
  Christianity and 189–91
  of Japan 54
  meditation 63–4
  no killing of sentient beings 106
Buddhist Lamas, reincarnation 147
Buddhist Pali canon on marble slabs 222–3
Buddhist texts, written by followers
Buddhist Vesak Day 55
burial of dead, not done by Zoroastrians 30
Butler-Evans, Kenneth, paintings 222

Caddy, Peter and Eileen, Findhorn Community 70, 107–8
Canterbury Cathedral 72
Capra, Fritjof, *The Tao of Physics* 50–1
Carpenter, Joseph Estlin 102–3
cat's behaviour at times of death 185
Catholic high school students, Australia 95
CE (Common Era) 4
Chad Varah 196, 208–10
chanting 74, 110
charismatic churches, power of 143
charitable organizations 2
charities 223– 6
childhood brainwashing 2
childhood, spiritual experiences 93–7
China 2
  research on spiritual experiences 234–5
Chinese New Year 55
choosing of Dalai Lama 213–14
Chopra, Deepak, *How to Know God* 51, 59
Christian Ascension 148

Index

Christian evangelicalism, conversion to, Wilberforce 202
Christian humanism 25
Christian Parapsychology 166–7
Christian Science 43
Christianity 19, 35–6
  founded by Jesus, a Jew 22
  growth away from Judaism 36
  missionary's experience 85–6
  teacher in India, Mother Teresa 206
  worship 54
Christmas 54, 55
Church of Jesus Christ of Latter Day Saints 44
Church of Scientology 43
churches, and mystical experiences 244
clairvoyance 14
Clapton, Eric, rock star 196, 218
Cloud of Unknowing 62
communal settings for religious experience 110
communication with God 50
communist countries 2
compassion 3
concentration camps 210
'Confessing Church', against Nazism 207
Confucianism 32, 33
consciousness
  after clinical death 17
  reality of 238–9
  studies 238–9
contemplation 62–3
conversion 99–102
conversion experiences 244
  Judaism to Christianity 101–2
Cornwell, John, *Darwin's Angel* 253
cosmic consciousness 16
Cosmic Rose 65
counter-culture 23
creative spirituality 23
crucifixion of Jesus 36
Cruise, Tom, actor, a Scientologist 44
Cupitt, Don
  Mysticism After Modernity 253
  The Sea of Faith 253

D'Aquili, Eugene, *The Mystical Mind* 254
Dadi Prakashmani 40
Dalai Lama, His Holiness 148, 171, 213–14
  and Buddhism 99–100
  exile 213
  inspiring leader 196
  on meditation 63
  world-wide influence 18
Damascus road conversion of St Paul 198–9
Daoism (Taoism), China 32–3
Dark Night of the Soul 138–9
Darshan, Mother Meera 67–8
Darshan, silent communication of light 49
Darwin, Charles, Theory of Evolution 254
Dawkins, Richard, atheist, 253–4
  The God Delusion 253–4
  taught by Hardy 3
  website 143–5
De Klerk, F. W., Nobel Peace Prize 215
Death Bed Visions 17
death, prospect of, as trigger 79–80
decline of religious observance 252
de-conversion 143–5
Dennett, Daniel, atheist, *Breaking the Spell* 253
dependence, feeling of 241
depression 83–5
despair 82–3
Dionysius the Areopagite 62, 243
  converted by St Paul 199
  Syrian monk 173–4
direct experience 23
dreams 125–7
drink, drugs, smoking, Eric Clapton 218
drug-induced trips 131–2
Durkheim, Emile
  Elementary Forms of Religious Life 22
  strength from God 220
dying and death 146–70

Index

Eastern Orthodox Christianity 36
ecstasy 15
  of Sri Ramakrishna 192
Eddy, Mary Baker 43
Eid-al-Fitr 73
  end of Ramadan fast 55
Einstein, Albert, Theory of
    Relativity 137
Eliot, T. S., poem, *Four Quartets* 177
'Emanation' doctrine 244–5
emotional dimension 12
empiricists 16
End of Life Experience (ELE) 151–3
energy in universe 33
Enlightenment of Buddha 31–2, 213
enlightenment, *kevala*, in Jainism 31
essentialists 16
Eucharist celebration 54
exceptional human experience
    (EHE) 15
execution of Dietrich Bonhoeffer 207
Exodus of Jews 34
experience In depth 12
  effect of 221, 222
  of Hajj 71–2
  when clinically dead 17
experiential dimension 12

faith in drugs, cure by 43
faith-inspired works of art 2
fasting 73–4
  and meditation 177
Fatima, Portugal, Virgin Mary 111
fear 85–6
Feast of the Passover 36
feng shui 33
festivals 54–5
Findhorn Community, Moray Firth,
    Scotland 70, 107–8
fire sacrifices 28
Five Pillars of Islam 38, 71
five-fold path 47
flowers in nature 10
football as religion 25
founders of religion 18–19
Fox, George 42–3
Francis of Assisi 18

Franciscans, founded by St Francis 228
Franks Davis, Caroline, *The Evidential
    Force of Religious
    Experience* 249–50
Friedrich, Caspar David, Romantic
    painter 87
funeral of young girl, Chad Varah 209

Gandhi *see* Mahatma Gandhi
Ganges river at Banaras (or Varanasi) 71
garden at Findhorn 70
Genesis, Book of 33–4
German bombs in war 9
German Theosophical Society 46
Gifford Lectures 3
Gita *(Bhagavad Gita As It Is)* English
    translation 49
glossolalia 122
Gnosticism 45
God
  description of 173
  in everyday life 252
  as Mind 43
  as religious ideal 253
God-consciousness 192
Golden Rule of *jen* (virtue) 33
Golden Rule, 'do as you would be
    done by' 18
Golden Temple at Amritsar 39, 71
gongs 90
good and evil forces in world,
    choice 30
Gopin, Marc, Rabbi 229
Gospels
  and Hebrew Scriptures 36
  illuminated manuscripts 19
  written by followers of Jesus
Great Renunciation of Buddha 31
greed, hatred, delusion 32
Griffiths, Fr Bede
  mystic experience 186–9
  Prison Phoenix Project 225
  on religious text 21
guidance 107–8
  from Christian God 8
Guru Gobind Singh 38
Guru Granth Sahib 19, 39

Index

Guru Nanak 18, 38
gurus (teachers) 2
   Hindu tradition 47
Guyana jungle, Jonestown 142

Hajj (pilgrimage), Mecca 37, 71–2
Handel, Georg Friedrich, 'Messiah' 89
Hardy, Sir Alister 96, 224, 231–3
   The Spiritual Nature of Man 5, 232–4
   contact with power 220–1
   Darwinian biologist 3
Hare Krishna 29, 49, 74
harmony with nature 32
harmony with others 12
Harrison, George, (Beatles), *My Sweet Lord* 49
Harvey, Andrew, and Ramakrishna 194
Hasidim of Judaism 16
Hay, David
   Religious Experiences Today 233
   The Spirit of the Child 94
healing 23, 103–4
   in Japanese religion 106
   powers of Shaman 129
   prayers for 60
   spring water 112
Hick, John, valid paths to same goal 64, 250–1
   meditation experience 64
Hijra 37
Hindu Goddess Kali 49
Hindu gods and goddesses 28
Hindu teachings, *sanatana dharma* 188
Hindu Thaipusam 55
Hindu Unitarian, Rammohun Roy 41
Hinduism 27–9, 47
   and Christianity 186–9
   merging with absolute 148
   and yoga 172
Hindus and Muslims, killings at Partition of India 205
Hindustanis, India 28
Hinton, Walter, mystic 175
holistic education 46
holistic health 106
homeopathy 43

Hospice Movement founder, Cicely Saunders 211
Hubbard, *Dianetics: The Modern Science of Mental Health* 43–4
Hubbard, L. Ron (Church of Scientology) 43–4
human suffering, roots of 32
humanism as religion 25
humanity as responsible for species 25
Hunt, Holman, 'Light of the World', painting 113
Husayn Ali, Mirza 41–2
Huxley, Aldous
   The Perennial Philosophy 172, 240, 245–6
   on effect of mescaline 131
Huxley, Julian 3

I-Ching (*Book of Changes*) 33
illness as trigger 79–80
'Immanence' doctrine 244–5
implicit religion 252
Independence of India, Gandhi fought for 205
India 4
   research on spiritual experiences 234
Indra's Net 4
Indus River, India 27
Inge, Dean W. R., on mysticism 16
initiatory experiences 99
interfaith 23–4, 75
International Society for Krishna Consciousness (ISKCON) 49
interpretation
   of mystical experience 240–55
   of religious experiences 240–55
   of spiritual experiences 240–55
intuitive insights 239
irreligious experiences 143–5
Islam 36–8
   message of Qur'an 19
   'submission' 37
Island of Shikodo, Japan, sacred place 71
Israel, twelve tribes of 34

279

Index

Jainism 30–1
  no killing of sentient beings 106
Jalaluddin Rumi, Islamic
    mystic 177–80
James, William 18, 108, 231
  *The Varieties of Religious
    Experience* 11, 100, 243
  on *fruits for life* 220
  on renunciation 68–9
Japan 4
Jerusalem 71
Jerusalem Peacemakers 229
Jesus Christ 5, 18
  George Fox, relationship with 42
  life, death and resurrection 19
  nothing written by him 20
  Sermon on the Mount 13
Jewish Kabbalists 172
Jewish praying 60
John the Baptist 35
Jones, Jim, drug addict, The People's
    Temple 142
Judaism 33
  law giving in 19
Julian of Norwich, Dame, Christian
    mystic 174–7
Jung, Carl Gustav, Swiss
    psychiatrist 196, 200–2
  Memories, Dreams Reflections 132,
    200
  on 'active imagination' 128
  difference with Freud 200
  Near Death Experience 201

Ka'aba, holiest shrine in Islam 71
Kabbalists 16
kami, Shinto 21
karma, freedom from 31
Katz, Steven, *Language, Epistemology
    and Mysticism* 247
King Mindon, and Dharma 223
King, Martin Luther 125, 189
Kitab-i-Aqdas 42
Koresh, David, leader of Branch
    Davidians 142
Krishna 5, 28–9
Krishna Caitanya 48–9

Krishnamurti, Jiddhu, Theosophist 45,
    193–4
Ks, five, Sikh religion 39
Kübler-Ross, Elisabeth 196, 210–12
  On Death and Dying 154, 210
Kuthodaw Pagoda, world's largest
    book 222–3

Lahore, Punjab 38
Langar, community kitchen 39
language, limitations of 21–2
Laoze (Lao-Tsu), 'Old Master' 32
Laski, Marghanita, *Ecstasy in
    Secular and Spiritual
    Experiences* 16
Latin chants 110
Leadbeater, C. W., Theosophist 45
Lent fasts 73
Lewis, C. S.
  Narnia 150–1
  Surprised by Joy 102
Liberation Theology, Latin America 25
liberation, *moksha* in Jainism 31
life after death 146
life changes after Near Death
    Experiences 17
life-enhancing experience 6
light, experiences of 113–18
Lord Sri Caitanya Mahaprabhu 48
'Lords' Prayer' 35, 61
Lourdes 71, 111–12
love 118–19
Lutyens, Mary, on Krishnamurti 194

Maclean, Dorothy, Findhorn 70
Madinah (Medina) 37
Mahabharata 29, 54
maha-mantra Great Chant for
    Deliverance 49
Maharishi Mahesh Yoga 18, 48
Mahatma Gandhi 18, 180, 205
  assassination by Hindu fanatic 205
  inspiring leader 196
Mahavira, founder of Jainism 30–1
Mahayama school of Buddhism 32
Main, Dom John, Christian
    meditation 64

Index

Makkah (Mecca)
  Muhammad born 37
  pilgrimage to 71
  (qibla) 60
Mandela, Nelson, President of
    South Africa 196, 214, 229
mantra (sacred word(s)) 48, 193
martyrdom of Christians 42
Marx, Karl 25
Marxism as religion 25
McCarthy, John, despair of,
    in kidnap of 82–3
McGrath, Alister, *The Dawkins
    Delusion* 253
Mecca *see* Makkah
Mediators 19
medical cures at Lourdes 112
meditation 12, 23, 48, 63–6, 171, 193–4
  in a mountain cave 37
Medjugorge,
    Bosnia-Herzegovina 111–12
megalomania 142
Meister Eckhart, mystic 172–5
Messengers 19
Metropolitan Anthony of Sourozh 53
metta (loving-kindness) 217
Mevlana Jalaluddin Rumi 137
military intelligence, Germany 207
military junta in Myanmar
    (Burma) 215
mind and body interconnectedness 106
mind and brain, relation between 239
Mind Life Institute 214
mind over matter 43
miracles 107
Missionaries of Charity 206
missionary work of St Paul 199
Montefiore, Hugh, Bishop of
    Birmingham 101
Mooney, Bel, *Devout Sceptics* 154–5
Moore, Thomas, poet, 'The Scent of the
    Roses' 165
moral order 9, 18
Mormons 44
Moses 18
  founder of Jewish religion 34
  and Muhammad 38

Mosque, prayer location for
    Muslims 60
Mother Meera, avatar 49, 67–8
Mother Teresa 206–7
  inspirational leader 196
Mount Carmel Centre, Waco 142
Muhammad 18
  instruction to read or recite 20
  last of prophets of Bible 36
Muhammad Ibn 'Arabi, mystic 172
Müller Orphan Houses 223
Müller, George, convertion to
    Christianity 223
murder 142
music 6, 88
Muslims
  daily prayers 60
  esteem of Moses (Musa) 35
  experience of interfaith 75
Mysteries of the Greeks 172
mystical experience 11, 16, 171–220
  within all religions 191–220
mystical traditions of world 195
mysticism 2, 16, 51, 242
  without religion 193

National League for Democracy
    (NLD) 215, 216
natural beauty 6
nature 86
  presence of God in 88
nature of religion, enquiry into it 253
Nazis, resistance to 207
Near Death Experience (NDE) 15,
    90–2, 146, 149, 155–62
  research, pioneer Kübler-Ross 17, 210
  scientific research 162–3
Nehru, Jawaharlal, announcement
    of Gandhi's death 205
Neoplatonic work 173
Neo-Platonism 198
neurotheology 17
New Age movements 23
Newberg, Andrew, *The Mystical
    Mind* 254
Nicholson, Ben, on painting and
    religious experience 87

281

Index

Night of Qadr' (Power or Glory) 37
Nirvana 31, 54, 148
Nobel Peace Prize 189
  awarded to Aung San Suu Kyi 217
  awarded to Dalai Lama 214
  awarded to Mother Teresa 206
  awarded to Nelson Mandela 215
  Thich Nhat Hanh nominated
    for 1967 125
Noble Eightfold Path 32
Noetic Training 59
numen (holy power) 136–8, 241
numinous, experiences 136–8
Nye, Rebecca 94

occult, interest in 23
Oglala Sioux tribe, North America 86
Olcott, Henry Steel 44–5
Om ('aum'), mantra, Sanskrit for
  God 194
oral traditions 21, 86
Order of the Star of the East 193
'other power' (*tariki*) 54
Otto, Rudolf
  The Idea of the Holy 136–7
  on religious experience 241
Out of the Body Experience (OBE) 17,
  149, 154
Ox-Herding pictures 76

paganism 23
Paramahansa Yogananda, yogi 180–2
Paramatman Light 49, 67
paranormal experience 14–15
parapsychology 15
Parliament of the World's Religions 24
Partition of India 205
Pascal, Blaise, French mathematical
  genius 173
  wager 173
Passover (*Pesach*) 34
patients' recovery and prayer 60
Peace Medal 40
peace near lake shore 87
peacemaking 189, 190
peak experience, secular 15
Pentateuch 33

Pentecost 36
Pentecostal movement 122
People's Temple 142
perception of *invisible* world 12
Persia 30
personal faith 12
physics and Eastern Mysticism 50
Pilgrim's Way, Winchester to
  Canterbury 72
pilgrimage 71–3
place triggers 78
Plagues of Egypt 34
Plato 196
  The Republic 155, 197
  and Christianity 198
  Near Death Experience in *The
    Republic* 198
  pupil of Socrates, *Phaedo* 196, 197
  story of Er, in *The Republic* 198
Plotinus, mystic 172
pluralism 250
Pontius Pilate 36
Poor Clares, founded by St Francis 228
Pope Pius X, cures at Lourdes 112
Pope, world-wide influence 18
positive thinking 106
Post Death Appearances 17, 164–70
post-traumatic Stress Disorder 244
power of spiritual movements,
  dangerous 141–2
Prabhupada, writer on Vedic
  scriptures 49
prayer, and power of 56–9
prayers of penitence, Christian
  churches 61
predestination 43
presence sensing 133–6
priesthood, calling 76–7
Principle of Credulity 249
Principle of Testimony 249
Prison Ashram Project 225
Prison Phoenix Trust 224
prisoner of conscience, Aung San
  Suu Kyi 216
prisoners, conversion 224–5
protection of all life 31
promise to God 9

Index

prosperity and religion 25
Protestant Christianity 36
Pseudo-Dionysius 173–4
psychical experience 14–15
pyramids 146

Qi (Chi) 33
Quakers 42–3
Quasi-religions 24–5
Queen Victoria 42
Quimby Phineas, magnetic healer 43
Qur'an (recitation) 37
   Arabic from angel Jibril (Gabriel) 20
   decorated copies 19

Rabi'a of Basra, prayer 54
racial prejuice in South Africa 205
Radhakrishnan, extrovert experience 171
Raja Yoga 40
Ramadan, fasting 38, 73–4
Ramakrishna, ecstasies 172
Ramana Maharshi 48
Rammohun Roy 40
rational analysis 239
Real as unknowable 250–1
Reformation of Manners, Wilberforce 202
Reiki healing 104–5
Reincarnation, Buddhist belief 147, 213
religion
   based on feeling and intuition 241
   as fever 12
   as 'opium of the people' 25
religions
   of the East 23
   proselytizing 99
religious appearances 226
religious belief 2
religious ceremonies 54–5
   in Turkey 236
Religious Experience Research Centre 3, 4, 231–3
Religious Experience Study Project, Tamil Nadu, South India 237–8

religious experiences 2, 11
   in Glasgow street 6
   profound 22
religious fundamentalism 25
religious humanism 25, 26
religious movements 23, 27
religious orders 226–7
Religious Society of Friends (of the Truth) 42–3
Renaissance Humanism 25
renunciation 68–9
repentance and forgiveness 228–9
Religious Experience Research Centre (RERC) 232–3
   archive, religious experiences 94–6, 108, 140–1, 182–3
Religious Experience Research Unit, later RERC 3, 225
revelation of texts 20
reverence for all living beings 18
Ricoeur, Paul, philosopher, on Taizé 111
Rig Veda 28
risk in Bonhoeffer's life 207
Robben Island imprisonment of Nelson Mandela 215
Robinson, Edward
   Director of RERO, after Hardy 232
   The Original Vision 94
Rolle, Richard, mystic 175
Roman Catholic Christianity 36
Roman Empire, Christianity, official religion 36
Rosicrucians 46
Rothenstein, Sir William, painter 87
Rousseau, Jean-Jacques, *Le Contrat Social* 87
running water in nature 10
Russian Orthodox Patriarchal Church, Britain 53
Ruysbroeck, John of (Jan van Ruysbroek) 228

sacred feminine 49
sacred places 69, 71
sacred power 21

283

Index

sacred texts 19
Sai Baba, *guru* 47
saints 2
Salt Lake City, Utah, USA, Mormon Church 44
salt tax protest by Gandhi 205
Sama 28
Samadhi, meditative absorption 65
Samaritans founder, Chad Varah 208–10
sanatana dharma (eternal truth) 28
Sangha, community of Buddhist monks 20
sannyasin 68
Santiago de Compostela 71
Sanyama 65
Satya Sai Baba 47
Saunders, Dame Cicely 196, 211–13
Schleiermacher, Friedrich, theologian 19
  The Christian Faith 241
  on religion 241
Scholastica, sister of St Benedict 227
Schucman, Helen, *A Course in Miracles* 20
science and spirituality 239
Scientific and Medical Network 239
Scientology, Church of 43–4
seal of the prophets, Muhammad 36
Second World's Parliament of Religions 24
secular humanism 25, 26
secularity of contemporary society 252
'self-power' (*jiriki*) 54
Self, release from 48
selfish desire 32
Self-Realization Fellowship, USA 181
Sermon on the Mount 13, 35
Service of Remembrance, Cenotaph, London 24
Seventh Day Adventists 142
sexual abuse 142
Shabbat (Jewish Sabbath) 55
shamanism 21, 23
  drumming 89
  healing, and by internet 106, 129–31

initiation 148
journey 127–9
rituals 122
Shams of Tabriz, dervish 178–80
Shantiniketan, abode of peace 41
Sharf, Robert, on religious experience 248
Shari'a law 38
Sheldrake, Rupert
  A New Science of Life 239
  on mind and brain link 238–9
  Prison Phoenix Project 225
Shema ('Hear') first prayer of Jews 60
Shi'as, led by Imams 38
Shiite Muslim, experience 144–5
Shinto Waterfall ceremony, Japan 21, 55
Shirdi Baba 47
Shiva 28
shoe removal, before prayer 60
Siddhartha Gautama, Buddha, Nepal 31
Sikhism 38–9
  bridge between Hindu and Muslim 38
  holy book, Adi Granth 19
silence 67
slave trade, Atlantic 202–4
Smart, Ninian 12
  The Religious Experience of Mankind 247–8
Smith, Joseph, founder of Mormon Church 44
  The Book of Mormon 44
Smith, Wilfred Cantwell, *The Meaning and End of Religion* 12
Society for Psychical Research 45
Socrates and ancient Greece 25
  drank poison 196–7
solitary religious experience 108–10
soul and superhuman force 9
soul retrieval 129–31
sound 89–90
South America 4
Soviet Union 2
'speaking in tongues' 121–3
spirit in laws of universe 137
spiritual consciousness 146

Index

spiritual nature of man 232
spiritual reality in many guises 250
Spiritual Science 46
spiritual search for self 75
'spiritual wives' 142
spiritualism 1, 2, 15
spirituality
  and consciousness 3
  convergent within religions 251
  and modern physics 51
Sri Ramakrishna, Hindu 191–2
St Augustine 121, 198
St Benedict, founder of Western
    monasticism 227
St Christopher's Hospice,
    Sydenham 213
St Francis of Assisi 227–8
St John of the Cross, mystic 138–9, 172
St Paul 36, 196, 198–200
St Stephen Walbrook, Chad Varah 209
St Thomas Aquinas 198
  Summa Theologica 221
St Thomas Becket 72
Stace, W. T., extrovert and introvert mysticism 247
Starbuck, Edwin, *The Psychology of Religion* 100, 231
State Law and Order Restoration Council (SLORC), Myanmar 216, 217
Steiner, Rudolf, schools 45–6
stigmata 172
  received by St. Francis 228
stress and trauma 17
suffering in life 32
Sufi poet and mystic 137
Sufis of Islam 16, 38, 172, 177
suicides 7, 142, 209
Sunni Muslims (majority) 38
supranational manifestations 172
suttee, (Sati) campaign against 41
Swami Order, monk 181
Swami Vivekananda 192
Sweeney, Allan 225–6
Swinburne, Richard, *The Existence of God* 248–9

synchronicity 132–3
Syria, Rabbi Marc Gopin's reconciliation with 229

Tagore, Debendranath 41
  experience by the Ganges 108
Tagore, Rabindranath, poet 41, 180
  Asian Nobel Prize Winner 108
  on watching the dawn 108–9
Taizé, France 110
Tamil Nadu, India, religious experiences 237–8
Tavener, John, 'Beautiful Names' 88–9
Teilhard de Chardin, Pierre 79
telekinesis 14
telepathy 14
Temple Mount, Jerusalem 38
temple worship for Zoroastrians 30
Teresa of Avila
  account of angel 124
  contemplative prayer 61
  ecstasies 172
  Spanish mystic 113–14
terminally ill patients, treating 210–11
terrorism 2
'The Hardy Question' 3
Theosophical Society 44–5, 193
Theravada school of Buddhism 32
Thich Nhat Hanh, Zen Buddhist monk 125
  The Miracle of Mindfulness 189–91
Thompson, Francis, 'The Kingdom of God', poem 78
Tibet, taken by China 213
Tibetan Book of the Dead 148
Tibetan Government in exile, Dharamsala, India 213
time, outside of 16
Tiruvannamalai ashram 48
Tolle, Eckhart 50
  The Power of Now 83–4
  Stillness Speaks 50
Torah, first five books of Bible 19, 33, 34
Toronto Blessing 111
Towers of Silence, for leaving corpses 30

Index

Transcendental Meditation 14, 18, 48
translation of texts 20
transmigration of souls 29
Truth and Reconciliation Commission 215, 229–30
Turkey, research on spiritual experiences 234, 236–7
Tutu, Archbishop Desmond 215, 230

ubuntu (African brotherhood) 214, 215
Ultimate Reality 250, 251
unconscious mind 132
Underhill, Evelyn, *Mysticism* 244
Unitarianism 46, 102
United States of America 4
Unitive State 244
unity with the divine 16
Upanishads (hidden teachings) 28, 41

Vaishnavism 49
Vajrayana school of Buddhism 32
van Ruysbroek, Jan, mystic 175
Varah, Chad 196, 208–10
Vedas, revelatory texts in Sanskrit 4, 20, 28
vegetarianism 106
Vietnamese War 189
Viking wisdom 128–9
violin music in church 88
Virgin Mary 49, 111
Virtual Jerusalem, requests for prayers 60
Vishnu 28
vision of cross 111, 113
  changes to original 22
  of Julian of Norwich 174–7
Voice of God 107
voices, hearing 119–21

Waheguru, Sikh God 38
Wailing Wall, Jerusalem 71
  prayers in 60
Waldorf schools 46
Walsch, Neale Donald
  Communion with God 50, 86
  Conversations with God 50, 86, 133
  Friendship with God 50

Ward, Keith 251–2
warfare 2
washing before prayer 60
Webb, Beatrice socialist reformer 6, 9, 231
Weil, Simone
  Jewish, and Christianity 99
  on love of God 119
West Indian slaves 202
Wetherall, Ann 224
White, Rhea, parapsychologist 15
Wilberforce, William 196, 202–4
Winchester cathedral choir 89
wisdom 3
Woods, Christopher, experience of light 114–15
Wordsworth, William, 'Tintern Abbey', poem 14
World Community for Christian Meditation 65
World Congress of Faiths, (Younghusband) 204–5
World Fellowship of Faiths 24
World's Parliament of Religions, Chicago, 1893 24
world peace 42
World Trade Centre, attacks against 218
worship 53–4

Yajur 28
Yang 33
Yin 33
yoga 23, 74–5
Younghusband, Sir Francis 196, 204
Yusuf Islam (Cat Stevens), rock star 196, 218

Zarathushtra (Zoroaster) 30
Zen Buddhism 172
  Japan 32
  mystical experience 185
Zen Buddhist monk, on dreams 125
Zoroastrian priests, Magi 30
Zoroastrianism 30